"This book is a page-turner that '...' end. It is a puzzle of family secrets, '...' in a community that is so well d'...' there."

TERRI BLACKST'...'
AUTHOR OF THE BESTSELLING SUN COAST CHRONICLES SERIES

"Susan Bauer has linked a gripping tale with characters drenched in human emotion. This book should be labeled with a warning: 'Contents are hot. Open with extreme caution!'"

HARRY KRAUS JR., M.D.
BESTSELLING AUTHOR OF *LETHAL MERCY* AND *THE STAIN*

"There's a quiet renaissance astir in Christian fiction, and Susan Wise Bauer is one of its freshest voices."

JOHN WILSON
EDITOR, *BOOKS & CULTURE*

"Susan Wise Bauer shows herself to be a master of the craft of fiction, blending vivid Southern tradition with the suspense of a mystery tale. *Though the Darkness Hide Thee* goes deeper than superficial affirmations of Christian happiness to uncover the rewards of a faith that perseveres."

FREDERICA MATHEWES-GREEN
AUTHOR AND COMMENTATOR ON NPR's *ALL THINGS CONSIDERED*

"Readers looking for high-quality Christian fiction that doesn't cheapen God's grace should try Susan Wise Bauer. She's a keeper. *Though the Darkness Hide Thee* is a refreshingly soul-satisfying read."

EDWARD E. ERICSON, AUTHOR

"*Though the Darkness Hide Thee* is a fascinating combination of two time-honored genres: the clerical novel of manners and the murder mystery. The style is vividly descriptive, the theology is tough-minded, and the story is hard to put down."

"The story enthralled me. The characters intrigued me. The mystery kept me on the edge of my seat. Susan Wise Bauer's tale of a young seminary couple's first pastorate in the Virginia countryside and the surprises they encounter is the best novel I've read in years."

"Bauer tells us a cracking good story of sin and grace and of the places they meet. The author respects her characters, and she presents them with a wonderful blend of judgment and love. Some of the scenes are heartbreaking in their depth of understanding. And the narrator is so attractive that you want her to step out of the novel and show up for dinner."

Though the Darkness Hide Thee

A NOVEL

SUSAN WISE BAUER

Multnomah Publishers *Sisters, Oregon*

THOUGH THE DARKNESS HIDE THEE
published by Multnomah Publishers, Inc.
and in association with the literary agency of
the Richard Henshaw Group

© 1998 by Susan Wise Bauer
International Standard Book Number: 1-57673-237-1

Cover photograph © 1998 Kevin Laubacher/Photogroup/FPG

Printed in the United States of America

For information:
MULTNOMAH PUBLISHERS, INC.
POST OFFICE BOX 1720
SISTERS, OREGON 97759

Library of Congress Cataloging-in-Publication Data:

Bauer, S. Wise.
    Though the darkness hide thee/by S. Wise Bauer.
        p.   cm.
    ISBN 1-57673-237-1 (alk. paper)
    I. Title.
PS3552.A83638T48   1998   98–10258
813'.54—dc21   CIP
     98 99 00 01 02 03 04 — 10 9 8 7 6 5 4 3 2 1

For Peter
we are the exiles, living as listeners
with hearts attending to the skies we cannot comprehend
yet waiting for the first far drums of Christ, the coming King

Acknowledgments

Thanks to Marilyn Helms and John Wilson for reading early drafts and commenting wisely on them; to Rod Morris, whose patience has finally paid off; and to my agent, Rich Henshaw, for always keeping my best interests in mind. As writer, mother, teacher, and member of a community of faith, I'm always aware that any creative work of mine is a collaborative effort: I owe my parents, Jay and Jessie Wise, all my thanks for baby-sitting, brainstorming, fact checking, cooking, laundry folding, and above all for showing me what it means to live in God's presence and (often) in his apparent absence.

My greatest gratitude and all my love go to my husband, who has taken on himself much more than his share of responsibility for our home and children, and who continues to do the hardest job on earth with grace, compassion, and wisdom.

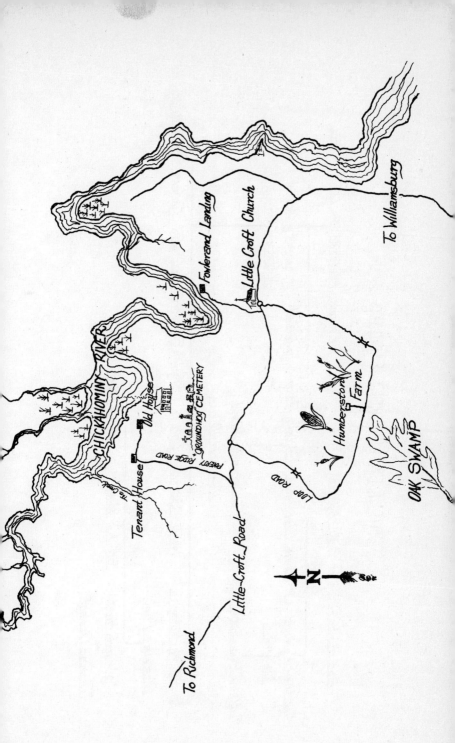

THE LITTLE CROFT FAMILIES

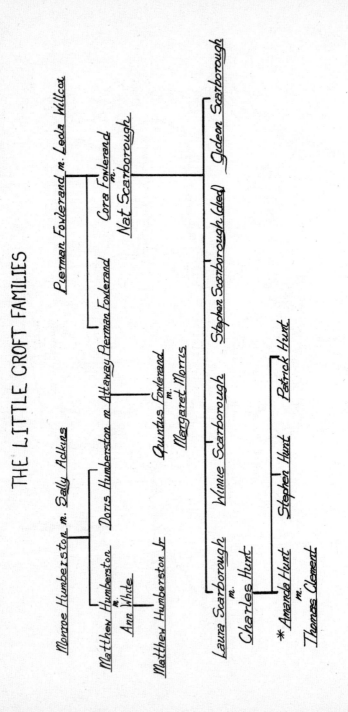

Chapter One

I wanted to go home.

Even the word was sweet, like candy in the mouth. Thomas and I had married in Philadelphia, among his friends; they were grad-school friends, closer than brothers until May, when they all scattered from the little ivy-covered campus like siblings escaping a tyrannous parent and never, never saw each other again. Thomas's family was salted thinly through the Midwest, and mine had suddenly shifted and changed and become unrecognizable. I'd grown up in Little Croft, Virginia, and when I thought of the fields and the black star-filled sky and the patches of old pines, I felt the warmth of a child, curled under the comfort of her nursery blankets after a long and noisy trip to an unfamiliar place.

I dreamed about Little Croft the night before we came back. I saw the white dust lanes between the ancient leaning maples, the wide brown stretches of plowed field, a hawk circling overhead with its wild adventurous shriek drifting down to earth. The pictures of my childhood came back to me in my dreams, like beautiful flat images in a mirror.

We drove into Little Croft on a scorching August evening with two Saint Bernards bulging out of the backseat of Thomas's tiny hatchback. Corn stood high on both sides of the unpainted blacktop road. Little Croft was steeped in sunset. A morning rain had washed the fields and trees, and now the red sun dazzled us, glowing back from every smooth surface.

Thomas rolled his window down and shoved his sunglasses up onto his head. It was a wide gesture of content. Hot air flowed in around us.

"Let's go to the church first," he suggested.

"Mr. Whitworth said people would be waiting at the house to help us move in."

"Just for a minute?"

I grinned at him. The new church was the start of a brand-new adventure, the first page of an unknown story, and much more exciting than the narrow two-story frame house we'd be moving into. The Saint Bernards were fighting to get their huge damp heads out of Thomas's window. I rolled my own window down, and Chelsea plunged over to my side of the car.

"Do I keep going straight? Last time we came from the other direction."

"It's up on the left, just past Fowlerand Road."

We drove past the dangling brown sign that marked the entrance to my grandmother's farm. A little farther on, a paved turnoff led onto the Loop Road, where Matthew Humberston reigned over a thousand acres of farmland. A mile past the Loop, a cluster of little gray houses gave way to larger homes with screened-in porches and multiple chimneys. A patch of woods, a wheat field, and then a grove of ancient maple trees surrounding the tiny white-board church: Little Croft Church, two hundred years old. The congregation had dwindled to a handful.

We parked on the packed dirt of the front lot and climbed out, pushing the dogs back in and slamming the doors against their eager noses. Above the church's double front doors, a faded white sign read Little Croft Church, Established 1792.

Thomas stood, tilting his head back to look up at the facade. He was tall, lean and light-haired, Ivanhoe with a flat Midwestern drawl. He'd spent the last five years directing a bustling young-adult program at a prosperous Philadelphia church, a majestic old building with a huge pipe organ and a huge charity mission and far, far too much political maneuvering.

I went up the steps and tried the doorknob. The doors swung inward at once. Clear light fell through the plain arched windows, onto the old red runner between the pews. There were twenty pews with straight walnut backs, cushioned in faded red that matched the carpet. A tiny gallery above our heads held three more rows of seats, reached by a breakneck spiral stair. The smell of bare polished wood and old cloth instantly brought to mind vacation Bible school: juice in a paper cup and two cookies that tasted vaguely of almond. Behind the tiny choir loft, red curtains masked the baptistry. Little Croft Church had been founded by English nonconformists on the run from the established Church. It remained prickly with independence, even as it wasted away.

Thomas walked up the aisle and disappeared through the door behind the small organ. I wandered up to the choir loft and peeked through the baptistry curtains. A spider had built an elaborate web in one corner. Above the dry tiles, someone had painted a dreadful mural of an enormous blue-eyed Christ with the sun rising behind him, welcoming scores of tiny men and women into his Godzilla-sized arms. I drew my finger through the dust along the near side.

"Amanda?"

I let the baptistry curtains close and scrambled down from the choir loft. Thomas had discovered the pastor's office, set at the end of an old white-plastered hallway at the back of the church. The room was tiny, with bookshelves apparently designed for miniature commentaries and a desk that Thomas could barely fit his long legs beneath. But the window looked out over a great golden field behind the church lot, and an oak tree five feet around shaded the back steps.

The window frame was swollen with heat and age. Thomas put his shoulder into it. The sash lifted with a jerk. The hot smell of brown-tasseled corn curled in and around us; a breeze stirred the dust on the desk and lifted the edges of a yellowed bulletin.

Thomas stood in the middle of the room and spread out his arms.

"On Sundays I can bring a Sunday school class back here," he said, "and we can have another one in the sanctuary, and put the children in that room across the hall."

He turned his head and grinned at me, and suddenly I felt the old lifting of the heart that used to come at the sound of his voice, a glimpse of his tall figure at the other end of a hallway, back in the days when we lived apart. Even after three years of marriage, I could never find the words that would give life to the sheer drowning love I felt for him. He put his hand out, and I twined my fingers through his.

"Are you happy?" he said.

"Yes," I said, truthfully enough. If I peered beneath the surface, I knew that Little Croft seemed oddly empty. I hadn't suggested yet that we drive by the house where I grew up, now sold to married lawyers who practiced in opposite directions and didn't tend the garden.

"I want you to be happy here."

"I know."

"Well then," he said, "let's go move in." He closed the door behind us and we walked down the steps together, his shoulder warm against mine. Daphne and Chelsea threw themselves against the windows of the car in frantic slobbering welcome.

We drove back along Little Croft Road to my grandmother's dirt lane. The brown sign swung just behind the mailbox: Poverty Ridge. An ironic name for the sprawling family farm, but it had been called Poverty Ridge when my grandfather was struggling to scratch a living from the red clay, and he'd refused to change the name even when the farm crawled across Little Croft County and into the surrounding counties. After his death, my grandmother had turned the running of Poverty Ridge over to her youngest son, my Uncle Giddy. The farm prospered, but the sign remained.

My grandmother, Cora Scarborough—née Fowlerand— had offered us a rent-free living, in the white Tenant House at the bend of Poverty Ridge Road. In exchange, I would help her with her housekeeping and shopping, cook her two meals a day, balance her checkbook, and put her hair in curlers. I'd been making a reasonable salary working for a north Philly advertising agency, but five years into my chosen profession, I knew I'd made a mistake. Writing ad copy tires the soul. The continual appeal to all that is shallow and self-centered gave me a mental rash; I always seemed to be scraping grime away from my imagination. The Little Croft salary was far from princely, but we thought that with careful management I could take at least a year off from ad copy and meditate on other careers.

When the firm offer from the Little Croft deacons arrived, I found myself shaken with a sudden, unexpected longing to go home. I'd been away from Little Croft for ten years. I could remember early-morning walks through the dawn fogs, the smell of fresh earth rising up and meeting the overlying warmth of the rising sun, beauty that swelled my heart until I thought it would burst with longing.

Home. I said the word out loud in the shower, in my car, in the beige-walled cubicle where I sat in front of my computer keyboard. Philadelphia became intolerable, a huge grimy waiting room one door away from a cool green field.

Poverty Ridge Road headed almost straight north for a mile and a half. The packed dirt lane cut narrowly through field after field of corn, took a sharp right turn at the edge of the Chickahominy River, and then ran another quarter mile before dead-ending at my grandmother's frame house. The Tenant House sat at the curve. The dirt road lay fifteen feet from its front porch; a steep bluff dropped down to the river behind. It was a tall skinny house, only one room deep but three rooms wide and two stories tall, with a kitchen lean-to on one side. Two children, sunburned from the summer river light, were racing up and down the road on muddy bikes. Someone was shaking a cloth out of an upstairs window.

We parked in the tiny backyard. A round placid man was sitting on the back steps, smoking a cigarette. He was short and plump and unworried, like a balding Fisher-Price figure. He got to his feet, dropped the cigarette without haste, and ground it out under his heel.

"I forgot," Thomas hissed. "Which deacon's that?"

"Ambrose Scarborough."

"Your—"

"Third cousin."

"Right." Thomas got out, deftly slamming the door against Daphne's lunge, and extended his hand. "Mr. Scarborough?"

"Reverend Clement," Ambrose said. His voice was unexpectedly high. "Glad to see you. Have a good drive?"

"Pretty good, thanks."

"Your movin' van came, round about noon. Put the stuff in all the wrong rooms. M' wife and me, we been movin' it to the kerrect places and doing some cleanin'. Amelia Whitworth came over for a little bit, and your Uncle Giddy was here for an hour or so." He smiled kindly at me as I emerged from the car. "An' a couple of Humberstons from down on the river are still 'round. Harold's wife and sister and a cousin. Place is in right good shape, now. You want to let them dogs out?"

"May as well," I said, answering Thomas's questioning look. He turned back and opened the driver's side door. The Saint Bernards catapulted themselves from the car, made three full-speed circuits of the yard, and then dove under the back porch and snuffled invisibly around.

"We should probably tie them up in the yard," Thomas said. "They're not used to all this space."

"Leave them," I said, wiping sweat off the bridge of my nose. "It's cool under there." A big swamp maple grew in the backyard, thrusting its top branches against the second-story windows and shading the whole back of the house.

"An' damp," Ambrose put in. "M' wife defrosted that there deep freeze for you an' it spread water everywhere. There was some deer in there that went back to Miss Clunie's time, so I 'spect the water smelled like rotten meat."

"Well," I said, "they ought to like that." The deep freeze

15

on the back porch was an ancient chest type, rusted around the edges. Bits of dirt flew out past the back steps; Daphne was making a nest. The shade under the back porch was cool, and the summer evening felt close to ninety.

"Come on in an' have a look at the place," Ambrose said, cheerfully, "an' then we'll be out of your hair."

He led us up the porch steps and in through the back door. We stood in a narrow central hallway that opened into large rooms on either side. The right-hand room had an old fireplace against one wall. Our sofa and chairs were jumbled in the middle of the floor. On the far side of the opposite room, a double doorway led into the lean-to kitchen. The stairway ascended on the left side of the hallway. Brown cardboard boxes lined every wall.

"You remember this house?" Ambrose inquired.

"Not very well," I said.

"This used to be the living room and Miss Clunie's bedroom, here with the fireplace." He jerked a thumb upwards. "Two smaller rooms and a bathroom, above. That there dresser, next to the fireplace, that's left from Miss Clunie's day. So's the little table in the east bedroom. Nothing in the kitchen, but Amelia unpacked some of your dishes before she had to go. Teakettle, fry pans, stuff she thought you'd need right away. There's m' wife, coming from upstairs."

Ida Scarborough was a vast woman, with a massive bust shrouded in a denim jumper and surmounted by a pink ceramic pin. She descended the narrow stairs with great care, shaking her head and clutching the rail until her feet were on flat boards.

"Afternoon to both of you," she said. "I see Giddy had that upstairs bedroom painted. That's the one where Miss Clunie

16

died, so it's good you got some fresh paint. Looks right nice now. I done unpacked your sheets and blankets so you can sleep tonight. An' Ambrose put in that window unit so you won't roast. It was mighty warm up there."

"Thank you," Thomas said, with real gratitude. "That's the one thing I was all geared up to do tonight. The rest can wait until tomorrow. Thank you so much."

Ida Scarborough smiled at him graciously. I'd known Ida since early childhood; she had sometimes come over to stay with us while my parents went out. She never would play games, but she would sit comfortably and tell stories for hours. I was conscious of a certain restraint in her welcome. When Ambrose led Thomas away to inspect the hot-water heater, she leaned forward so that her bosom brushed my shoulder. Her breath smelled of peppermints, and the scent of warm talcum powder billowed out from her folds and creases.

She murmured, "Mandy, darlin', I didn't want to say nothing in front of Reverend Clement, but I didn't unpack all them boxes. Thought it wasn't my place. I was surprised to see them, tell you the truth. In a pastor's house, too."

I cast rapidly back over the various intimate products I'd packed away. Silk underwear? Thomas's collection of Bloom County cartoon books? Birth control? Ida and Ambrose only had two children, spaced a careful three years apart, so that could hardly be it.

"All them liquor boxes," Ida said, dropping her voice another notch. "I mean, if a man has one beer, I guess that might be 'tween him and his God, and I won't say Ambrose himself hasn't succumbed to temptation a time or two, in his younger days. But there's all kinds of whisky boxes, dozens of 'em. Does he drink it all himself?"

"Oh, Mrs. Scarborough, those are all books. We had a liquor store just around the corner from us in Philadelphia, so we went and got all the empty boxes. They're just the right size for books."

"I see. Well, I'm right glad to hear it. My, you got a mighty big collection of books, don't you? You shoulda had Giddy build you some more shelves. But he's been spending all his time in the graveyard, I reckon. Well, let me round up my husband and shoo all them Humberstons out and give y'all some peace so's you can head for bed afore you collapse."

She recalled Ambrose from the pump house with some difficulty, and the Humberstons—three women whose faces were more familiar than their names, married to men I vaguely remembered—collected their children. They bumped away down the dirt road in pickups and compact cars, and Thomas and I were left alone in the Tenant House.

"I now know all that is to be known about pump houses," Thomas said.

"There's a cobweb in your hair."

He bent his fair head down, and I untangled the thick white strands. He said, his voice muffled, "What do we do now?"

"Go pay homage to my grandmother."

"Right away?"

"Oh, yes." Granny Cora was the matriarch of the family, and only a foolhardy Scarborough relation would dare to skimp on the proper attentions.

Thomas took my hand, lacing his long fingers through mine. His clear brown eyes were full of light. The slanting late sun came through the kitchen window and fell on him, illuminating the short hairs at the back of his neck so that each stood out, fine individual strands of gold.

"For the first time," he said, "I feel like I could settle in and find a home. Let's go see Granny Cora."

Chapter Two

We left the dogs snoring comfortably under the porch and walked down the dirt road toward the Old House. The lane was lined by a tumbledown wooden fence. Wild sumac grew all along the fence, its crimson leaves reaching up to the top rail. Halfway along the lane, the sumac had been trimmed away from a gateway, a gap that led onto a rutted road that ran away to the right: through the cornfield, up a slope, and into the ancient family graveyard. The stones were at the top of the hill, pale in the darkening air. Uncle Giddy was standing perfectly still in the middle of the graveyard.

"What's he doing?" Thomas murmured.

I shook my head, mystified. We walked on, past the chicken house and Uncle Giddy's kennel of hunting hounds, through the inevitable cluster of outbuildings that always surrounds old farmhouses. The Old House was famous for its view, perched on the high slopes of the Chickahominy above an emerald tangle of marsh. At the sound of our knock, Uncle Giddy's hounds erupted into howls.

"Come in!" Granny's voice ordered.

We stepped directly into the living room. Granny Cora was enthroned on her favorite recliner, her back to the river and her windows closed against the heat. "Well," she said. "Welcome back, Amanda. And you, of course."

Thomas bent down and kissed her on the cheek. She'd met him several times on our trips back to Little Croft, but it ill became a matriarch to remember the names of all her extended clan. Granny Cora was taller than I was, broad-shouldered and strong at eighty-one, with thin white hair pinned into flat coils all over her head. She fixed me with a steel blue gaze and added, "You're looking right puny."

"Thank you, Granny." I kissed her forehead. She never wore makeup, and the old skin was dry and clean. "What's Uncle Giddy doing?"

"Shooting a groundhog. Move that cat food and sit down." She waved the flyswatter in her right hand at the brown sofa across from her. Thomas shifted the greasy bowl of scraps from the upholstery and sat gingerly. My grandmother tended to live as though water still had to be hauled from the Chickahominy in buckets, up a seventy-foot hill.

A fat old hound uncurled itself from under the chair and wandered into the middle of the room. Granny said sharply, "Go lie down, Dog-dog!" The animal wiggled and grinned its way back behind her chair and flopped noisily onto the floor. Dog-dog had to be at least twenty; he'd been around since my childhood, growing fatter and slower every year.

"He's been after those groundhogs for a week," Granny went on, "and he hasn't shot one yet. They're coming up with bones again."

"Bones?" Thomas said.

"Giddy plowed over part of the old graveyard. Took up too much land. All that side of the field was old graves that he had to trim 'round every year. He left the newer ones. Put the rest in wheat. But the groundhogs have been coming up with bones. He's gone to try and shoot them."

Out of guilt, I imagined. The historical society would have a seizure. The Scarborough-Fowlerand graveyard predated the Civil War.

"The Tenant House looks good," I offered.

"Attaway told Giddy to paint it fresh for you. Mind," Granny Cora said, pointing the flyswatter at Thomas, "anyone who comes down from Philadelphia to live in the Tenant House at the bottom of my lane isn't wrapped any too tight. Why you'd come to preach out here in Little Croft, I can't imagine. Weren't you good enough to get a job at one of them fine city churches?"

I was never sure whether Granny's barbs were the result of a failing mind or sheer malice, but a glint in her blue eyes made the latter more likely. Thomas smiled at her, unruffled.

"I had a job at one of those fine city churches," he said. "I was spending all my time running parties and doing paperwork. Philadelphia has dozens of churches, and Little Croft only has one little church without a pastor. I thought I could be of more use here."

"Little Croft kills churches," Granny said. "Sucks the life out of them and spits 'em out."

"Did you ever go to Little Croft Church, Mrs. Scarborough?"

"Oh, I went long ago, back when I had four children 'tween two and eight and a husband workin' fourteen-hour days out in the fields. I was young then. Preacher told me to hold my tongue, I recall, and keep the meals warm so's my husband wouldn't feel like wanderin'."

"Did he start wandering?"

"Beg pardon?"

"The warm meals—did they work?"

"Never you mind," Granny said, her ears turning slightly pink. "I reckon I hope things go well for you. But there's no preacher yet that's made any difference to this county. God's forgotten we're here, and we're doing just fine."

"You'll have to come hear me preach."

"Huh," Granny said. "Let's see if you last, first. If you're still preaching in a year, I might believe there's something in it. Soon's you get yourself unpacked, Amanda, you c'n come balance my checkbook and clean out the basement for me. Both in a mess. And ain't no one been to see me for two whole days. I might as well be dead."

We came back to the Tenant House in the August twilight. The dogs had disappeared, venturing out to explore their new kingdom in the feathery darkness. Upstairs, the overhead lights cast a harsh white glare over our room: boxes and scattered packing paper and bags bulging with miscellaneous possessions. But Ambrose had put our bed frame together, and Ida had found the linens box and put fresh sheets on the mattress. She'd even dug out our towels and left them folded neatly on the end of the bed.

We took turns showering; the old porcelain tub in the bathroom was surrounded by a circular rod with a battered curtain on it, and Thomas had to duck his head to fit underneath the showerhead. Years of mineral-rich well water had left a deep pitted ring around the drain. When we were finally clean, we cut off the lights, fell onto the mattress, and let the blast of cold air from the little window unit wash over us. Rich dark silence lay all around us.

"Want to celebrate?" Thomas suggested.

"After nine hours in the car and half an hour with Granny Cora?"

"We survived both. All the more reason to celebrate."

I laughed. His skin was fire-warm, welcome in the cold rush of air conditioning. I put Granny's grumpy skepticism and the narrow musty halls of the Tenant House away from my mind. This was our own place, a sphere of intense and private belonging. The moon was rising; the glass panes had begun to shine with silver, patching the walls in squares of pure shadowy light.

I woke, just past midnight, to the familiar sound of Uncle Giddy's hunting hounds howling at the wind. Thomas shifted beside me, pulled the pillow over his head, and subsided back into sleep. I lay listening to the hounds, to the low chanting sound of frogs in the Chickahominy marsh, to the scrape of the swamp maple's branches against the wooden siding. I was wide awake and restless.

I got up eventually, pulled on shorts and a T-shirt, and wandered around the house in the moonlight, thinking about our furniture. We needed a new bed if we were going to have a spare room, but maybe we could use Miss Clunie's old dresser for visitors. It was a nice piece of walnut with a tilting mirror attached to its top; when I opened the top drawer, dust and faded lavender breathed out at me. The mirror was wedged at a funny angle. A wad of paper had been thrust into the joint to keep the glass tilted downwards. I worked the paper out and straightened the mirror so that I could see the dim reflection of my face.

I unfolded the paper a little later, while I was standing in the kitchen waiting for the teakettle to boil. It was a page torn from a notebook, and the writing on it had faded to pale yellow.

Desperate. Desperete. You made me desperate. You
never loved me, and I only loved you out of desperation because he never looked at me, never touched me.
Out of desperetion.

The letters were round and childish; it was the handwriting of someone—a woman?—who did not write often. I
formed a picture in my mind. Miss Clunie, young and darkhaired, sat writing a last despairing note to a lover, wondering
how to spell a word; she reached for a scrap piece of paper, jot-
ted it down, wrote out a sentence to see whether it looked right
in context. She'd sent the letter, thrust the scraps into a drawer,
and later crumpled them into a ball to wedge her mirror. I was
having trouble with this picture; Miss Clunie had been a thin
silent bitter woman, as far back as I could remember. The kettle
was boiling. I put the paper down and saw in the slanting light
fainter letters, farther down on the page, scrawled sideways
across the lines as though running unheeded over the edge of a
page that came before.

...*will kill me.*

Chapter Three

I slept late the next morning and woke up to find Thomas's pillow empty. When I went down the narrow staircase, I could see him through the windows of the front room; he was sitting on the top step of the porch, watching the green fields glitter under the morning sun. I went into the kitchen and dug through boxes until I found our coffeepot and the half-can of coffee. Ida Scarborough had left us a coffee cake in a Tupperware container: cream cheese, brown sugar, eggs, and lots of butter. Ah well, I thought, cutting lavish slices. The first breakfast in a new house ought to be luxurious.

I made coffee and took a tray out onto the porch. Thomas turned his head. He'd been reading Thomas à Kempis, as he often did in his morning silences; opening the day with the Christian mystics was a habit he'd developed in seminary, as a way of balancing out his reasonable Presbyterian education.

"Coffee cake!" he said, pleased.

"Have you seen the dogs this morning?"

"Yes, they're asleep on the back porch. Caked up to the eyeballs with river mud."

I put the tray on the top step and sat down next to him. Fresh morning air blew the steam from the coffee cups into wisps. Boats were already on the river; the distant burr of motors was joined by a tractor starting, the rattle of a combine trundling its heavy way down Poverty Ridge Road, Giddy's rooster vocalizing in the chicken yard.

"I thought I might go over to the church this morning and

unpack my books," Thomas said.

"Okay."

"You don't mind if I take the car for a couple of hours?"

"No, I'll start opening boxes."

"I can't wait to get started here," Thomas said. He sat with his elbows on his knees, gazing out across the fields. *The Imitation of Christ* lay on the porch beside him.

"Really?"

"Yes, of course. Why?"

"I'm still surprised you wanted to come to Little Croft at all."

"Why?"

"Well, it's not really a plum job, is it? Remember the placement office told us, back when we were working on your résumé, that churches were getting sixty and seventy applications for every opening? And Ambrose told me last night that Little Croft Church heard from two other candidates. One was eighty and the other was twenty-one and straight out of Bible college."

"I saw something, when I was working in Philadelphia," Thomas said. "We started out, all of us on staff, trying to be like Christ, but something happened in that church; we were remaking Christ in our own minds, turning him into a picture of our own wants. Mike wanted to be like Christ the wonder-worker, Joshua wanted to be like Christ the judge…and I wanted to be like the Christ who rode into Jerusalem while everyone shouted Hosanna. I needed to get away from big crowds, Amanda, away from people who told me what a wonderful job I was doing and what a great future I had. I thought that maybe, out here, I could understand who Christ really is; not the Christ that I wanted him to be."

He ducked his head away from me, suddenly self-conscious, and ate a piece of coffee cake.

"I didn't know," I said.

"Well, I was working on intuition. When you heard from your relatives about this job, I knew it would be good to try to find a place where we could put down roots. But beyond that, I thought: Little Croft would be good for me. I wasn't really sure why, though. Not till now, when I've had a chance to think."

He stood up, dusting crumbs from his hands.

"I can come move furniture for you as soon as I get back," he said.

I rose as well and wrapped my arms around him. He bent his head down and kissed me. Over his shoulder, I could see the silos in a gleaming silver row, and the green-gold field of corn beyond the white curve of the lane. The sky was impossibly blue. The whole scene was like something out of a medieval book of heraldry, like the enameled crest of a noble family: Gold and silver rampant against an azure field.

He drove off to the church; I went back into the kitchen to wash the breakfast plates. A truck motor putted past the house, but I paid no attention until the kitchen telephone began to ring. When I picked up the receiver, Granny Cora's voice said, "Amanda? Come over here. I want to see you for a bit."

The dial tone buzzed in my ear. I hung up with a grimace. We had agreed that I would start working for Granny the following week, after we were unpacked. But having a poor relation just down the road was likely to prove far too tempting for her. I ran my fingers through my hair and decided not to bother with a shower.

A flock of crows in the tops of the oaks chuttered and scrambled above my head as I went up Granny's front steps. Inside, Granny had turned on her window-unit air conditioning. The room was cool, and dog hair moved in faint swirling eddies across the linoleum. Dog-dog uncurled from the mat and wandered arthritically away into a bedroom.

Giddy was sunk disconsolately in a green plush chair. My uncle, Gideon Scarborough, had my grandfather's thin height and craggy features and Granny Cora's blue eyes. He was ten years older than his youngest sibling, my mother; his eyes had faded to a dull watery blue.

Granny was enthroned on the sofa, and across from her sat her older brother, Attaway Pierman Fowlerand, the patriarch of the clan. Great-uncle Attaway was a Little Croft icon; beyond him lay an entire invisible world, a maze of intricate genealogical loyalties and ancient obligations and hostilities. At family gatherings, I'd sometimes heard dark mutterings about Attaway's ruthlessness as he built a Little Croft empire; he had a passion for land that came from innate greed and (in my mother's opinion) from a scornful father who had always insisted he'd amount to nothing. Attaway was a clean-shaven, heavy man with a face full of complicated folds, sparse white hair brushed straight back, and light blue eyes almost lost in the cleft of a farmer's squint. He never wore a farming coverall; for sixty years, he'd put on a clean shirt and bow tie every morning before heading out into the fields. Little Crofters laughed at him, but rarely to his face.

He sat with his hands folded on the head of a cane and his blue Ford cap centered on his knees. Today, the shirt was light blue and the bow tie was a tasteful contrast in maroon and cream. His dark green pickup was parked behind Giddy's, visible through the side window above the kitchen sink.

"You remember Amanda?" Granny said. "Laura's girl. Just moved back with her husband. Clement, his name is. Thomas Clement. He's at Little Croft Church."

Great-uncle Attaway nodded. He didn't bother to get up.

"Haven't seen you since you were in school," he said. "You look like your mama. How's she doin'?"

"Very well," I said.

Attaway sniffed skeptically. My parents had moved to Montana two years ago to be near my brother Stephen, who was alone with two-year-old twins after his young wife walked out. Stephen needed them more than I did, and much more than they needed to keep the old tin-roofed farmhouse on Fowlerand Lane. They had sold their piece of family property for a hugely inflated price and bought a house at the foot of a mountain. In Little Croft, this was considered roughly equal to pitching diamonds into the nearest swamp and moving to Nepal.

"So she tells you, anyway," he said. "Hear your husband's not getting paid enough to keep a fly in molasses."

"Well, just about enough. We're hoping the church will grow."

"Huh," Attaway said. "Not with them Humberstons in charge."

I scratched my nose, which was beginning to itch under the combined insults of dog hair and dust. Great-uncle Attaway was slightly demented on the subject of the Humberstons. He had married one, years ago, and after her untimely death the Humberstons and Fowlerands had mutated into deadly enemies. Matthew Humberston was Great-uncle Attaway's personal Lucifer. He also happened to be one of the deacons who had hired us. I said, "You'll have to come to church, Uncle Attaway, and show them how it's done."

Attaway snorted. "Last time I went to church was thirty years ago. Preacher kept talking about the rich man and Lazarus, so I got up in the middle and left and never went back. Isn't moral to put beggars into Abraham's bosom and hard-workin' men into flames. I'm right certain that's not what Jesus meant to say."

"Hah!" Giddy said suddenly. Two brown dots were moving cautiously between the stones of the distant graveyard. Giddy rose up out of his chair, grabbing his rifle.

"You open the front door and they'll go back underground," Great-uncle Attaway warned.

"I'll go out the back," Giddy said. He clattered through the little kitchen toward the back porch. We heard the screen door creak open, very slowly. A moment later the top of Giddy's feed cap crept silently by the kitchen window. The brown splotches sat up on their hind legs, sniffed the air, and dove underground. Uncle Giddy swore. The feed cap reversed directions.

"He oughta poison the creatures and be done with it," Attaway said. "Well, let me get on my way, Cora. I'll be in Richmond till late. Meeting my lawyer. Need anything?"

"You might send Quintus over with his rifle," Granny Cora suggested. "Giddy's eyes aren't good enough to hit a barn these days."

The screen door banged and Giddy reappeared. "Dratted rodents," he said, and settled gloomily back into his chair.

"I'll tell Quintus to come by later," Attaway said.

"Don't need 'im," Uncle Giddy snapped.

"You do," Granny retorted. "You're blind as a mole."

"I hit that grackle on the wing last week!

I ventured, "I've got to go finish unpacking—"

"Giddy, you jumped in the middle o' them grackles and sprayed the yard with enough shotgun pellets to choke a mule. Somethin' was bound to come down."

"Well, I sure don't need Quintus. I've got them traps out in every burrow."

"Granny—" I began again.

"Those groundhogs ain't going anywhere near your traps. They got more sense than you do."

"Mama, you ain't been out in the field for twenty years. Them groundhogs got so many escape holes—"

"Tell Quintus I'll give him dinner if he comes up," Granny said to Attaway.

"But Mama—"

I gave up and retreated through the back door. Poverty Ridge Road led back to the Tenant House, but to the east a narrow footpath led down a slight ridge into a thick wood. As children, we had used that path to cut across to the farm from Fowlerand Lane. The Chickahominy glittered in front of me; the path wound away to my right. A breeze blew up off the river. Eventually I turned left and walked away from the shaded path, back down the warm white dust of the road, towards where the Tenant House stood in the shade of the big green maple.

Chapter Four

I wandered through the rooms in the dim indoor daylight, wondering where to start unpacking. I hadn't been in the Tenant House since just after my college graduation, when it had been occupied by an elderly cousin universally known as Miss Clunie. Her lime green curtains still hung at the upstairs windows, and the faint reek of illness lingered in the fireplace room where she had spent her days. I stuffed the curtains into the burn barrel in the backyard and opened all the windows. Old houses in the country smelled different than old houses in the city; in Philadelphia, the lingering scent of years of living bore traces of mothballs and cooked cabbage. Here, the familiar mustiness was overlaid by decades of drifting wheat dust and the tang of fertilizer.

I decided to unpack all the books in the fireplace room. We could build bookshelves beside the fireplace; the mantel was an old oak beam, and the front window overlooked Poverty Ridge's great spreading fields. The movers had piled Thomas's old wooden desk and our reading chairs and bookshelves into a heap in the middle of the floor. I pushed furniture around, unrolled our faded crimson-and-blue study rug, and started unpacking books. All our old favorites: my Southern writers, Thomas's Christian mystics, the Victorian poets, Jane Austen, and Charlotte Brontë. I dipped into the books at random, sitting cross-legged in the middle of the rug with stacks of books all around me. Sun slanted through the window, turning the old dim rug on the floor into a square of deep glowing color. A warm breeze blew through the window. At the Big Barn, halfway down the dirt road, several men were climbing over a harvester with tools in hand. When I leaned forward, I could see Uncle Giddy, trudging empty-handed back down the graveyard road.

I settled back and felt something crumple in my pocket. I'd shoved the wad of paper from Miss Clunie's dresser into the pocket of my shorts the night before and hadn't taken it out. I flattened the paper on top of Eudora Welty's collected short stories and again read those sprawling words: ...*will kill me.*

For a moment, I had an odd prickle down my spine, as though two separate worlds were about to rub catastrophically together. I shook my head impatiently, and as I did so I felt that someone was standing behind me. I turned my head sharply and heard Ida Fowlerand's voice in my memory: *That's the room Miss Clunie died in, so it's good you got some fresh paint.* But the Tenant House foundations were Civil War era; I doubted that Miss Clunie was the only person who'd ever died here.

I got up with a shiver and went to the kitchen to make a pot of coffee. Another pickup was driving up the dirt road. It slowed at the curve of the road and pulled into the Tenant House yard. I went to the back door and saw Quintus Fowlerand unfolding his long frame from behind the wheel.

"Hey, Quintus!"

"Hey, Amanda!" he called back.

I went across the grass to hug him. Underneath the denim shirt, his shoulders were hard muscle and bone and not much else. He'd always been thin, but I thought he'd lost weight since my last visit. He blinked down at me, half smiling. Quintus was Attaway's only son, which made him (I thought) my first cousin, once removed. He was in his midthirties, tall and mournful and dry-humored; in his face, the heavy Fowlerand features were pared down to spare elegance. His hair was bleached almost white by long summer days, and his big hands were stained. Quintus and I had always been good friends. He'd taught me to cast overhand, when I was seven and he was a lofty fifteen. Ten years later he had let me drive his stick shift up and down Poverty Ridge Road until I figured it out. I'd seen him infrequently since his wedding five years ago. He'd been shining with happiness, untouched by Attaway's dour face and silent disapproval.

"I'm glad to see you," I said. "Come in and look at my house."

"Well, I'm supposed to go shoot a clutch of groundhogs for Aunt Cora. But I reckon another half an hour of life won't make no difference."

"You're not going to shoot them anyway. Uncle Giddy's already been out there this morning and scared them all underground. Want some coffee?"

"Sure," Quintus said, following me into the Tenant House. "Daddy said he read Giddy the act about gettin' this place painted. Looks good. Smells better too."

"What did it smell like?"

"Miss Clunie, mostly." Quintus sat down at my kitchen table, an ancient meat-cutting table I'd scrounged from Granny Cora's attic and refinished long before I met Thomas. I handed him a cup of coffee and said, "You ever heard of a ghost in this house?"

"You got the creeps already?"

"Just an occasional shiver. Does Miss Clunie haunt it?"

"Huh," Quintus said. "I reckon Miss Clunie had plenty

enough of this house whilst she was livin'. No, I ain't never heard of any ghosts around Little Croft. Exceptin' the Loop Road lady, of course, and the soldier on Fowlerand Road."

The Loop Road ghost was a woman in white who'd been murdered by her husband back in 1920, because he found her with a lover. The lover fled; the husband cut his wife's throat and set out for Richmond on foot. The woman's brothers caught him a mile from the courthouse, dragged him back to the Loop, and hanged him on an old oak beside the house. The house had long fallen down, but the old oak still stood. The hanging limb jutted out across the first curve of the road.

"I seen her once," Quintus said, solemnly.

"Sure you did. Wringing her hands and wailing?"

"No, just standing there beside the tree, lookin' up. I never seen the soldier, but Peggy saw him once on her way home from work. Walking along with a black dog at his heel. She said he was whistlin' and looked happy as a dead man can look."

"How's Peggy doing?"

"Peggy's okay," Quintus said. "She's not been…real happy. She wants a baby, and nothin's happened in five years."

"I'm sorry," I said.

"Yeah." He turned the mug around and around, absently. "How long you been married now, Amanda?"

"Three years."

"Well, it'll hit you soon then."

"Maybe."

"I never thought I wanted kids either, when we got married. Never was gonna get married, either, so that don't say much. But Peggy always wanted a baby. She's been to three specialists in Richmond and had two operations at MCV, and still nothin'."

He took a swig of coffee. I sat down and had a good long

look at him from across the table. The bones of his face stood out underneath the skin, and the corners of his mouth were drawn down into sharp grim lines.

"What's in this stuff?" he asked.

"It's angelica. Hazelnut coffee."

"You been gone too long," Quintus said.

"How's the farm?"

"Busy. Daddy deeded half of it to me last month."

"That's good news, isn't it?" I was surprised. Relations between Quintus and Attaway must have warmed considerably since I'd last visited.

"Tryin' to avoid estate tax, that's all."

"But he trusts you."

"He don't have no choice. He's eighty-five and movin' slower these days. He brought Roland and Pierman into the farm two years ago—"

"Harold's sons?"

"Yeah, and a couple of lazy triflers they are, just like Harold. I think Daddy meant to cut me out, but Roland and Pierman can't run the place. They spend most of every day propping up the barns in the company of a six-pack. Less than worthless. He knows it, but he won't say so."

"Here," I said, helplessly. "Have a cookie." I pushed the plate towards him, and he grinned slightly and took two.

"It ain't any worse than usual." Quintus heaved himself up, cramming the last bit of cookie in his mouth. "Well, guess I better get goin'. Aunt Cora's not so patient as she once was." His tall head nearly brushed against the low old ceiling. With the light behind him he looked impossibly thin, a cardboard cutout of a man. He added suddenly, "I'm glad you're back, Amanda."

"I am too. I wanted to come home."

"Pity you have to live here, instead of on Fowlerand Road. Miss your old place?"

"I haven't been to look at it yet."

"I don't blame you. It ain't always good for you, starin' at what could be, but isn't."

"Quintus, is there anything I can do?"

Quintus shrugged. His voice was casual, but there was a deep puzzled unhappiness behind it.

"You could go visit Peggy for me," he said. "She quit her job last month." He hesitated, and then added in a rush, looking out the window, "She has spells where she sits an' stares an' won't wash her hair or talk or eat."

"I'll call her today," I said.

"We're livin' at the old place, you know."

"With Attaway?" I said, startled. "No. I didn't know."

"Yeah. Me, I'd rather live in a swamp and swat mosquitoes. But I've been puttin' money away. We'll be able to build our own house without borrowing, when the land's mine. I promised Peggy when we got married that I wouldn't never get in debt. Well, I'm off. I'll see you later, Amanda."

I stood at the window and watched him pull away down the dirt lane. He parked in front of the Old House, climbed out of his truck, and went up the steps of Granny's house, rifle in hand and his fair head lit up by the hot August sun.

Late in the afternoon, I called Peggy. The old Fowlerand place was on the river, way at the end of the long winding road that led from the blacktop down through hundreds of acres of Fowlerand farmland. It was a big sprawling shabby place with lots of large, dusty rooms. Attaway had always lived in the kitchen and den just off the back door, letting the rest fall into disrepair. I imagined the telephone ringing through those dark empty spaces, Peggy hurrying down the big bare stairs to answer it, her blond head shining against the stained wallpaper.

But eventually an answering machine clicked on. Peggy's light sweet voice said, "This is the Fowlerand place. If you want to speak to Quintus, Peggy, or Attaway, leave a message and we'll call you back."

I said into the receiver, "Hi, Peggy, this is Amanda Clement—Amanda Hunt that was. Quintus's cousin. We've just moved back to Little Croft, and I thought maybe we could get together. Have lunch in Richmond, or something. Call me when you get a chance."

I left my number and hung up, deciding to try her again later if I didn't hear back. Peggy was from a well-to-do West End family, and her devout Catholic mother had practically disowned her for marrying a Protestant farmer who'd never finished high school. Peggy had been working at a Richmond bank, but if she had quit her job as Quintus said, it would do her good to get out of Little Croft for an afternoon. Attaway's constant company would be depressing for even the soundest of minds.

Thomas came home shortly after. He had unpacked his books and gone over tomorrow's sermon, and he was pleased with life and ready to make the Tenant House comfortable. We spent the rest of the day moving furniture and unpacking boxes. I forgot about calling Peggy again until long after dark. I sat on the edge of the bed and thought: It's way too late now. I'll call tomorrow after church.

Thomas went almost instantly to sleep. I lay next to him

with my eyes wide open. My muscles ached with effort, but the unmade phone call niggled at my mind. The maple branches tapped against the side of the house, and the low moan of Giddy's hounds rose and fell in the distance. I cut on the little bedside lamp and read Jane Austen until the words blurred and staggered in front of my eyes. When I finally slept, the lines of that old faded letter interwove and doubled persistently through my dreams.

Chapter Five

Thomas got up at six Sunday morning and went over to the church to deliver his sermon to the empty pews. This had been his pattern, on those rare occasions when he was allowed to occupy the Philadelphia pulpit. I heard him leave, squinted at the clock, and went gratefully back to sleep.

When the door slammed again, I thought in a rosy pink fog: He's forgotten something. His feet sounded on the steps.

"Amanda! It's five minutes after ten!"

I sat straight up in broad daylight. Thomas was standing in the door, divided between amusement and irritation. He was wearing his Sunday suit and his light hair was brushed into shining smoothness.

I leaped out of bed and charged into the shower. From underneath the running water, I heard the bathroom door creak open.

"Coffee's in the kitchen," Thomas said.

"No time for it!"

"Didn't you hear the alarm?"

"No, I slept right through it. I had a terrible night last night. Couldn't get to sleep."

"Why?"

"Miss Clunie's memory was bothering me, I think. Will you go find my blue dress?"

Footsteps receded down the hallway. I lathered my hair frantically. A hand appeared above the shower rail, and Thomas's voice inquired, "This one?"

"No, no, there's a slit in the back of that one, it's too high for Little Croft Church. The blue one with the white vine pattern around the collar."

He retreated. I shaved my legs with skin-ripping speed and dried myself off.

"Can't find it," Thomas said, returning.

I ran back down the hallway to the bedroom and dug through the pile of unpacked clothes. The blue dress was all the way at the bottom, far too wrinkled to be worn, and I hadn't found the iron yet. I tried on three different outfits (too short, too form-fitting, too much collarbone) and finally stuffed myself into a black skirt and white blouse; unexceptionable, unflattering, and dowdy. I followed Thomas down the porch steps, tugging irritably at the waistband. His mouth was twitching with suppressed laughter.

"You look very nice," he said, starting the car.

"I look like my Aunt Winnie."

"Maybe we should discuss the reasons your subconscious doesn't want to go to church."

"Wasn't my subconscious. I think we have ghosts."

"Oh, sure." Thomas slowed at the end of Poverty Ridge Road and turned left onto the blacktop. I picked lint industriously off the front of my skirt. We drove past the turnoff to the Loop, where the road dropped away down a low hill. I glimpsed the hanging oak, standing starkly at the bottom. Clouds were beginning to coat the rim of the sky, and the air was still and damp; an August thunderstorm was on its slow way in.

The Little Croft congregation numbered around forty, scattered through pews designed for two hundred. Ambrose

Scarborough and the other two deacons—a tall silent man named John Whitworth, and Matthew Humberston, brother to Great-uncle Attaway's dead wife—had warned us of this. The previous pastor had carried a bitter soul underneath a smiling face, and attendance had dwindled to a handful even before he delivered his final biting sermon. But new families were moving to Little Croft, which stood halfway between Richmond and Williamsburg, convenient for two-career couples driving to different cities. The congregation was bound to grow again.

A cluster of familiar faces occupied the pews: Fowlerands, Humberstons, Watkinses, Whites, Scarboroughs, and Mileses. I'd half hoped to see Quintus and Peggy, but Quintus had never been a churchgoer, and if Peggy went at all I imagined she drove down to the Catholic church at Northend. Ida Scarborough was there early, handing out bulletins in a billowing cloud of lemon scent. Matthew Humberston and his son arrived five minutes before the call to worship, both of them wearing dark suits without ties. I sat on the left front pew, in lonely splendor. The third deacon, John Whitworth, arranged himself on the right-hand front pew and promptly went to sleep, sitting straight up and silent between his wife and her sister.

The pianist was seventy-five and well meaning. We creaked through two hymns and sat down for the offertory: a slightly uncertain rendition of "Work, for the Night Is Coming" by the choir, three sheepish men and seven women. I'd never heard the hymn before. The All Saints repertory tended towards the triumphant and optimistic.

Work till the last beam fadeth, fadeth to shine no more;
Work, for the night is coming, when man works no more.

The melancholy lines twined around me. Thomas was sitting in the pastor's chair, up on the dais; an elegant carved-wood throne with forest green cushions. I couldn't see his face. I bent my head over the bulletin, reading the announcements to block the hymn from my mind. Clouds had sealed over the sky; the air inside the church had gone gray with the coming storm. The dark velvet curtains of the baptistry absorbed the light from the recessed bulbs over the choir loft so that the singers were lost in shadow.

> Work when the day grows brighter, work in the glowing
> sun,
> Work, for the night is darkening, when man's work is
> done.

I progressed from the midweek prayer meeting, through the list of shut-ins, to the final bulletin announcement. *The new pastor and his wife will be pounded in the fellowship hall, directly after the service. Bring a potluck dish and stay for Sunday lunch!* I adjusted the syntax in my mind while the last minor chords dragged to an end. The choir closed their books and sat down. I shivered, ridding myself of the lingering sense of catastrophe. I'd had premonitions of disaster all my life; never did they come true.

Thomas stood back up. He had decided to preach all the way through the gospel of Luke. Thomas had been wasted in youth work; he could make a genealogy seem full of mystical meaning. I listened to him explain, clearly and forcefully, how God broke into the human sphere. When he bent his head for the final prayer, I sneaked a look over my shoulder. Here and there, in the faces of his listeners, I saw a glint of understanding.

"God the Father," Thomas said, "God the Son, and God the Holy Spirit bless you and keep you. May the Lord make his face to shine upon you and be gracious to you. May the Lord lift up his countenance upon you, and give you peace. Amen." A sudden escaping ray of sun illuminated his hair, the white collar of his shirt, the glint of gold on his fourth finger.

The fellowship hall, built in 1959, was a little white-board building at the back of the church property. It was connected to the church by a brick sidewalk, and the graveyard lay just behind it. Children ran around the building, skirting the graveyard, while the women laid out the food inside.

Thomas and I stood together on the sidewalk, smiling and shaking hands. Clouds had thickened across the dome of sky, and thunder rumbled faintly down on the river. The leaves on the maples were whipping back and forth, showing their pale undersides. The afternoon had taken on a strange, backlit doubleness; the grass summer-bright and dry, the air darkening with fall storm. Inside the fellowship hall, someone was hurrying to close windows.

We stepped through the door into a comfortable chattering of voices. A window air conditioner was going full blast. People were already moving by us with paper plates full of food, and dishes lined a folding table along one wall. Corn pudding, string beans, roast, macaroni and cheese, pans of biscuits, baked tomatoes, chicken oven fried and covered with rich buttery gravy, gallons of iced tea. Across the front of the room, another table was hung with crepe paper and loaded with goods: flour, sugar, shortening, canned goods, jam and peaches, and a mop bucket full of brand-new cleaning supplies. Little Crofters hadn't restricted themselves to a pound of food each. There was enough there to keep us for weeks.

"Well then," John Whitworth said, just behind us, "help yourselves. We saved you a place down there."

He pointed down towards the end of the room, where several tables had been set up in front of a cold fireplace. Ambrose and Ida were already seated and eating hard. Another grumble of thunder rattled along the river, coming closer.

"Better get it quick," John said, "'fore all them people outside come runnin' in."

He moved on ahead of us, collecting a plate and starting to fill it. John Whitworth was lanky, solemn, slow talking, and slow moving. His wife Amelia had organized the potluck and was now busy running the show; I could hear her sharp decisive voice clearly through the happy hum of conversation. The familiar Little Croft voices lulled me into pleasant security. I kept seeing familiar faces, smiling and greeting us as we moved along, scooping food onto our plates. Old neighbors, school friends, childhood acquaintances; I'd swum in the Chickahominy or played raucous birthday games with half the people there. Three times, I thought I heard my mother. Each time I turned to find a second cousin or distant aunt, standing and chattering in that distinctive Scarborough voice. I'd never been at a Little Croft gathering without my parents there: my mother the center of a listening group, my father leaning against the door, his gray eyes amused and distant.

We carried our sagging plates to where Ambrose and Ida Scarborough sat, and a moment later Matthew Humberston arrived with his son.

I set my plate down and said hi to Matt Jr. He was younger than I was, a tall dark boy with a perpetual slouch and an unshaven chin. Matt jerked his head in greeting and devoted himself to his bacon and sausage. His father looked down at him severely.

"Be civil, Matt," he said.

"Hey," Matt mumbled.

I sat down across from Matthew Sr. Since my Great-uncle Attaway had married Matthew's oldest sister, I was a relative of sorts, but we weren't well acquainted. Matthew Humberston was built slender, but his forearms were thick and blue veins stood out along his arms and his long-fingered hands. He had thick curly dark hair, long enough to tuck behind his ears, and a neatly trimmed dark beard. He'd always reminded me of a landlocked pirate; there was a certain lawless quality about him, and an eye patch would have suited him down to the ground.

"How's Dr. Hunt doin'?" Matthew inquired, buttering a biscuit.

"Dad's fine, thanks. He joined a family practice in Montana. He likes it out there."

"Well, we miss him here," Matthew said. "Dr. Hunt always told the truth. And we ain't had a family practice here since he left. Got to go to that clinic in Mercysmith."

Ambrose took a swig of tea and said, "I went to that clinic once. Ain't goin' again."

"Why not?" Matthew asked.

"All women there. Three of 'em. One I saw was called Gabriella. I ask you. Gabriella Jones-Boston. With a hyphen."

"Huh," Ida said, piling inch-thick butter on a biscuit. "You looked white as a haunt when you went, an' that stuff she gave you turned you pink and put you on your feet. I been goin' to her for two years now."

"Suit yourself," Ambrose said, amiably. They went on eating side by side with mutual satisfaction.

Matthew grinned across at Thomas. "So, Reverend," he said, "you got any plans for growin' this church?"

"I thought I'd go door to door, get a feel for the neighborhood. I'd like to start a summer youth camp. And expand vacation Bible school from one week to two. Maybe look into beginning a three-day preschool in the Sunday school rooms."

"That's a right good idea," Ida said, brightening. "Lots o' new families round here with small children."

"And I'd like us to join the Central Virginia Foodbank. Amanda tells me there's a section right down the road where people need help."

There was a short thoughtful pause. John Whitworth had settled himself at the far end of the table and was eating his way through an enormous chunk of roast.

"Winnville, that area's called," Ambrose said finally. "Black folks mostly."

"Yes?" Thomas said.

"Well, the black churches generally take care of their own. Rising Mount Zion, Little Elam, they go out to Winnville all the time."

"If there's still need, then the black churches can't do it alone."

"I reckon they help everyone that wants to be helped."

"You think no white folks out here are on food stamps?" Matthew asked.

"Didn't say that. Just don't want us to waste the reverend's time."

"Let him do what he wants," Matthew said. "I got a farm-hand living down in Winnville. Sister's got four boys and no husband. I'll give you her address, Reverend."

"Reverend Norris never went down that way," Ambrose offered.

"All th' better," Matthew said. "That man was pure poison. Maybe the reverend will find some ears he didn't drip all his sorrows into. I want me some more tea. Get you another glass, Reverend?"

"Thanks," Thomas said. Matthew collected his cup and walked away.

I heard an energetic clicking of heels behind me. Amelia Whitworth appeared at my elbow with one chicken leg and a single dab of potato salad on a virgin plate. She settled into the empty chair beside me: small, sharp and thin, with ash brown hair drawn back into a gold clip and quick brown eyes.

"So many people!" she said brightly. "All come out to honor you, Reverend Clement. My goodness, Amanda, haven't you gotten pretty! Pass me a napkin, would you, John? John!"

John, shaken out of his happy absorption, passed a napkin to his wife. She dabbed at her mouth daintily.

"An' have you settled into your grandmother's house?" she asked. "I'm right sorry I couldn't stay longer yesterday. Sure was plenty to do, getting the place clean and all."

"We're slowly unpacking," I said. "Most of our stuff is still in boxes."

"You miss your old house, I reckon."

"Yes, Mrs. Whitworth." Under the table, Thomas moved his foot to rest against mine.

"Place in good shape?"

"Uncle Giddy had it repainted and cleaned before we came."

"That's good," Amelia said, "but you make sure you air

them closets out good before you put anything in them, you hear? Miss Clunie, at the end, she couldn't keep herself clean for more than ten minutes at a time, an' that help they had in used to stuff everything in the closet instead of washing up. Left it all for your Aunt Winnie to do at the end of the week. House smelled like a public bathroom after a busy day. 'Spect it's still lingering in the wood."

"'Melia!" John Whitworth said, faintly shocked.

"Now, John, I'm sure Amanda wants to know all there is about her house."

"Maybe," Matthew said, returning with two glasses of iced tea, "but tell her after dessert, will you, Amelia?"

Miss Clunie's accidents had already infringed on the appeal of my potatoes and gravy. I drank some iced tea and tried to think of another topic of conversation. An occasional drop of rain pinged gently against the tin roof of the fellowship hall.

"So, Reverend Clement," Amelia Whitworth said, "can you baptize folks?"

"Yes, Mrs. Whitworth."

"That church you were at—what was it called, John?"

"Can't remember," John said.

"What was it, Reverend Clement?"

"All Saints," Thomas said.

"What kind of church was that again?"

"Interdenominational, Mrs. Whitworth."

Amelia Whitworth's lips worked. For a moment I thought she was going to have a go at it, but at last she cleared her throat and said, "Well, that's pretty close to a Bible church, right?"

"Yes, it is."

"An' did you baptize folk properly?"

"We sprinkled adult converts, Mrs. Whitworth."

"Like Methodists, that would be?"

"Yes, that's right. The method isn't as important as the symbolism. They knew that they were buried with Christ and raised to new life, and so did everyone else."

"But no one ever told you how to get someone down in the water?"

"I practice on Amanda when I get a chance," Thomas said.

Matthew Humberston chuckled, deep in his throat. "Let's worry about baptizing people after we get 'em into the pews, Amelia," he said. "Haven't noticed no sinners beatin' down the door to get dunked."

"Huh," Amelia Whitworth said. "Well, Reverend Clement, we're right glad to have you anyway. John never has told me much about where you come from an' all that. Where's your family?"

"I grew up in the Midwest, but my sister was killed in a car accident several years ago, and the rest of my family scattered afterwards."

"I'm right sorry to hear it."

"I'm looking forward to living here in Little Croft. I guess I feel like Amanda's family can be mine, too. It's been a long time since I had family around."

Amelia looked across at John. Ida paused with a forkful of pie hovering in front of her mouth. Ambrose cleared his throat.

"You met them yet?" Ambrose asked. "Cora and Giddy, and Attaway Fowlerand and the boys?"

"Well, not all of them—"

"Hear that rain?" Amelia Whitworth said. "Startin' to come down hard. I reckon we better help you get all that stuff in your car dry. John, you want to go rustle up a couple of umbrellas for the reverend?"

Chapter Six

I n the end, we couldn't even fit all the goodwill offerings into the hatchback; we hadn't gotten around to unpacking the minuscule trunk yet, and the car floor was covered with dog hair. We stacked food along the backseat and left the rest for Amelia, who promised that John would bring it along later. We pulled out of the church lot, waving good-bye to the die-hard potluckers who remained. Between the presents and the royal send-off, I felt as though we were beginning a second honeymoon.

Our Sunday afternoon tradition was to lock the doors, take a long nap, brew a pot of coffee, and play Scrabble until evening service. Saturday's broken night and Sunday's long morning had worn me out; I was staggering with sleepiness. The dogs were snoring under the back porch, and when we went up to our room the rain drummed down against the tin roof, steady and soporific. I changed into jeans and an old shirt and collapsed into bed. Water streamed against the windows. A clap of thunder hit the house like a blow.

Thomas, flopping on the bed in T-shirt and boxer shorts, said, "Is it going to hit us?"

"Storms follow the river," I murmured, sinking further towards oblivion. I'd lived near the river all my life, and no thunder was going to keep me awake this afternoon.

"We're on the river."

"It'll travel down to the flat places, down to Fowlerand Landing. It always does. If you go down there after a storm you can see great plowed furrows in the dirt, where the lightning strikes." I turned over and nestled into the warm curve of his body. He put his lips against the back of my neck. I roused myself enough to add, "And it was a good sermon."

"Such enthusiasm," Thomas said, but his voice was tired. We'd both of us been strung up for the first morning at Little Croft Church. I could feel the tension running out of him, like the water flowing gray outside the windows. His arm was loose and relaxed around me.

Drifting in the indistinct haze that comes just before sleep, I thought of Thomas's scattered family: Jane, dark and intelligent and wrong-headed, dead at nineteen on that Chicago freeway; the father who'd left for the far ends of the earth; the mother who went in and out of private clinics and didn't always remember her son's name.

I'd met Thomas Clement in a Hebrew class, three years ago, at the end of a very bad summer. My car had died in the spring, in south Jersey, so I spent the hot months working overtime and squirreling my fees away for a down payment. In August I finished up a whole series of ads for a Philadelphia muffler company, threw the folder of design specifications at the far wall of my cubicle, and stomped down to the local seminary to register for a class. Any class, I thought, as long as it engaged the part of my brain that was slowly withering away.

I ended up in beginning Hebrew. The Hebrew Bible I bought at the seminary bookstore looked as though a bird had done a fertility dance on the page. I sat in the back row, surrounded by men, wondering what I was doing. But the lecturer—a big gentle man with a sandy mustache and a diffident grin—came in and wrote out the words of Deuteronomy on the board, in the oldest Hebrew script known. These were the shapes the I Am himself might have used as he wrote on the stones of Sinai:

Have no other gods before me. I was enthralled.

Thomas sat in the far corner, his shoulders hunched slightly, his forehead in his hand as he wrote. I watched him sometimes from behind my Hebrew flash cards. He was about thirty, I thought, too thin for his height, and the wrinkles at the corners of his eyes belonged to an older man. I hadn't seen him in the first weeks of class, and eventually someone told me that he'd been away, taking care of family: his younger sister had died in a Chicago pileup, his father had decamped to Alaska, and his mother had been hospitalized with depression. He disappeared promptly after class every day, and I probably never would have spoken to him if I hadn't run into him in front of the little used bookstore around the corner from my apartment.

The weather was October cool, with a hint of warmth still lacing the fall air, and the bookstore owner had put a rack of paperbacks out on the sidewalk. I was collecting Agatha Christies, and the rack contained a few of the British-published paperbacks with their original titles.

I felt someone watching me and looked up. He was smiling at me from the other side of the rack. The lines at the corners of his eyes and mouth had relaxed; he looked younger and less grim.

"Hi," he said.

"I've seen you in class," I said.

"Yeah. I work at the church right around this corner. All Saints." He put out his hand. "Thomas Clement."

"I'm Amanda Hunt."

"Yes," he said. "I know."

I was almost asleep when a car door slammed in the yard, a fraction of a second before Daphne and Chelsea sent up an alarm. I jerked upwards and said with heartfelt woe, "What is it now?"

Thomas rolled over on his back and said, "Tell me that isn't the Whitworths with the rest of our stuff."

"It is indeed," I said, peering into the dim stormy air. "John and Amelia and—hold on—yes, Matthew and Matt, and Ambrose and Ida, all of them with boxes and umbrellas, headed for the back porch. You better get dressed."

He groped around for his clothes, muttering. I went down the steps and opened the back door. They stood on the porch beside the rusty freezer, shining with goodwill and rain; except for Matt, who bore his armload of canned goods with sulky reluctance.

I invited them in. I could hardly claim that I didn't have anything to offer them, after all. They clustered into the kitchen and deposited the goods on the kitchen table. I put on some coffee, and the men stood in a cluster next to the refrigerator, waiting for the coffee to drip. I could hear Thomas's feet, creaking on the boards of the hallway overhead. My mouth tasted like cold metal with exhaustion.

"We can help you put this stuff away," Amelia offered. Her fingers were already twitching towards the handles of the kitchen cabinets.

I had vacuumed them out the day before, so I said, "That'd be fine, Mrs. Whitworth."

"Look here," Ida Scarborough said, displaying two cans of water chestnuts, tied up in a net bag along with a package of noodles, a bottle of soy sauce, a jar of bean sprouts, and a recipe card. "That's right cute, isn't it?"

I thought it was faintly unusual for Little Croft. I leaned over to read the label, which bore the name "Joe and Jenny Morehead."

"I'll make up the list," Amelia said, rubbing her hands together.

"The list?"

"For thank-you notes."

"Of course," I said.

Thomas appeared at the door in jeans and bare feet. His fair hair was rumpled up, and his eyes were heavy.

"Afternoon," he said.

I saw Matthew Humberston's dark eyes flick towards Thomas's toes, and then take in my untucked shirt and hasty ponytail. "Maybe we could come back another time?" he suggested. "Bound to be a busy weekend for y'all, movin' and all."

I cast him a grateful glance. But just then, a motor idled around the side of the house into the yard. The dogs started yelping again from the pen. Another car door slammed.

"I'll get that," Thomas said. He padded away through the cluttered living room. A moment later I heard Great-uncle Attaway's voice at the front door and his heavy tread in the hallway. Thomas came back through the living room with Attaway behind him.

"You all know Amanda's great-uncle, don't you?" Thomas asked, stepping into the kitchen. "Want some coffee, Mr. Fowlerand?"

Attaway filled the rectangle of the kitchen doorway. He was capless, and his straight white hair nearly brushed the top of the frame. At the edge of my field of vision, I saw Matthew Humberston's wire-thin body tense and straighten. His shoulders went back. The heads of the other two deacons turned towards him, drawn by an invisible strand of tension.

"No coffee, thanks." Attaway's narrow glance moved to Ambrose, then to John, then away again. "Came to see that you were settled in, that's all. I told Cora I'd manage the place for her. Giddy's got no head for landlording. So you let me know if you have any troubles, and we'll get 'em straightened out." He cleared his throat. "After all, Clement, you're family now, ain't you?"

The floor creaked under Matthew's feet. He shouldered his way past Thomas and stood for a moment with his face six inches from Attaway's. They were much of a height, but Matthew Humberston was half the other man's weight.

"'Scuse me," he said. "I'm feeling like this room might need some airing out."

Attaway stepped aside. Matthew strode away through the living room. His son shambled after him. I heard the door slam twice.

Thomas's face had closed into sudden wariness. "Everything looks fine right now, Mr. Fowlerand," he said, "but I'll let you know if the house needs any work."

"Right," Attaway said. "Just wanted you t' know." He stood for a long moment, looking around him. "I ain't been in this house for years."

Amelia Whitworth slammed a cabinet shut with unnecessary vigor. Attaway blinked at her, slowly coming out of his abstraction.

She said tartly, "Ain't no use going into raptures in the kitchen, Attaway. You never spent no time in here."

"Huh!" Attaway said. He stumped away through the living room, thumping his stick ahead of him. Thomas followed him, shutting the front door behind him and then returned to the kitchen. A thick awkward layer of silence had dropped over the room. John Whitworth was scarlet with embarrassment, shuffling his long feet on the floor. Amelia tutted twice under her breath and slammed another cabinet door.

Thomas said at last, "I gather that Mr. Humberston doesn't like my wife's great-uncle?"

"You might say," Ambrose Scarborough agreed, rubbing his jaw with a pudgy hand.

"Is it going to be a problem that we live here?"

"Well, I reckon we'd all feel better if Attaway weren't acting as your landlord. But we know you can't afford much else, with what we c'n pay you."

"What do you think he wants to do? Control the church?" Thomas's voice was skeptical.

Ambrose blinked at him and said, "What good would that do him? No, the only thing that troubles him 'bout Little Croft Church is that Matthew's on the board. He just wants to have his thumb in anything that might do Matthew some good."

"Well, you can tell Mr. Humberston that I'm not going to let any petty hatred interfere with my church duties."

"Petty hatred?" Ambrose said. "Hate ain't never petty. And 'specially the hate between those two. Reverend Clement, next to Attaway an' Matthew, Cain and Abel were right good friends."

"Doris Humberston—that's Matthew's older sister—married my Great-uncle Attaway and died when she was in her early thirties," I said, much later. We lay in the Sunday night dark, limp with weariness. The storm had rained itself out by late afternoon, and the thunderheads had blown away in great gray puffs. By the time evening service was over, stars glinted from the blackening sky.

"She took too much of something one night," I went on. "I can't remember now whether it was sleeping pills or tranquilizers or aspirin. But Attaway found her dead the next morning. He was away hunting."

"How old would you say Matthew is?" Thomas asked. His face was invisible in the dark.

"Forty-five? Fifty? Matt's five years younger than I am, so he'd be…twenty-two. Doris was fifteen years older than Matthew."

"Your great-uncle was a cradle robber."

"She was twenty years younger, and he was well-off. Wasn't all that uncommon."

"So why does Matthew hate Attaway for that?"

"Well, she'd been depressed for months, and the Humberstons insist Attaway should've done something about it. So there's always been bad blood between Matthew and Attaway, but it looks as though things have gotten a lot worse. Oh, darn it—"

"What?"

"I meant to call Peggy Fowlerand again. I'll have to do it in the morning."

"Peggy's your cousin's wife, right?"

"Yes. Quintus is Attaway and Doris's son."

Thomas sighed and turned over. I thought he was meditating on the spider's-web complexity of the Scarborough-Fowlerand-Humberston relationships, but when I touched his face gently a few moments later, I realized that he was asleep.

I lay open-eyed in the dark. I'd grasped Amelia Whitworth by the sleeve, as she and John went out the door a bare hour before the evening service was due to begin.

"Mrs. Whitworth," I'd said, "what did you mean? What

you said to Great-uncle Attaway, I mean."

She looked at me, puzzled. She had to tilt her head up to look me in the eyes.

"'Bout the kitchen?" she said.

"Yes."

"Well, Doris and me was friends, back when she was alive. She was always limp as a rag 'cause he never did help her out none, that's all. She did all the work for him and for the baby, cleaned up after all those big Fowlerand boys that used to tramp through in their muddy boots, and he sat in the livin' room with his shoes off. Guess I just got exasperated with him, that's all. Pretendin' the kitchen was so full of memories. That man couldn't boil water 'thout somebody filled the pan for him."

"Here?"

"What do you mean, darlin'?"

The rain had slackened to a drizzle. John and Ambrose and Thomas were out in the yard, having a second look at the well pump. I said, "In this house? I thought Great-uncle Attaway had always lived down in the old Fowlerand place."

"Oh, he did. 'Cept when Quintus was about two. Him and Doris came up here and lived for a bit, 'cause the whole roof on the old place was goin' and had to be fixed. Stayed here quite a while. She died here, you know."

"In the Tenant House?" Doris's death was family legend. When I'd heard the story told, I'd always pictured her lying stiff in that high-ceilinged old bedroom, just off the main hallway of the old Fowlerand place, at the end of Fowlerand Landing Road.

"Oh, yes. Right in that room where y'all put your bed," Amelia said. "I remember, 'cause I came over that morning and stood in the yard and watched the sheriff go in and out. They had all the shades drawn, an' your grandma and Attaway were the only folks they let in. I could hear Quintus wailin' all the way through the walls."

She patted my hand.

"Don't worry about that none," she said. "That's been thirty years or more. I don't think Attaway thinks about it much himself, not any more. All old houses got stories, Amanda."

Maybe so, I thought, lying awake and listening to Thomas's quiet breathing. But we hadn't come back to Little Croft to wrestle with old ghosts. Thomas wanted a family, a home, a place to perfect his service to God; and I wanted something more elusive. I wanted reassurance, reassurance that I could still find a place where God was as real as the sunlit fields, as easy to hear as a hawk keening overhead. Somehow I'd lost that certainty in my Philadelphia years, and I'd come home to find it again in the perfect beauty of Little Croft.

Chapter Seven

I got up early Monday morning and made coffee and sat down in front of Thomas's desk in the fireplace room. My job with Granny Cora began at nine. I was determined to get up in the mornings and spend two good hours reading and working on my laboriously acquired Hebrew. I opened my *Biblia Hebraica* and started on the first chapter of Genesis.

In the beginning, God created the heavens and the earth. I could hear Moses in the desert, repeating to the rebellious Israelites the ancient words that lingered on the lips of Adam himself: *B'reshiyt bara Elohim et hashama'im v'et ha'aretz.* As I read the words out loud, I felt their familiar mysterious pull, the sense that for a moment I could look directly at the instant when chaos and emptiness straightened themselves into order and time began its endless tick.

The sensation—God as close as the written page—lingered as I showered and dressed and saw Thomas off to his church office, as I stepped out on the back porch to begin the walk towards the Old House. The morning sun flooded down on the backyard. Beyond the bank, the Chickahominy shone sapphire blue. The branches of the old maple shifted above me. Every leaf stood out, sharp-edged shadow battling with strong fresh light.

"This is why I came home," I said out loud.

At the sound of my voice, the dogs erupted happily from underneath the porch. Quintus had potted at least one groundhog; they were wrestling a fresh hide between them. Chelsea had a hind foot, and Daphne was chewing on one ear. I leaned over the porch rail and said, *"B'reshiyt bara Elohim et hashama'im v'et ha'aretz.* Same words that came out of Moses' mouth. What do you think of that?"

Daphne sat down on the hide and yawned. Chelsea leaped on Daphne's back and tugged at the groundhog's tail; Daphne flopped over and rolled on it defensively. Flies hovered around them. So much for transcendent beauty.

I tramped on down Poverty Ridge Road. Beside the lane, Granny's sweet corn waved its tassels in the slight breeze off the river. A wide swath had been trampled right through the middle of it. Uncle Giddy was sitting on the front porch of the Old House, looking out across the corn with his rifle over his arm.

"Mornin'," he said peevishly. "See what those groundhogs have done to the corn? Quintus only got one the other night, and I've been sittin' out here ever since just before sunup and haven't seen a whisker. Dang things won't go near my traps, either."

"Sorry, Uncle Giddy." I squeezed past him and went in the front door. Granny Cora was standing at the stove, frying two eggs and a thick slice of ham in about three inches of butter. This was contrary to doctor's orders. According to written instructions from my mother and her sister, my Aunt Winnie (now in North Carolina with her fourth husband), I was supposed to enforce the cardiologist's restrictions on Granny's meals. This was a mighty challenge, second only to balancing her checkbook. Granny never recorded her checks.

"Granny," I said, "you're not supposed to fry things."

"I'm not fryin'. I'm just sauteein' them in a little butter."

"Is that the low-salt ham Aunt Winnie sent over?"

"Oh, yes," Granny said, dropping one eyelid slightly.

I sighed and looked around for the paper towels to sop some of the grease off. She arranged herself at the table, and I put the plate in front of her.

"You c'n pour me some coffee," Granny said, "an' do my hair."

"Want me to say the blessing?"

"Nope." Granny picked up her fork. I poured her a cup of the thick strong coffee perking on the back of the shabby old stove. It had chicory in it. I poured myself a cup, too. The acrid sting on my tongue brought a whole welter of memories. Once I'd stayed a whole week with Granny Cora, right after my youngest brother was born. She had fixed pancakes every morning, and at breakfast I'd been allowed to have tiny cups of chicory-flavored coffee, sweetened almost to a syrup with sugar.

"What are we doing today?" I asked, unrolling her thin white hair from the bristly curlers.

"Need you to balance my book."

"Let's clean out the basement instead. There's canning jars up on those top shelves that have been there since I was little."

Granny licked salt off her fingers. Dog-dog stuck his nose out from under the table. She dropped a piece of bacon rind down past the tablecloth, and he snapped it up and disappeared. I could hear his tail thumping on the linoleum.

"Okay," she said, "after you balance my book."

I started to brush her white curls out. "I saw Quintus yesterday," I said after a while.

"Looks drawn up, don't he?" Granny said, sopping up bacon grease with a piece of toast.

"A little. How's he getting along with Great-uncle Attaway?"

"'Bout like always."

"That bad?"

"Well, Attaway's been givin' him a bit more rope. He's sendin' him off to that big farm show at the fairgrounds to buy equipment today. Gave him the checkbook, no less."

"When's he leaving?"

"Oh, this afternoon, I reckon. He said he might stay overnight. Why?"

"Doesn't matter." I decided that I'd call Peggy as soon as I got home and invite her over for the evening. I went on brushing, thinking about Peggy sitting motionless and depressed in the Fowlerand house, and from there, by a natural association, to Doris's long-ago death. I wished I could remember more of the details.

"Granny," I said, idly, "how exactly did Doris Fowlerand die?"

Granny reached for her coffee cup and knocked over her glass of water. I sopped the mess up with a dish towel and wrung it out over the sink, draping the towel neatly over the edge to dry. When I turned around she was scraping up egg yolk with her toast.

"Want some more water?" I said.

"No."

"I haven't heard anyone talk about Doris since I was small. I haven't seen a picture of her in years. Did she look like Matthew?"

Granny took another swallow of coffee. Her old eyes were on the empty road out front.

"Not much like Matthew," she said at last. "He's a strong man, Matthew is, and sure of himself. Doris was quiet. Never spoke her mind."

"What happened to her?"

Granny thought this over. Finally she said, "Took too many pills one night. Attaway found her dead in the bed. He came back from a hunting trip late that night. He had Giddy with him and a couple of Humberston boys, and it was so close to dawn that they didn't go home. They all sprawled on the living room floor and slept there."

"In the Tenant House?"

"Yes," Granny said, apparently assuming I'd known this all along. "An' next morning, Attaway woke up and went in to see why she wasn't up. An' there she was, cold and gone."

"Yes, but why'd she do it? Was it on purpose?"

"Well, there ain't no knowing another mind. Giddy helped clear out the house after she died. There was whisky under the sink. She'd been drinking that night, with Attaway gone. Maybe she forgot she'd taken her pills and took some more by accident. Quintus was with her. He was just a little fellow. She put him to bed before she died. Attaway heard him wailing the next morning and got up to see why Doris hadn't fed the baby his breakfast. An' there she was. Oh, there was a ruckus, all those Fowlerands in the house, and Doris lyin' there dead. There was police cars and ambulances and Fowlerands everywhere, and Attaway stormin' up and down in the middle of it. I walked over and held Quintus. He couldn't talk much; just kept saying 'Mama? Mama?' over an' over."

The back door banged. Uncle Giddy was unloading his rifle in the laundry room. He came in on the end of Granny's sentence and looked at her glumly.

"I'm gonna get me some of that poison gas and do them dens with it," he said. "What accident you talking about?"

"Doris Fowlerand," Granny said.

"Been a string of days since that." Giddy settled himself in a chair. "I was there, y'know. I was a deputy. Coulda stayed with it, but Daddy needed me to help out on the farm. Yeah, Attaway always felt real bad about that. Never wanted to talk about it. Told me never to talk about it either."

"Why?" I asked.

"Ah," Uncle Giddy said, "I reckon he wanted to stop the gossip. Them Humberstons was always black-tongued. They woulda said he killed her, 'cept he had me and Tom Humberston and Leland Humberston all with him, all that day. So instead they started saying that Doris took them pills 'cause Attaway beat her. And they still say so."

"Did he beat her?"

"No," Granny said.

Giddy raised a lean eyebrow at me. "Maybe," he said. "Mama, you finished your books yet? I got to get down to the feed and seed. I'll go to the grocery for you if you send me some money."

"Amanda'll do 'em now," Granny said. "And we'll clean the basement after." She hauled herself up from the table and hobbled towards her room to dress. I cleared her plate away.

"Any bacon left?" Giddy asked.

"One piece. Uncle Giddy, did Matthew like Uncle Attaway when he first married Doris?"

"I don't reckon Matthew'd have liked anybody who showed up to marry Doris."

"Why?"

"Thought she hung the moon, he did. She was fifteen years older than him, you know, and she practically raised him after his mama died. Uncle Attaway got married when I was ten or 'leven. 'Twasn't till after that the Fowlerands took a dislike to him. Old Monroe Humberston—Matthew's father—started to go soft in his head round about the time your mama got married. He used to sit on the porch and call out everything that came into his head, at the top of his lungs. He got a complex, they call it, about Uncle Attaway. Every time he came over Monroe'd go into a fit. Finally Matthew had to put him away in that home in Williamsburg. He was courting Ann at the time—Matt's mother—and Monroe used to yell names at her when she went by. Biblical names, you know."

"But Matthew and Ann got married anyway?"

"Well," Giddy said, "she were a sensible girl. They never went to see him much, though."

Granny Cora came hobbling back out of her room, buttoning up her polyester shirt.

"We got work to do," she said sharply. "Go to the store if you're going, Giddy, and quit your chattering."

"Huh," said Giddy. He accepted the bills she held out to him and stalked out the back door. I sat down to the mess that was Granny's checkbook.

"Granny?" I said.

"What?"

"What happened to Ann? Matt's mother?"

"Oh, she died."

"Car crash? Overdose?"

"Lung cancer. Quit digging up cold corpses, Amanda, and tell me how much money I got left."

Chapter Eight

I called Peggy as soon as I got back to the Tenant House, but the phone rang on and on without an answer. The answering machine didn't even cut on. I hung up, feeling vaguely uneasy, and started to thaw chicken in the microwave. We had plugged it into a countertop outlet, but two minutes into the defrost cycle all the kitchen circuits blew, and I spent half an hour in the fuse box figuring out which switch connected to which part of the house. The written labels had faded into pale unreadable lines.

Thomas arrived in time to make the salad for dinner. He'd spent the day sorting through his predecessor's files, which showed a depressing lack of interest in the congregation.

"No wonder people have been leaving," he said, energetically chopping lettuce. "The man never visited the members, never counseled anyone, never did any kind of outreach. Even the directory's two years out of date. It's a wonder the church is still alive at all."

I listened to him and felt reassured. He was planning on visiting all the families in Little Croft Church in the next few weeks; he had enlisted Ida Scarborough to help him contact the Little Croft families with young children; he had already set up appointments with the county authorities to discuss the technicalities of running a three-day preschool on church property. The Fowlerand-Scarborough-Humberston spiderweb hadn't entangled him at all.

We ate the chicken and salad, and watched a movie and

went to bed early. Thomas was reading his way through the *Lord of the Rings* for the third or fourth time. I curled up next to him and opened my Jane Austen. The yellowed paper marking my place fell out. I picked it up and looked again at the fading letters.

You never loved me, and I only loved you out of desperation because he never looked at me, never touched me.

Maybe they weren't Miss Clunie's words. Doris had lived here, too, with Great-uncle Attaway; lived and died here. Were those final ambiguous words a threat, or a plea for protection?

When I walked into the Old House the next morning, Granny was sitting bolt upright in the green plush chair, still wearing her nightgown, staring at the door with her blue eyes stone-hard and her face as white as down. As soon as I put my foot past the threshold she said, "Did you hear?"

"What, Granny?"

"Peggy. Peggy's dead, that's what. Attaway called me this mornin' from the sheriff's office."

I thought at once of Doris and her sleeping pills, and of my promise to Quintus, and a huge sickening wave of guilt crashed over me.

"She killed herself?" I said wildly.

Granny stared at me. "Killed herself?"

"Peggy. Quintus said she'd been depressed—"

"She crashed her car. Last night, drivin' to Richmond. She was goin' in to meet Quintus at the fairgrounds, and she went off that big curve on Winneck Road. They been trying to get hold of Quintus all morning."

My first, inexcusable reaction was sheer relief; I hadn't been responsible for Peggy's death, she hadn't killed herself in despair while I snuggled contentedly up to my husband in a warm and private bed. A second later, I thought of Quintus sitting in my kitchen chair and saying wretchedly, "She has spells where she sits an' stares an' won't wash her hair or eat." Quintus, with his blue eyes puzzled under the shock of fair hair and his big hands flat on the table. Quintus, with his soul bound up in Peggy's happiness, putting his pennies away to build her a new house.

"What's he going to do?" I asked.

"He's tryin' to arrange for Miz Morris to come take care of the funeral."

"Quintus?"

"Course not. He ain't got back from the fairgrounds. Attaway's takin' care of things. He saw her last."

I walked past her, moving automatically to the refrigerator. "What do you want for breakfast, Granny?"

She didn't answer. I turned my head. Her fingers dug into the chair's overstuffed arms.

"Granny?"

"Why'd you say that?"

"Say what?"

"That she killed herself?"

"Oh, Granny, I don't know. You want eggs?"

"Okay."

"Scrambled? Fried?"

She didn't answer. She stayed in her chair, staring out the window. I had to call her three times before she rose and hobbled to the table.

~ ~ ~ ~ ~

We went through the morning in a daze. I snatched a moment to call Thomas, midmorning, while Granny was taking a leisurely visit to the bathroom. The church phone rang unanswered; the little car was gone from the Tenant House yard.

Attaway came stumping up Granny's steps around noon, when I was cutting out buttermilk biscuits on the countertop. He was wearing a crisp striped bow tie and was immaculately shaved. I had a nasty picture in my mind of Attaway, roused from sleep by the phone call everyone dreads, shaving in front of the mirror with his lips pursed in a whistle. I could hardly believe that no trace of the tragedy lingered on the heavy folds of his face.

"Well," Attaway said, settling himself on the sofa, "we done found Quintus. Shut himself up in some little motel off Laburnum an' didn't leave me with no phone number. I reckon he called Peggy, though. He kept sayin', 'But I just talked to her. I just talked to her.' As though that would keep her from bein' dead somehow."

"When's the funeral?" Granny asked.

"I left that to Miz Morris. She showed up an' made a scene just as I was goin'. Jimmy White's on vacation, so they got Emory Watkins handling the wreck. He had a couple of mechanics goin' over that car with their glasses on. Reckon he's got to earn his money somehow. He let me have a look at it. Crumpled up like a ball o' paper."

I gathered up the scraps of biscuit dough and patted them out into a fresh square. Jimmy White, the Little Croft sheriff, would have turned Attaway out without a second thought, but Emory Watkins was young and uncertain.

"I guess she went to sleep," Attaway said, scratching Dog-dog absently behind the ears. "She went off the road at that big curve just afore Winnville. Straight into that old tree. It was mighty late at night to be drivin' around."

"Amanda," Granny said abruptly, "you done over there?"

I slid the pan of biscuits into the oven and wiped my hands on a dish towel. "Yes, Granny."

"You want to go start on that back flower bed? Attaway can get them biscuits out when they're ready."

"Okay," I said. I wanted to ask Great-uncle Attaway why Peggy had set off to Richmond in the middle of the night when she knew Quintus wouldn't be coming back until the next afternoon. Granny's voice held an unmistakable note of dismissal. I went out the back door, feeling Attaway's eyes follow me.

The beds were entwined with a summer's jumble of weeds and volunteer plants, but I couldn't fix my mind on what I was doing. I kept picturing Quintus, hearing the worst possible news from Attaway; Attaway who hated him. The sun was hot on the back of my neck.

After half an hour, I heard Attaway's truck motor start and fade away down the long dirt road. Granny came out and enthroned herself on the steps to watch my progress. Dog-dog wobbled out behind her and went to sleep on a sunny patch of grass.

"You want some lunch?" Granny said, eventually.

I shook my head. The back garden lay at the very edge of the hill, and the Chickahominy snaked below us in a wide silver band. The late summer wind brought the smell of river mud up the hill and across the garden.

"Did Great-uncle Attaway say where Quintus was?"

"Said he was with Miz Morris. They were goin' on down to see the Northend priest 'bout funeral arrangements."

I rooted up a tangle of spearmint that had spread unruly tendrils across the sweet william.

"Granny," I said, "what was Peggy like?"

"You never met her?"

"I just saw her once or twice. That was all."

"Margaret Morris," Granny said.

"What?"

"Margaret Morris was her true name. But everybody called her Peggy. Nobody ever gave that girl her full name."

"Where did he meet her?"

"Attaway's farm. She was at some tip-nosed school in Richmond, and she was supposed to be working on the school paper. They came out for a visit to Little Croft to write it up for the paper. All about how the other side lives." Her voice held a deep and momentary scorn. "So there they were, playin' farmer for the day, chasing chickens around and squealing, and around a corner comes Quintus, all blue-eyed and bright-haired. She fell like a rock from a high place. Her mother created a fuss, but Quintus was stronger than Miz Morris in the end."

"What about Peggy?"

"She was a pretty girl," Granny said, poking at an encroaching strand of wire grass with her cane. She seemed to have recovered from the news already; her strong old face was placid, and her hands were steady. "Pull that up 'fore it creeps into my pinks. Pretty, but a lost soul. Like a dust mote in the wind. She swayed back and forth, wavered around, swung here and there, until they got married and Quintus gave her a spine. Even stood up to Attaway, after that, she did."

"Didn't he like her?"

"Attaway never liked anything Quintus did or said. He'd have liked her fine if some other Fowlerand had married her. But he used to rile her something awful." Her voice trailed away.

I dug down to the roots of the wire grass. It clung hard to the ground, resisting my fingers. After a moment I said, "Attaway saw her last night?"

"He says he brought home a batch of venison, round nine or so, an' she was in the kitchen cleaning up and singin' to herself."

A sudden racking shudder seized me. I shrugged it off, annoyed, and said, "I thought he didn't like her."

"That's as may be," Granny said. "But she was cookin' for him while she and Quintus lived there. He says when he left her, she was gettin' ready to put it in the freezer. Next thing he knows, Emory Watkins is callin' him, asking where Quintus is, 'cause he's standing at the tree that Peggy's car is wrapped around."

I worked my way carefully around the roots of the pinks, which were entwined with wire grass, and wondered whether Peggy could possibly have been drinking. I looked up to ask Granny and caught her staring out over the Chickahominy. The placid face was creviced, carved into deep lines, and the steady hands were white around the nails and knuckles. Her distress was as clear as the sharp scent of spearmint rising up from the warm ground beneath my hands.

"Granny," I said gently, "what's the matter?"

Granny shook her head. "I never thought she mighta killed herself," she said at last, in a voice I could barely hear.

"Granny, I didn't mean that. I was just thinking of Doris, that's all. I was telling Thomas all the family stories last night, and Giddy said Doris might have killed herself…and Peggy's death is the same, in a way."

"How so?"

"Well…their husbands were away for the night, and no one really knows what happened next."

Granny said nothing. I looked up at her where she sat, with the afternoon shadows beginning to slant towards her. She didn't meet my eyes. She thrust the cane into the ground and hauled herself up by the wrought-iron step rail.

"I thought you were gonna say that Attaway'd been with them both, just before they died," she said. She limped back into the house. I dusted my hands off and followed her; but by the time I got into the kitchen, she'd shut herself in the bathroom.

"I got me a chocolate pie pain," the old voice said through the door. "I'll be in here a while. Put my sheets in the washer for me and take yourself on home."

I stripped her bed, hauled the linens down to the washing machine in the basement, and made the bed up with fresh sheets. When I was ready to leave she was still in the bathroom, barricading herself behind the locked door.

"Granny?" I shouted. "I'm going home."

"Righty." Slight pause. "Mandy?"

"Yes?"

Another pause.

"Nothin'," Granny's voice said eventually.

I had a dreadful headache by this time. Quintus's face haunted me; I kept hearing Peggy's high frail voice on the answering machine, assuring me that I would hear back from her. I was in no mood to play guess-my-mind with Granny Cora.

I yelled back, "I'm going now, Granny."

"Wait up," Granny ordered through the bathroom door. I paused with my hand on the door. After another long moment, she said, "Never mind."

"I'm going," I said. I closed the door firmly behind me and walked down Poverty Ridge Road. The late sun glanced off the windows of the Tenant House, filling them with flat deceptive fire. I quickened my step. Thomas was home; I could see him standing on the riverbank, watching the boats go by. He turned his head and said, "Amanda!" with the familiar delight in his voice.

I wrapped my arms around him. He smelled of soap and shaving cream and, very faintly, of coffee. He kissed the top of my head and said, "What's the matter?"

I told him, in disjointed sentences, of Peggy's death and Quintus's disbelief. Thomas's arms tightened around me.

"Poor Quintus," he said. "To lose your family, so suddenly…"

I laid my cheek against his chest, hearing the reassuring thump of his heart. A deep thread of uneasiness ran beneath my words; it had to do with Attaway, cold and oddly satisfied. We stood together for a long silent time, while boats roared by on the river and the sun dropped slowly down behind the pines.

Chapter Nine

Peggy's funeral was held Friday morning at eleven. At ten, Thomas and I walked up to the Old House in our best subdued clothing. Rain threatened in the distance; the sky was coated with black-bottomed clouds.

I left Thomas waiting next to Granny's car and went up to the house. At my knock, Granny Cora emerged from her tiny back bedroom dressed in her funeral outfit: a black polyester skirt and her solemn-occasion hat, a black bowl with a spray of artificial violets on one side of the brim. Under the hem of her skirt, her ankles bulged out over the tops of earth-crusted canvas shoes.

I came inside and closed the screen door behind me.

"Granny," I said, "don't you have another pair of shoes?"

"My feet were so swole this morning I couldn't get them in nothing but my garden shoes."

"Can't I at least clean them off?"

"We're goin' outside. There's dirt in the graveyard. They'll be dirty enough by the time we get to the gravesite. Here." She handed me the keys to her navy blue Granada, an ancient car driven twice a month. "An' put Dog-dog down in the basement before we go."

"Do you mind if Thomas drives over with us?"

"Suit yourself. Here's my umbrella."

"Don't you have a black umbrella?"

"This one's the biggest, so I'm takin' it. Here."

I took the umbrella, which had CLYDE'S SEEDS printed in

big purple letters across the panels, shooed Dog-dog into the basement, and walked Granny down the front steps. Thomas was waiting by the car in his impeccable black city suit. I waited for Granny to make a sharp comment, but she folded her knotted old hands in her lap and we drove to the funeral in relative peace.

Peggy Fowlerand was to be buried at Northend Catholic Church, at the far end of the county. The church had survived the Civil War flames that consumed Northend Plantation, and the tiny gray stone building was one of the oldest in a county full of ancient foundations. The local funeral home had erected a canopy and thrown green indoor-outdoor carpeting over the mound of dirt beside the grave.

We got out of Granny's car and walked towards the canopy. Fowlerand relations already occupied most of the folding chairs. They were, oddly, almost all men. Attaway wore a blue suit with a yellow bow tie. His head was bare, his face immobile, his knuckles clamped over his cane.

Quintus sat beside him. I had called him twice, and Thomas had driven down to the old Fowlerand place on Wednesday, but Quintus refused to speak to anyone. He had spent the three days since Peggy's death entirely alone. He was visibly thinner, and his blue eyes were staring blindly ahead of him.

"Who's that?" Thomas murmured. I followed his discreet finger. A well-dressed woman in her sixties sat small and very upright at the far end of the chairs, wearing a black hat and white gloves and grasping a patent leather purse. She had the face of a china doll, perfectly painted, her light gray hair in flawless curls on a well-shaped head.

"That's Quintus's mother-in-law," I said softly. "Mrs. Morris."

"Let's go sit in the back row," Granny said, pointing.

"Look, there's Giddy. I told him to drive me, but he was out fussing with those blamed groundhogs this morning and said he didn't want to leave 'em. Guess he finished early."

I looked around and located Uncle Giddy, morosely smoking a cigarette on the other side of the graveyard wall. Giddy would never step into the territory of a church for some complicated reason of his own. We started to make our way through the polite cluster of Little Croft residents. I could hear the Northend priest clearing his throat from his place on the far side of the coffin.

"'The LORD is my shepherd; I shall not want....'"

Granny went on, loudly, "Giddy thought he saw a mama with two babies, and they move slow, so he said he could shoot 'em without too much trouble."

I cringed. The priest, unfazed, intoned, "'He leadeth me beside the still waters....'"

"But they moved faster'n he thought, and he lost 'em. I see Attaway brought himself out. He said he might stay home."

She whooshed herself into a back chair with a great sigh of relief. I caught the resigned eye of Mr. Adkins, the elderly black owner of the funeral company. He stood at his usual ceremonial post at the edge of the canopy. He wouldn't shush Granny Cora, though; his grandmother had been a slave, and the Scarboroughs had fought for the Confederacy. The graves lay up on the hillside, underneath the newly plowed field. I made an apologetic face, and he inclined his head slightly.

Granny remarked, "Didn't know they'd use Adkins. Thought Miz Morris didn't like black folk."

Thomas murmured, "The priest's reading, Mrs. Scarborough."

"Ain't deaf yet," Granny said tartly.

The priest raised his voice. "'He leadeth me in the paths of righteousness....'"

I sat down hurriedly, hoping I'd be less visible. Thomas folded his tall body into the chair next to me. Granny subsided, and we listened to the rest of the service in relative peace. Halfway through the final prayer, she began rummaging noisily through her purse. I peered over at her through my fingers. Candy wrappers rustled, change jingled, balls of Kleenex appeared and disappeared.

"Amen," the priest said, finally.

"Thomas," Granny whispered, quite loudly. "Got something for you."

Ahead of us, the Fowlerands were standing for the benediction. Quintus got slowly to his feet, his thin shoulders hunched beneath his jacket. Attaway put a hand on his arm, and Quintus jerked as though an electrical current had gone through him. He threw Attaway's hand away and pushed his way from the row of chairs, heading unseeing across the graveyard. He stumbled against a leaning stone, veered away, and disappeared through a gap in the old brick wall, into the trees that fringed the graveyard's edge.

The priest concluded his benediction while the heads of his listeners all turned in the direction of Quintus's fleeing figure. The crowd of Fowlerands beneath the canopy shuffled and broke into uncomfortable knots. Granny heaved herself up to her feet.

"Here you go," she said. "Found these in the bottom of a drawer. Thought you might like to see 'em."

She thrust a crumpled heap of paper squares into Thomas's unready hands; old photographs, brown and crumbling at the edges.

"Ah," Thomas said. "Thanks."

"Wait up. There's a couple more in here." Granny shook the bag impatiently. Attaway was leaning on the head of his cane, watching the trees where Quintus had disappeared. His face showed pure scorn. He turned his head at Granny's voice, and his light blue eyes settled on her black purse. He hobbled back toward her and stopped, two feet away.

"What's that?"

Granny Cora shoved another picture onto the top of the stack in Thomas's hands. "That's Doris," she said to Thomas. "Doris. Attaway's wife."

Attaway's eyes dropped to the photo. Doris, in faded brown and white, stood in front of a white-board house in a checked frilly apron, young and wide-eyed, her lips parted slightly. It was a sweet face, pretty and not very bright.

Attaway hissed, "What are you doin', Cora?"

"Clearin' out my drawers." Granny looked away, refusing to meet her brother's eyes. Attaway thrust the tip of his cane fiercely into the ground and limped away from the grave.

"He doesn't like to talk about Doris," Granny said.

"Why?" Thomas asked.

"'Cause of the way she died," Granny said. She snapped her purse closed, and I saw with surprise that her old hands shook.

"You know," Thomas said, "they never told us about this kind of thing in seminary. Fighting demons would be a heck of a lot easier than coping with your grandmother and your great-uncle and his brother-in-law and all the dead people they seem to have accumulated between them."

A thunderstorm had rolled down on us at dusk. We sat in the bright little kitchen of the Tenant House with water pouring down the dark windows and the electricity flickering at every howl of the wind. Thomas had excused himself directly after the funeral to go work on his next sermon, but I'd ended up driving Granny to Attaway's house, where every Fowlerand and relation by marriage in the county had spent the afternoon eating and drinking and not mentioning Quintus or Peggy at all. By the time I got home, I was too tired to think of anything more original than grilled cheese for supper.

So we ate sandwiches and pushed the plates away and spread Granny's old photographs out between us. She had scrawled names on the soft backs with a lead pencil.

"Doris at the old Fowlerand place," Thomas read out loud.

"Attaway's wife, who also happened to be Matthew Humberston's older sister."

"Yes," Thomas said, "the girl he robbed the cradle for." He examined the picture, tilting it towards the light. Doris in her apron was standing on the front porch of the old Fowlerand place. Sun washed down over her smooth dark head and the boards sparkled white and spotless under her feet. I pushed another picture over.

"Here's Quintus and Peggy, at their wedding."

"Must be genetic," Thomas said, looking down at Peggy's round immature face topped by lots of white net.

"She was eighteen and he was twenty-eight. Here's Granny when she was young—oh, look, Thomas, here's my mother, and Aunt Winnie, the one who lives in North Carolina now, and Uncle Giddy…"

The label read: *Me and children, 1948.* The edges of the photo were crumbling away into dark dust. Granny Cora sat on a wicker chair, slim and smiling, her smooth brown head bent over a chubby blond baby on her lap: my mother at the age of two. Her older sister Winnie stood beside her, thin and solemn with her fair hair in corkscrew curls. Giddy at seven leaned his arm on the back of his mother's chair. A white-headed child of four stood beneath Giddy's protective arm.

"Who's that?" Thomas asked.

"The baby between Giddy and my mother. His name was Stephen. My oldest brother's named after him. He pulled a kettle of boiling water over on himself when he was five. That was 1949, I think."

"Look how blond his hair is."

"My grandfather was so blond that his hair looks white in pictures. Here he is." The picture read: *Nathaniel Scarborough and Matthew Humberston hunting.* I barely remembered my grandfather. He was in his midforties in this picture, standing beside a hanging deer. He was straight and taut-bellied and handsome; a shock of fair hair fell over his forehead, and a triumphant grin split his face. A thin dark youth scowled from the animal's other side.

"They don't like each other much, do they? Who's this in the sheriff's uniform?

"Uncle Giddy. He was a deputy for years."

"Who's next to him?"

"Great-uncle Attaway, in his forties."

"Handsome guy," Thomas said.

I took another look at the picture. Forty years ago, Great-uncle Attaway had been dark and hawk-nosed with broad, straight shoulders. Giddy was still in his teens, and the new uniform sagged across his narrow chest. Thomas turned over the next photo.

"Here's Peggy and Quintus again. In color, this time."

"That's just a year or so ago," I said. They stood on the Fowlerand dock, the wooden walkway that led from Fowlerand Landing out into the Chickahominy. Quintus's blond head and Peggy's dark one were close together; he was laughing, and she was staring up at him with a look of pure adoration.

"Mm," Thomas said. The handwriting on the back of the last picture read, simply, *1955*. I turned it over. It was an old black-and-white family portrait. Nathaniel Scarborough, my grandfather, stood with his arm around his wife's shoulders. Her head was turned slightly away from him, and the tendons in her neck stood out. My mother, nine years old, leaned against her protective hand. Giddy and Winnie at fourteen and sixteen stood beside their father. Winnie was smiling, but Giddy was regarding Nathaniel Scarborough with a hooded secretive stare.

"Your grandmother doesn't want him to touch her," Thomas said, studying the images. He was right; her reluctance at his touch was visible in every strained muscle. Thomas laid the pictures out in front of him in a block, a squared carpet of the living and the dead.

"Your grandmother and Giddy and Attaway are still alive," he said. "Your grandfather—"

"Heart attack. Salt pork and cigars."

"Why did Attaway get irritated when your grandmother brought the pictures out?"

"He doesn't like to talk about Doris."

"Yes, but why?"

"He loved her?"

"Well," Thomas said, "maybe. Why does your grandmother

think it's so important for me to have all these pictures of dead people?"

"I don't know."

He shuffled them together into a neat pile. "If you can bring it up without being obvious," he said, "find out what happened to Doris, will you?"

"Why?"

"Because your grandmother's hands shake when she talks about her. I'd like to know why, that's all."

I bent my head down, tracing the borders of the picture in front of me. Thomas had spent four years working at All Saints while he finished his master of divinity, one slow class per semester. He'd graduated with the degree, a good résumé, and no debt. He could have applied to any church, in any city; and he had chosen to come home with me. He reached out and covered my hands with his.

"Amanda," he said.

"I wanted it to be the way I remembered it," I said, clenching my fingers up into a fist beneath his hands.

"I miss your parents too," Thomas said. "But we still have family here. They're not exactly what I expected, but that's all right. I need to…adjust, that's all."

I raised his hand to my lips and kissed it. "Well," I said, "there's one comfort. You've already seen them all at their worst."

Chapter Ten

I woke up early Sunday morning, our second at Little Croft. Thomas was over at the church, and the farm was grave-still. I put on my robe and went out onto the back porch of the Tenant House with my coffee. The sun was halfway above the dark fringe of pines, and gold morning light washed over the Tenant House yard.

There is, in everyone's inner world, a green place where life is as it should be. For me, that place had always been Little Croft itself; not the Little Croft of the Fowlerands and Scarboroughs, but a place where the clear beauty of the countryside gave a glimpse of something greater. I wanted not just the Little Croft I loved, but the Little Croft that had always been intended. A place without corruption, without sin, without death; a field where God could walk in the mornings. That reality was almost present in every curve of ground, almost behind every tall tree, almost seen in every shadow. And the screaming of the distant hawks was the sound of the land crying out to be reborn. I held on to those glimpses; shadows that were more real than the sun that cast them. I stood on the back porch and prayed for Thomas and the Sunday morning service and the Little Croft congregants; I put them all together and held them up to the God who lingered just out of sight and pleaded, Break through to us.

The Sunday morning crowd had enlarged itself. Last week's congregation had returned in force to hear the second installment of

Luke. Matthew sat in a back pew. Matt slouched next to him, staring at his feet. Ida Scarborough beamed through the sermon with her hands folded across her ample stomach. Ambrose sat beside her, fidgeting. His round unwrinkled face was worried; the expression sat oddly on it, like anger painted on a balloon.

John Whitworth fell asleep halfway through Thomas's third point. I was sitting right behind him. He slept unobtrusively until just before the benediction, when he let out an unfortunate snort and Amelia planted her elbow in his ribs. He came awake and sat straight up.

"I waren't sleeping!" he complained, loudly enough to turn heads.

"Let's stand for dismissal," Thomas said. The Little Croft congregation rose with a rustle. I made my way to the back door, trying not to giggle. Two new families occupied the back row: a young man, broad shouldered and red faced, with a thin dark wife; and a straight-backed graying man with a pillowed wife and four solemn children.

Thomas and I stood together at the door, shaking hands as the congregation filed out. The graying man hustled his four children out. His wife followed obediently. He grasped Thomas's hand with great firmness.

"Remember me?" he said. "You came by my house last week. George Rainey. Here's m' family. The wife. You preach the Word, young man, but you don't use it."

"Beg your pardon?"

"The Word. The Word of God to the English-speaking people."

I greeted someone else, hoping that Mr. Rainey would move along. Thomas said, "Ah, the King James. Yes. I decided to use a more modern translation. It's easier to follow and more accurate in many places. If you'd like to discuss it some time..."

"Discuss it?" George Rainey said, indignantly. "Did the apostle Paul discuss his letters? Did the prophets discuss the messages God gave them? No sir. You don't discuss the Word. It governs you." The four children—all boys, ranging in age from twelve down to about three—were staring at Thomas with wide wondering eyes.

Thomas said, "We can certainly agree on that, Mr. Rainey. But the whole issue of translation—"

"'Tisn't an issue," George Rainey said. "Just a matter of obedience. We'll come on back next week and see whether you've answered God's call. Hope so. Nice church, this. We'd like to be part of it. Let's go, boys."

The children filed out behind him, with Mrs. Rainey trotting after. Thomas grimaced at me under cover of a yawn. Mr. Whitworth shambled by, sheepishly, under the stern guidance of his wife. Ambrose Scarborough followed him. He leaned forward and said in a low voice, "Can I come by this week? Talk for a minute?"

"Sure," Thomas said. "I'm in my office most mornings."

"Okay. I'll come on by, later this week." Ambrose hurried over the threshold. Thomas watched him go, a crease forming between his eyes.

The young red-faced man with the thin wife came near the end of the procession. "Joe Morehead," he said, putting out his hand. "My wife Jenny. We were out of town last week, but we sent a present to the pounding. Glad to meet you."

Thomas shook hands, the crease smoothing slightly.

"I remember—the Chinese food," I said. "It was different.

I wondered who you were."

"I thought everyone else would send shortening and canned goods," Jenny Morehead said lightly. She was attractive, wearing subdued and sophisticated makeup, and I envied her thick sleek haircut. I invited them to dinner, impulsively, and they looked at each other and agreed. Joe owned a little contracting business in Williamsburg; Jenny was a nurse in Richmond. They were the first couple of our age we'd seen in Little Croft. We settled on Friday night for dinner.

"We'll look forward to it," Jenny said. She smiled back over her shoulder as they went out.

The church had taken on the disheveled look of a sanctuary at noon on Sundays. Bulletins littered the floor and someone had crumbled a cracker into the back pew. I put my arm around Thomas's waist and said, "You went door to door this week, didn't you?"

"Wednesday, yes."

"Looks like it's working."

"I visited the Raineys," Thomas said, rolling his eyes. "Hadn't gotten to the Moreheads yet."

"What does Ambrose want?"

"I don't know." We wandered out onto the porch to watch cars pull out of the lot. Thomas said after a moment, "Did you see Matt, in the back row?"

"Yes."

"He's in trouble. I've seen that look on a kid's face before."

"It wouldn't be the first time."

"What's he done?"

"When he was in high school, he was arrested for smacking mailboxes with a sledgehammer while driving a stolen car. He was charged with about seven different offenses, but after a week or so the charges sort of melted mysteriously away."

"Then what?"

"My freshman year of college, he beat up one of my cousins—Pierman Fowlerand, who was ten years older than he was but about five inches shorter. Pierman needed twenty stitches in his face. Matt got arrested for that too, but nothing ever came of it."

"What's the matter with the police department out here?"

"Nothing. Pierman went in and told them he was drunk and took the first swing and he wasn't going to press charges. Two weeks later Pierman started driving a new pickup truck. Great-uncle Attaway just about burst a blood vessel."

"Matthew buys him out of trouble?"

"No matter what."

"He seems like an honest man."

"He is. Matt's his only son."

I spent all day Wednesday cleaning Granny Cora's basement: taking cobwebbed jars off the shelves and arranging them on the floor, scrubbing the shelves where they'd sat, and wiping thick layers of dust off the glass. By five, when I trudged back across the field, I was hot and sweaty and thirsty, my hair was caked with dust, and black rimmed my fingernails. I climbed into the shower and stayed there until the smell of Granny's basement washed away.

I heard Thomas's car pull up while I was drying my hair. His feet thumped across the landing to the bathroom door. The door swung open.

"I visited four families today," he said triumphantly. "And I got the final list of building modifications that we need for the preschool. It's not going to be much work at all. And I'm almost finished with my sermon. And I went to tea with the Women's Missionary Society. What is that smell on the back porch?"

"Daphne and Chelsea have a dead groundhog under there."

"You're joking."

"No, Quintus gave it to them. At least they're not out raiding the neighbors' trash cans."

"That's not going to be much comfort when that thing gets really ripe."

"So did Ambrose come by yet to talk to you?"

"Late this afternoon."

"What's bothering him?" I hung my towel on the rail and started to dress.

"He says Attaway's been going around the congregation, family by family, asking people how they like me."

"Why?"

Thomas straightened out my towel where it hung crooked against the wall. "Ambrose thinks it has something to do with Matthew Humberston," he said at last. "Matthew's been a big man at Little Croft Church for years. People in the church don't seem to think much of Matt Jr., but they like Matthew, they respect him. Attaway's reminding people that I'm living on his sister's property, by his suggestion, and that I'm married to his great-niece. And the funny thing is, it's not doing Attaway any good. Matthew's about to blow his top, and everyone else is getting progressively madder at Attaway, not at me or at Matthew. Your great-uncle's not real popular around here."

"No, I know. He's a slumlord, for one thing. He owns all those houses along Winneck Road and charges too much for rent."

"The shacks before the curve?"

"Yeah. Some of them don't even have indoor bathrooms. The people who live there have nowhere else to go."

"Amanda, I don't think I like your great-uncle much."

"Whatever you think of him," I said, "he isn't stupid, and he isn't careless. I wish I knew what he was up to."

Friday afternoon, I left Granny's early and drove into Williamsburg to shop for dinner. I had put myself out for Joe and Jenny; I'd cleaned house late into Thursday night, hanging pictures and arranging books and unpacking the remaining boxes. The Tenant House looked cozy and picturesque, and Thomas had promised to scrub off the back porch where the dogs had been sleeping.

I came home with a basketful of meat and produce from Williamsburg's upscale Fresh Market, ready to cook dinner for Joe and Jenny at top speed. Thomas was home, obediently washing dog hair and caked mud off the painted boards. He got up, wiping his hands, and followed me into the kitchen.

"What's that?"

"Sirloin. There's French bread and fruit salad, and the chocolate cake over there. Will you set the table?"

"Gee, this is like Christmas." He took the plates and went into the living room. I started to scoop seeds out of the red peppers. I was arranging vegetables on my one nice platter when a brown sheriff's car idled its way up the lane, turned right at the corner, and then left into the Tenant House yard.

I went to the back door, wiping my hands. Thomas stood behind me, and together we watched the Little Croft sheriff climb out of his car: Jimmy White himself, back from vacation.

"Evening," I called.

"How you doing, Amanda?" Jimmy White said. "Haven't seen you for years. This your husband? Nice to meet you, Reverend Clement."

He came up the steps and shook hands with Thomas. The two men were almost the same height; Jimmy White was a tall and solid black man in his fifties, graying at the temples. He was out of uniform, his jacket and hat hanging in the back window of the brown car.

"Sorry to bother you in the evenin'," he said. "I been out of town. Visiting my daughter at college. Missed a mess, didn't I? Mind if I talk to you for a minute, Amanda?"

"If you don't mind me cooking at the same time. We've got company coming."

"You mind, Reverend?"

"No, of course not."

He followed us back to the kitchen. James White had been the Little Croft sheriff for fifteen years, and a deputy for fifteen years before that. He was direct and forceful and incisive, a direct contrast to the drawling white deputy who had handled Peggy's death. He accepted a cup of coffee and stood looking down the dirt road. I went back to chopping fruit. Thomas stood in the kitchen doorway, watching us.

"We got a new pastor last year down at Little Elam," Jimmy White said. "Hard settling in sometimes. Y'all doin' okay?"

"It's not as though we're coming to a strange place," I said.

"No, but family can be a problem too, an' you got lots of family here." He set his coffee cup down on the counter. "So. I'm just tryin' to satisfy myself about Peggy's accident. I been down talking to Quintus already. You seen him?"

"Not since the funeral."

"He's not making much sense. Can't string more than two or three words together at a time. I told him to go see a doctor, but I don't know if he will. We miss your dad down here. Anyway, he saved the answering machine tape. Got Peggy's voice on it. Attaway was gettin' ready to record over it when I went in, and Quintus grabbed it. He was sittin' in a corner holding on to it. I sent Attaway out and got Quintus to play it for me. Had a couple messages from you on it."

"Quintus told me she'd quit her job and gotten depressed. I promised him I'd have her over."

"But you never did?"

"No, she never called me back. I meant to call her again but…I forgot."

I half expected Jimmy White to offer some sort of comfort, but his mind was elsewhere.

"So you never got to talk to her at all?" he asked.

"No. Sorry."

"What exactly did Quintus say to you, 'bout her state of mind?"

I cast back to Quintus, drinking coffee at my kitchen table with boxes stacked all around us. "He said, 'Peggy's okay, but she's not been real happy. She wants a baby, and nothing's happened.' Then he told me she'd been to specialists and to MCV, and then he said, 'She quit her job last month. She has spells where she sits and stares and won't wash her hair or talk or eat.'"

"Okay," Jimmy White said. "Well, I'll go on up and talk to your grandma. Quintus said he'd been up there just before. See you later." He straightened up, hiking automatically at his belt.

"Is there something about the accident…"

"Just gettin' the details straight in my mind," Jimmy White said politely.

We followed him out onto the porch. As he walked to the car I called, "Mr. White?"

"Yeah?"

"How fast was she going, when she went off the road?"

He stood with his hand on the door for a full quiet minute. "She went right off Winneck Curve into that big old gum tree," he said, finally. "Turned the car into a pile o' metal. No brake skids, but we tested the brakes and they worked just fine. I reckon she was going forty or so, and never bothered to put her foot on the brake. You two have a good weekend. Hope the church goes well for you, Reverend."

Chapter Eleven

J oe and Jenny arrived half an hour later. They brought flowers, complimented the food, and told stories about their jobs. It was midnight before they took themselves reluctantly away, promising that they'd see us Sunday.

Thomas and I talked Jimmy White's visit over, after they had gone. For several weeks we waited for some new development in Peggy's death, but nothing ever happened. Attaway spent his evenings sitting in Granny's living room, complaining loudly that Quintus had withdrawn from the farming just at the busiest time. But Granny Cora had gone silent on the subject of Peggy's death, and Quintus himself had disappeared from view. No one answered the Fowlerand phone. Quintus stayed in his room or went down (as Attaway grumbled) to the Catholic church to sit by Peggy's grave. Pierman and Roland were driven to actual work. Even Attaway was out in the fields, driving a combine in his bow ties and collared shirts and swearing at his son under his breath.

October wore on, and Matthew Humberston took in his cotton. The huge white bales sat at the edge of the road with canvas stretched over the top. Matt drove his trucks for him, and in the mornings I often saw him, rumbling down Little Croft Road with his cap pulled down over his eyes. Uncle Giddy harvested his corn, planted his winter wheat, and spent his mornings pinging away at the groundhogs from Granny's front steps.

Thomas enlisted the church in the Central Virginia

Foodbank, stocked a food pantry, and got Ida Scarborough elected the director of the Little Croft Preschool, due to open the following fall. He worked his way steadily down a visitation list of church members. Half the time, he found that Attaway had been there before him, asking harmless questions and making it clear that the new pastor was living on Fowlerand land.

This pinprick annoyance seemed to accomplish nothing, apart from throwing Matthew Humberston into a helpless rage. We had Matthew up several times for lunch—Matt never would come with him—and found him good company: an intelligent man, almost illiterate but sharp-minded and shrewd, with a pleasant dry humor. He would not speak of his son at all. Thomas tried twice to talk about the Fowlerand-Humberston hostilities, but each time the muscles in Matthew's face froze and a black curtain dropped down behind his dark eyes. The old resentment was a bleeding wound, too deep for any human remedy.

Despite all Thomas's efforts, attendance had dropped off slightly. We counted a growing number of the congregation as personal friends; we saw Joe and Jenny often, Ambrose and Ida clucked over us like the children they'd never had, and even John Whitworth managed to stay awake through a good majority of the sermons. The Raineys—returning to see whether we had burned our modern translations—swept out of Little Croft Church with magnificent condemnation. "And good riddance," Thomas said afterwards in an unpastoral moment.

But with curiosity satisfied, the Little Croft parishioners went back to daily life. The congregation puttered along as it had for the last two hundred years. Thomas worked doggedly, preaching and counseling and knocking on doors, taking food down to Winnville and hope up to the big new houses being built along Route 5. Visitors came, and rarely came back. Fishing, hunting, the Sunday newspaper, Sunday morning sleep-ins; all rated far above the little rural church and Thomas's careful explanations of the gospel of Luke.

I saw Quintus again six weeks after Peggy's funeral. The October afternoon was sharp, and lemon-colored leaves were drifting steadily down from the big maple in the backyard. It was Thursday; Thomas had gone to tea with the Missionary Society again, and I'd been at Granny's all day. I came home and showered and was in the kitchen putting dinner together when Quintus's truck came over the little rise in Poverty Ridge Road.

I ran out the front door and stood beside the road. I'd called him over and over; eventually I'd given up leaving messages. He slowed, reluctantly, and rolled the truck window down and cut the motor. His movements were small and careful, as though every muscle in his body hurt. His blue eyes were sunk deep into their sockets and every vein stood out beneath papery skin.

"Quintus!" I said.

Quintus gazed back at me. He was wearing a heavy flannel shirt against the cooling air, but I could see that he was shockingly thin. Deep lines led from his nose to the corners of his mouth.

"I wrote you a letter," I said at last. I hadn't known what else to do.

"I got it."

"You're killing yourself."

"Don't pick at me, 'Manda." He turned his eyes away from me. After a moment he said, half defiantly, "I converted."

"Converted? To what?"

"To bein' a Catholic. Like she was."

"Really?"

"Daddy thinks I gone and lost my mind."

"You don't look as though it's done you any good."

"I can pray for her," Quintus said. "This way, I can pray for her. Reverend Norris, he told me once that anybody died without being a good Christian, they were prob'ly in hell, and I don't know what Peggy was. But Father Jarrow tells me I can still pray for her."

"God is merciful, Quintus."

"Huh," Quintus said. He turned the key and the truck motor started again. "Uncle Giddy called Daddy for some physotoxin. He sent me over with it, so I better get goin'."

I watched him drive away. If a child's first picture of God was his father, I didn't wonder that Quintus doubted the Almighty's mercy. He walked into the Old House with a cardboard box in his hand, came straight back out, and drove back down Poverty Ridge Road. He didn't turn his head to look towards where I stood in the Tenant House yard.

I saw Quintus that night, in a bright saw-edged dream full of light and air and wind. We were fishing off the banks of the Chickahominy. He was sitting beside me, his pole between his feet, tying a hook onto my line with strong thin hands. Warm summer sun lay all around us. I could hear my father's voice nearby, Giddy's slow drawl, and Uncle Attaway's sharp laugh.

Quintus towered over me. The river breeze blew strong across the water and stirred his blond hair against the tanned skin of his face. He was smiling. I could smell fish scales and river mud and the brackish scent of a tidewater marsh, thick in the warm air. The small washing waves of the Chickahominy sloshed against the bank. I said, hearing the small voice of an eight-year-old, "You should go away from Little Croft." He couldn't hear me; he went on knotting the transparent line, his face full of absent kindness.

I woke up suddenly with my heart pounding as though I'd dreamed of a monster. Soaking rain beat steadily down outside. The light and wind and air of the dream were gone; dark damp closed in all around me where I lay. The fall had been unusually wet. Corn still in the fields had begun to mold.

I got up and made hot chocolate and drank it in the kitchen, half reading an old Agatha Christie, watching water run down the black glass. Whatever dying sadness had soaked into the walls of the Tenant House didn't belong to Miss Clunie. When I closed my eyes, I saw Doris Fowlerand lying white upstairs, and Quintus in his crib, soaked and hungry, with no one to lift him up over the edge.

Chapter Twelve

Friday morning came up cloudy and chill, with a gray wind blowing up the Chickahominy River hill and a steady dismal drip of rain. I woke up late. My early-morning reading had slipped in the last weeks. I could feel a cold starting in the back of my throat.

I stepped out onto the porch to feed the dogs. Daphne and Chelsea had finished their groundhog hide and had now come up with a large beetle-infested section of deer hide in the woods, left there by some early hunter. They had dragged it up to the back porch. It still possessed one hind foot and a gnawed-upon head, and the combined smell of wet dog and deer rose up in a cold miasma around me.

Thomas had gotten up early for breakfast with the local chapter of the Ruritans. I left him a note, asking him to get rid of the hide when he had a chance, and went over to Granny Cora's. She was in a foul mood, and I rolled her hair and did her laundry to a grumbling stream of complaints.

Uncle Giddy drove up around ten and climbed out of his truck, looking gloomily triumphant.

"I got 'em now," he announced, coming in the door.

"Morning," I said from the kitchen.

"Huh? Oh. Good mornin'. I got poison gas for them groundhogs."

"Poison gas?"

"You block up the tunnels, see, and drop these pellets

down there, and the gas goes all through the den underground and kills 'em all."

"Yeah? And what does it do to your farmland?"

"Nothin'," Giddy said cheerfully. "Physotoxin. Quintus brought it last night. Same stuff I fumigate them silos with to kill the weevils. Don't do a thing to the wheat a'tall. Mornin', Mama."

"Huh," Granny Cora said, huddling into her shawl.

Giddy helped himself to coffee and headed down the graveyard lane with a shovel. The cold drizzle didn't seem to bother him at all; he was out there the rest of the morning, poking through the stones and the field in an enlarging circle, hunting for groundhog exits and shoveling dirt into the holes.

Granny demanded chitterlings and mayonnaise on Wonder Bread for lunch, so I didn't eat with her. I got back to the Tenant House around four, ravenously hungry. My note was gone from the door, but the bedraggled piece of deer still inhabited the back porch. Daphne and Chelsea lay on the damp boards, their noses pressed lovingly against the dirty hide.

I changed into old clothes, found my rubber gloves, hauled the deer hide out to the Chickahominy River hill, and threw it over. The Saint Bernards pranced around behind me, begging for their treasure. But they were either too large or too lazy to plunge down the vine-coiled slope after it. I went back in and changed for the second time. I heard the door slam while I was in the bathroom, scrubbing my arms up to the elbows.

"Thomas?" I called.

He put his head in through the bathroom door. His hair glittered with damp, and the shoulders of his coat were dark with water.

"What are you doing?" he said, eyeing the container of antibacterial soap.

"I just threw that old piece of deer over the hill."

"I pitched it over once this morning, but they had it back on the porch in twenty minutes."

"Maybe you didn't throw it far enough."

"Maybe not. I've been all around Winnville this afternoon. Went to every house in that dreary run-down section. I couldn't even get through the door most places." He stood and looked at me, his face drawn into lines and his hands jammed into his pockets. "People wouldn't even come to the door. I could see shadows behind the curtains, but when I knocked no one would answer. How am I supposed to make a difference down there, Amanda? I'm trying everything I know. I go to those big fancy houses and the people there are too busy even to hear what I have to say. That's okay, I keep going back to the Gospels in my morning reading, and I see that Christ spent most of his time with the poor. But when I go down to the poorer sections, I keep running headfirst into a wall as thick as stone."

He reached for a towel and started to dry his hair.

"These are Great-uncle Attaway's slums, right?" I asked.

"Yeah."

"Sounds like his visitations have done some damage."

Thomas hung the towel up, straightening the edges scrupulously. "I'm pretty sure Christ's great-uncle didn't wander around sabotaging his ministry to the poor."

"We could move out of this house."

"Then we'd have to pay rent; and you'd have to start writing ad copy again; and what about your grandmother? And I'll still be the guy that married Attaway Pierman Fowlerand's great-niece. It's not just the Winneck slums, Amanda. We haven't had anyone new come to the church in two months. I keep wondering how much that has to do with your great-uncle and his visits."

I gazed at him in distress.

"I was so sure I knew why we were here," Thomas said. "I thought this church was God's gift to me...a place where I could finally find a family. I don't understand why the family has now become the thing that holds me back."

"I don't either. Thomas, I'm so sorry..." I could hear the inadequacy of the words.

Thomas shrugged slightly, turning half away from me. "And I'm starving," he said.

"We have hamburgers. And chips and pickles."

"Good."

"And there's a pint of Ben & Jerry's in the freezer. So after dinner we can eat ice cream and watch TV."

"I'm sure that's what the Puritans did when they were disappointed with God," Thomas said.

He sat up late that night; when I went to bed he was still in the fireplace room with his New Testament and Thomas à Kempis open in his lap, gazing out the black windowpanes. I leaned my elbows on the sill of the bedroom window upstairs and prayed for him: wordless, desperate, feeling his helplessness in the face of my family's complicated quarrels. Cold struck in at me through the glass.

I woke at two, when the telephone downstairs rang. Thomas was beside me. He threw an arm out and mumbled, "Wha's that?"

"Telephone," I said. I put my head under the pillow, but the shrill noise went on and on and on. I threw the covers off and stumbled downstairs in the dark, banged my foot against the table, and hopped across the kitchen, muttering curses.

"Hello?"

I could hear scuffling and a heavy gasp. Someone was shouting in the distance.

"Hello?"

A male voice demanded, "This the new preacher's house?"

"The new—Yes. Yes, it is. The Little Croft Church preacher?"

"Can y' get him?"

"In the middle of the night?"

The voice shouted, "Is he like a priest?" The yells in the background were increasing in volume.

"What do you mean?"

"Can he do what a priest does?"

"What do you want him to do?"

"Man's dying," the voice bellowed. "Wants a priest. Can he do that?"

I heard the bedroom door open upstairs.

"Thomas!" I called. "Thomas!" I said into the telephone, "Wait a minute and you can talk to him—"

"No time, lady. He's bleedin' to death. Tell him to get down to Fowlerand Landing." The dial tone sounded in my ear.

I slammed the phone down and ran to the bottom of the stairs. The faucet was running in the bathroom. I scrambled up the stairs and found Thomas blearily drawing a glass of water.

"Thomas, someone just called and said there's a man bleeding to death down at Fowlerand Landing. They want a priest—"

"Did they have the wrong number?"

"No. There's no priest in Little Croft. Someone was asking for a priest and they thought to call you."

"Okay," Thomas said, looking around for his pants.

"Are you going?"

"Yes, of course. Why not?" He dumped the glass down and headed for the bedroom. The light came on, blinding both of us. He scuffled for his shoes under the bed.

I thought of the background of yells and loud scraping noises and decided to go with him. I pulled on jeans and a sweatshirt and dug through my purse for the cellular phone I carried with me when driving alone. Daniel might have gone into the lion's den with his trust in God alone, but that didn't mean we had to go waltzing down to Fowlerand Landing cut off from man's aid.

"What are you doing?" Thomas demanded, tying his sneakers.

"I'm coming too. Just in case."

Fowlerand Landing Road angled off from Little Croft Road just past the church, and the old Fowlerand house—Great-uncle Attaway's family home—lay at the very end of the road. All along Fowlerand Landing, lanes wandered off into the depths of the Fowlerand holdings, mailbox after mailbox plastered with Fowlerand names. Attaway's old white-porched house stood at the north edge of the vast tract of land, right on the banks of the Chickahominy.

Thomas drove recklessly fast, swerving to avoid ruts. We came around the final bend to find the front of Attaway's house lit up by a dozen sets of truck lights. Pickups had been pulled into a semicircle in the front yard. The windows reflected the headlights back. The house itself was dark, no lights inside, and on the front porch a man sprawled on his face in a black pool of blood. Another man lay propped on his back against the steps, his head sagging backwards against the top step and his face streaked dark red in the yellow truck lights. Two other men stood over him, one of them gripping a shotgun in both hands.

"This looks bad, Thomas," I said.

"Doesn't your great-uncle live here?" Thomas pulled the car over into the shadows. Two strapping Fowlerand men had seen us already and were running towards the little hatchback.

"Yes. Quintus too. But Attaway's truck isn't here. He must be away. Don't get out of the car—"

One of the Fowlerands hammered on the glass. His face was distorted with something stronger than fear. He bellowed, "Man wants a priest!"

"I have to get out," Thomas said. "You stay in here. Lock the doors."

He reached across me and pushed the lock down. The Fowlerands were waiting on his side of the car, hulking in the dim light. Thomas got slowly out of the driver's side, slamming the door hard after him. I groped for the cell phone. What was the emergency number on a portable phone? 911? I dialed it and listened to the maddening delay as the phone clicked over and over again. I could see Thomas between the Fowlerands, walking through the wall of trucks into the glare of the headlights. More men appeared from the darkness. I cracked the window slightly. I could just hear their voices, raised and slurred. I pushed the END button on the phone and dialed 0 instead.

"...chased him all the way down here. He never had a chance..."

"...came down and found him sneaking off. If he dies..."

"Got what he deserved, the crawling..."

"He was begging for a priest. Said he was dying and goin' to hell."

Thomas had stooped over the man who lay with his head on the steps. Someone spewed out a sewer-stream of curses, ordering him away. He straightened and stepped over the prone figure on the steps, bending instead over the man on the porch. James Earl Jones's recorded voice said sweetly in my ear, "Welcome to Bell Atlantic."

"I want a real person!" I bellowed. A female voice said, "How may I help you?"

"I need the Little Croft sheriff. It's an emergency."

"Hold for the number, ma'am."

"Not the number! I can barely hear you. You've got to connect me." The threatening half-circle was closing in around Thomas, kneeling next to the sprawled man on the porch. I put my forehead against the glass of the car window and felt my heart beating up into the back of my throat. After a century of slow time, I heard the telephone ring once, twice, three times. A welcome drawl said, "Sheriff's office."

"This is Amanda Clement—Cora Scarborough's granddaughter. I'm down at Fowlerand Landing, and there's a dead man down here and a big fight going on."

The voice said, reassuringly, "Hold on, Amanda." I recognized the timbre now: Helen Adkins, short and fortyish, a Little Croft deputy since my high school days.

"Okay," Helen said rapidly. "I'll get a deputy down there right now, and I've put out a call to the trooper who lives down on the state land. He can be there in five minutes. What's happening now?"

"My husband's with the dead man." Actually, I had seen the arm of the figure on the porch twitch, but I figured a dead man would get the state trooper out here sooner. "There's another guy all beat up, Helen."

"I'll get the rescue squad too. Want to stay on the line?"

Thomas, on his knees, had his neck craned up, talking to the Fowlerand who stood threateningly above him. I could hear the man's loud voice. "He's still moving. He ain't dead yet."

Thomas's voice, raised against the noise, "He's dead. Let me talk to that man."

The man on the steps raised his hand slightly, and someone kicked him in the ribs. The half-circle was closing in. Thomas was on his feet, backing up against the house wall.

"Helen!" I yelled.

"Hold on, honey. The trooper's almost there."

Someone was shouting again. Suddenly the yellow light was laced with red and blue. A state police car was easing down Fowlerand Landing Road. It idled past me and came to a stop. Immediately the tight cluster of men at the porch began to disintegrate. The man against the steps had slid down into a huddle in the grass. A state trooper climbed out of the patrol car, his hand on his belt, and a moment later another set of lights appeared around the bend in the wood-lined road. The Little Croft deputy sheriff had arrived, with an ambulance close behind him.

"Amanda!" Helen's voice said.

"It's okay, Helen. They're here."

"Your man all right?"

"He's coming now." Thomas was weaving his way back through the maze of police vehicles and indignant Fowlerands. I unlocked the door for him. In the dimness I could see every familiar line on his face, carved deep and grim. He slid into the driver's seat and folded his hands on the steering wheel. His voice was shaking.

"He was alive when I first got there," he said. "He was still breathing. He died while I was trying to talk to him. He was breathing blood, because the guy on the steps there shot him through the lungs."

I reached for his hand. His fingers were frost.

"Who was it?"

"Amanda—"

"Who was it?"

"Quintus," Thomas said. "Amanda, darling, he wanted a priest. He wanted absolution. I told him God would forgive his sins. His eyes were already looking into the pit."

"Quintus," I said, slowly. I peered through the fogging glass and saw a glimpse of matted fair hair disappearing under the Rescue Squad's concealing blanket.

"That's not all," Thomas said. "Matt Humberston shot him."

"Matt?"

"They're saying Quintus found Matt hunting on his land, and a fight started. Matt chased him all the way down this road, cornered him on the porch, and shot him in the chest. Then all these guys—are they your cousins too?"

"Very distant." I could hear my own voice, muffled as though it came through glass.

"Well, they caught Matt and beat him over the head with a shotgun barrel until we showed up. They were mostly drunk too. I don't know what they would've done, Amanda. They kept telling me that Quintus was alive because he was moving. He was, too; his fingers were twitching a little and every once in a while his foot would jump. But he was dead. He had blood coming out of his mouth. They wanted to know if I'd saved him."

I could feel water on my face. I was thinking of Quintus sitting alone in the old Fowlerand house, staring unseeing out the windows, while Thomas and I ate and slept in companionable warmth. Thomas gripped my hand.

"We have to stay," he said. "The police want me to make a statement. About what he said when he was dying."

"What did he say?"

"He said, 'Matt said he'd kill me. Told me yesterday he'd kill me. Tonight, said he'd been meanin' to kill me all his life and now he had the chance.' They want to write that down. Then I turned around to Matt. I wouldn't have recognized him, he had so much blood on his face, but he was yelling, 'Is he dead? Is he dead?' I was so mad I said, 'Yes, he's dead and you killed him.' And he said, 'Good!' and put his head back on the steps and passed out. I guess they want to write that down too."

I rubbed the persistent tears from my eyes. The limp darkhaired figure on the steps was being loaded into the ambulance. As the stretcher moved into the blazing lights of the police car, I glimpsed Matt's features beneath the streaks of dried blood. Thomas's face was papery white in the revolving lights from the trooper's car. I put my head against his chest, and he held me; there was blood smeared along the palms of his hands.

Chapter Thirteen

I woke up late Saturday morning in the warm circle of Thomas's arms. He was sound asleep with his face buried in my neck. I lay for a moment feeling his chest rise and fall. A mockingbird was calling just outside the window. Sun washed over the floor, and an October breeze rapped the maple branches against the roof. I stretched and then remembered, suddenly: Quintus Fowlerand was dead. His tall gangling body was stiff in a drawer. Thomas had spent twenty minutes hunched over the kitchen sink the night before, scrubbing caked blood from around his fingernails.

He woke when I moved, and his arms tightened around me. I could feel in his muscles the strong need for reassurance. Neither of us spoke; but it was as if our private place had been invaded, shadowed by violence. Even as I banished thought from my mind, I could see in uneven flashes the sprawled bodies, the faces knotted with anger, Thomas kneeling in the harsh headlights of the Fowlerand trucks.

I stood in the shower for a long time afterwards. The warm smell of coffee brewing floated into the bathroom, but I went on standing, watching water puddle around my feet. I could hear Granny Cora's decisive old voice in my ears. *There's no preacher yet that's made any difference to this county. God's forgotten we're here, and we're still doing just fine.*

I dragged up half-remembered words from the prayer book

and repeated them over and over in my mind, driving out the circle of despair.

Lord, have mercy upon us.
Christ, have mercy upon us.
Lord, have mercy upon us.

The bathroom door creaked open. Steam danced around me, driven by the draft. Thomas's hand came around the curtain, holding a mug full of coffee.

"I feel like someone hit me on the back of the head," he said.

I took the mug silently.

"There's water dripping off every flat surface in here," he said. "You going to get out soon?"

"In a minute."

"I'm supposed to go down to the sheriff's office this morning."

"Okay. I'll be out in a minute."

I could see Thomas's shadow through the blue-and-white shower curtain. He was rummaging for his razor, examining his face in the mirror.

"You okay?" I drank some coffee. I'd made it strong, and I could feel it, black and bitter, all the way down to my stomach.

"Yeah."

Silence. I heard his razor tapping against the side of the sink. I drank some more coffee. The razor chinked against the shelf of the medicine cabinet.

"Right," Thomas said. "Yell when you're done."

The door closed behind him. I put the mug on the edge of the tub and lathered up my hair. Matthew's son had killed

Attaway's son at the end of Fowlerand Landing Road, with Thomas as final witness. I could hardly believe it had happened.

I turned off the water, climbed out of the tub, and stood gazing into the mirror, absently toweling my hair. Blue Fowlerand eyes looked back at me. My father had given me his thick straight light brown hair. But the bones of my face, the curve of cheek and line of eyebrow, were all Fowlerand, pared down and free of Attaway's padding wrinkles.

I went back into the room to dress. Thomas's feet creaked up the stairs. The shower began to run again.

He didn't come home for lunch. I ate some soup and went back to bed. I'd spent the morning drifting around the house in a state of growing agitation, and by noon I was almost sick to my stomach with anxiety. I took two aspirin and lay down and forced myself into stillness. The buzzing restlessness in my arms and legs faded slowly into heaviness. I was hovering just above the abyss of deep sleep when I heard the tires of Thomas's car in the yard.

I lay where I was, listening. His feet sounded on the porch steps. The back door opened and closed. The refrigerator door opened and closed. The stairs creaked. The room darkened slightly as his body cut off the light from the hallway. He sat down on the foot of the bed, popping open a can of Coke. I felt my chest squeeze itself into a tight painful knot. His face was closed and dark.

"Matt's still in the hospital with a concussion," he said. "I saw Matthew walking away from the sheriff's office when I went through the doors, but he didn't see me. I don't think he knows yet that I was there. I've been giving statements since ten." He took a swig of his drink and stared out the window at the tangle of yellowing leaves. "They might subpoena me for the trial. Depends on whether Matt spoke to me as a pastor or as a witness. No one really seems to know... I think I'll take Chelsea out for a walk."

He looked at me sideways.

"You can go alone," I said. "I'm not going to be hurt."

"I'm sorry. I don't know what to do. I need to think."

I sat up and hugged my knees, watching him change into old shoes. I didn't know what to do either; but suddenly I felt responsible for this whole mess. My family, my home, my childhood church—my relatives, shooting each other in the fields I had played in as a child.

Thomas spent all of Saturday afternoon over in the church office, working on his sermon. I stayed home, stared blankly at a book, prayed for him in an agony that went beyond words, and listened to the phone ring. Granny Cora was dying to hear all the details. The answering machine contained eight hang-ups when I checked it just before bed.

We didn't discuss Matthew Humberston the next morning. In three years of marriage, I'd discovered that Thomas was a nervous preacher. If he went into a sermon preoccupied, he talked in endless jittery circles. He went back over to the church at dawn to preach his sermon to the empty pews, and came back to pick me up just before ten. I stood in the back of the church and watched cars pull into the packed-dirt lot. Matthew's dark pickup truck didn't appear, but the crowd had grown since last week. Curiosity or the hope of a good juicy gossip had brought out a large segment of Little Croft.

If they'd hoped for an eyewitness account of the local scandal, they were disappointed. Thomas preached on the fourth chapter of Luke, and we sang three hymns that were completely unconnected to death and hatred. Amelia Whitworth's sharp brown eyes were eager, but she said nothing. Ida clucked over us as though we'd suffered through a fire or flood. Ambrose and John flanked Thomas with bland indifference as he stood at the back door to shake hands afterwards. In the face of that incurious double stare, no one asked questions.

A new family had visited: a clean-cut man in his early forties with a blond wife and two beautiful little girls. They thanked us on the way out and invited Thomas for a pastoral visit. I saw the shadow lift slightly from Thomas's face, and I was grateful.

I couldn't face Granny Monday morning. I knew she wouldn't be satisfied until she had dug every detail of Quintus's murder out of me. The mild cold I'd been running since Friday obligingly developed into a racking cough and a fever, so I curled up under the blankets with a book and let Thomas call me in sick.

I could hear his patient voice down in the kitchen, fencing Granny's questions. "No, ma'am," he said, "Sheriff White asked me not to talk about it." Pause. "Yes, ma'am." Pause. "No, ma'am." Another pause. "No, she's coughing with every breath, so I don't think so." Short silence. "Yes, ma'am, I'll be sure to tell her so. Good-bye, Mrs. Scarborough."

He came back up the stairs and put his head through the bedroom door.

"Thanks," I croaked.

"Your grandmother says to rub Vicks on your chest."

"Oh, yeah. Right away."

"And she says you need to stop sneezing by tomorrow so you can drive her to Quintus's funeral at three-thirty."

I pulled the covers up to my ears. "Lord have mercy."

"I'll come keep you company."

"Do you think you ought to?"

"Yes. I watched your cousin die, I told him he wouldn't go to hell, and I'm going to his funeral. Jimmy White can't object to that. I won't talk to anybody, that's all."

"Not even to Matthew Humberston?"

Thomas said, "What's your uncle doing in the graveyard?"

"He's getting ready to poison the groundhogs. Did you ever read *Watership Down?*"

"Nope. Why?"

"You get a rabbit's-eye view of what it's like to be gassed in your own comfortable den."

"Am I supposed to feel sorry for the groundhogs?" Thomas asked. I realized that he was delaying, reluctant to leave.

"Want me to quote?"

"Go ahead."

"'All shall be well, and all shall be well, and all manner of thing shall be well.' Dame Julian of Norwich."

"Drat Dame Julian. I'm not worried about the eschaton. I'm a little concerned about the next six months."

"'The battle is not against flesh and blood, but against—'"

"Yes, I know," he said, "but the flesh and blood's pretty darn powerful, isn't it? Blast Matthew anyway. Why didn't he teach his son not to go shooting Catholics late at night?"

"I expect Matt was drunk."

"He smelled like the entire Busch brewery on a windy day, but if he threatened Quintus the day before, it's still premeditated.

They'll put him away for decades. Amanda, I think I might go see a lawyer. Do you mind? It'll cost something."

"No, I think that's a good idea."

I started coughing then, and Thomas took himself off to the church office. I never did say what I was thinking: that even if Matt's words were deemed to be words of confession to his pastor, Thomas would still have to decide whether to speak them. Quintus had died, after all, and Matt Humberston had killed him.

At three-thirty the next day, we were seated in the Northend graveyard once more. Red clay covered Peggy's grave. Quintus's coffin was covered with flowers.

Granny was wearing her funeral outfit again, umbrella and all. "It's not raining," I had whispered to her.

"It might," she retorted.

So we made our way through the crowd with the big purple-lettered umbrella hung over my arm. The same canopy stood over the same square of green indoor-outdoor carpeting. Mr. Adkins stood at his same sentry post, watching the proceedings with a sharp eye. Attaway was seated in the front row of folding chairs this time, and his bow tie was black. Quintus's cousins flanked their uncle; Roland was sniffing and wiping his nose, Pierman staring into the distance. A row of strapping Fowlerand cousins filled the row of chairs just behind them, scrubbed clean and newly shaved. Mrs. Morris sat at the far right-hand corner. None of the male Fowlerand heads turned towards her. I saw her eyes dart sideways once, twice.

"Well," Granny said, settling into her chair, "I reckon she's glad to have Quintus here. Me now, I think he ought to be back on the Fowlerand plot where he belongs. Don't know what Attaway was thinking of."

Thomas folded his tall body into the chair next to me. Cars were still pulling onto the grass verge on the other side of the low graveyard wall. A black pickup truck cut its engine at the corner of the road, and Matthew Humberston emerged from the front seat, alone.

"Look," I said softly into Thomas's ear.

"What?"

"Right there."

"Lord o' mercy," Granny said, "there's Matthew."

At the sound of her voice, the Fowlerand heads turned as one. Matthew Humberston was alone, wearing a black suit. On the other side of the coffin, the priest began reading.

"'The LORD is my shepherd, I shall not want...'"

I fixed my eyes virtuously on Father Jarrow, but I could tell Matthew Humberston was coming nearer by the growing silence at my back. He walked by my left shoulder, directly to the last row of chairs, and seated himself at the far end.

"'He leadeth me beside the still waters...'"

Matthew, suddenly struck by a thought, dug in his breast pocket, took out a pair of sunglasses, and began to wipe them with elaborate care. I could see a muscle start to twitch at the corner of Attaway's mouth. But he caught himself and sat perfectly still, staring straight ahead. Matthew dropped his sunglasses, apparently by accident, clicked his tongue and bent down to rummage beneath his seat. He hadn't glanced over at Thomas at all. Thomas was bouncing his knee up and down beside me. I put my hand on his knee and he stilled it at once.

"'Surely goodness and mercy shall follow me...'"

Granny leaned forward and said, quite loudly, "Hullo,

Matthew. Quit upstagin' the corpse and pay attention."

"'And I will dwell in the house of the LORD for ever,'" the priest said reprovingly. "Let us pray."

Thank God, I thought. Granny Cora folded her hands, temporarily silenced. Matthew Humberston bowed his head. We sat politely through the prayer and the homily, which I didn't hear; I was too busy picturing Matthew Humberston and my great-uncle slugging it out as soon as the priest said "Go in peace." When the words were finally spoken, I was ready to bolt for the car.

Thomas stood up, clearly intending to leave before Matthew could speak to him. The Fowlerands were getting to their feet, a solid wall of muscle right in front of Matthew's nose. Matthew leaned back in his chair. His glasses hid his dark eyes. The line of Fowlerands parted slightly, and Attaway appeared through the gap. He thrust his old head towards Matthew, and I barely heard the word that left his lips.

"Murderers."

Matthew Humberston said softly, "What's done in heat is no match for cold killing, is it, Attaway? You of all folk should know that."

He got suddenly to his feet. His eyes met Thomas's, briefly. He leaned forward. "My boy's still in the hospital," he said. "Won't be out till tomorrow. I been up there ever since." His voice was confidential. He nodded shortly and walked away.

Thomas looked at me. "He doesn't know yet," he mouthed.

I nodded. Matthew was making his way through the Northend graveyard, skirting the standing gravestones while the scattered funeral watchers scrambled out of his way.

~ ~ ~ ~ ~

Jimmy White had left a message on our answering machine. Matt was due to be released from the hospital on the following day and would probably be arraigned that same afternoon. He still didn't know whether Reverend Clement would be subpoenaed for the trial, so he'd appreciate it if Thomas would avoid any contact with Matt until further notice.

Thomas went off to meditate on his sermon. I decided to go for a walk. I was restless, and the fall air was sharp and liquid. I went out the back door and walked past the Old House, down the little ridge, into the thick wood that lay between the Old House and Fowlerand Landing Road.

The old footpath wound away through old pines bigger than my arms could circle around. Scrubby brush threatened the path's edges, but someone still used it; I could see a narrow beaten thread that persisted, under fallen trees and around soft marshy patches. I walked silently, hearing my feet crackle on pine needles and fallen holly leaves. The path crossed the remnants of an old barbed-wire fence, forded a little stream, and climbed an unexpected hill. I clambered to the top and found myself in a patch of beech woods. Wolf beeches, my mother had called them, big ancient trees that smothered all undergrowth and carpeted the ground with lemon-brown leaves. Stephen and Pat and I had called these our Robin Hood trees. They bore an uncanny resemblance to the towering oaks in the Wyeth illustration, Robin and his merry men half drenched in forest shade.

I turned abruptly and trudged back down the path, back towards the Tenant House.

Chapter Fourteen

I woke up early the next morning and went down to make coffee. An unseasonably warm wind was blowing leaves against the panes. I cracked a window for fresh air and sat down at my desk to do my Hebrew and reflect on the mighty acts of God.

But I couldn't concentrate on Exodus; I was suddenly impatient with all those magnificent miracles. I opened the book in front of me to the middle and read a psalm, trying to feel the shining phrases.

> One thing I ask of the Lord, one thing I seek;
> that I may dwell in the house of the Lord all the days
> of my life,
> to gaze upon his beauty and to seek him in the place
> where he lives.

I looked out the window. The sun was still below the horizon. River mist drifted in low wreaths across the fields outside my window; the white dirt road gleamed in the diffuse glow that comes just before sunrise. The breeze brought the clean wild smell of earth and leaves to my nose, and a hawk shrilled in the distance. I closed my eyes and tried to feel God's presence in all this beauty; but he was lost, somewhere, obscured by the Fowlerand-Humberston mess. And so I prayed: Son of God, have mercy on us. Clear this mess away so we can see your face again.

~ ~ ~ ~ ~

Thomas came down, shaved and dressed, and went out to feed the dogs. I fixed breakfast. When he came in, we ate at the kitchen table and discussed the fireplace. Soon it would be cold enough to light a fire, but something seemed to be blocking our chimney. I thought there was probably a dead bird in there. A foul smell was wreathing its way into the kitchen.

"Although," I added, "it seems to be coming in through the window, not from the chimney." I sniffed again. "Is it?"

"Is it what?"

"Coming through the window. That smell. It is." The kitchen window was cracked, and the putrefying odor seemed to be curling around from the back porch and creeping over the sill. I went into the hallway and peered out onto the back porch. Daphne and Chelsea were sprawled on the deer hide, nuzzling it with decadent affection.

"Phew! Didn't you see it when you fed them?"

Thomas looked sheepish. "I hated to take their new toy away from them."

"You should have pitched it over the hill again."

"They spent all day yesterday hauling it back up the hill. And I'm in my good clothes. I thought I'd do some more visitation today." He was wearing neat khakis and a sweater.

"Don't change the subject. They can't keep the deerskin."

"But they love it."

"They can't have it. It reeks. They reek. I'm in my old clothes, and I'm going to bury it."

So I went out with a shovel, while Thomas drove away towards the church, and dug a very deep hole in the rich dark dirt at the edge of the woods. I hauled the old deer hide over and tipped it into the hole, covered it up, and piled up heavy fallen branches into an impenetrable heap. When I came back up the path, I caught sight of the back of Great-uncle Attaway's truck, bumping away down Poverty Ridge Road.

I walked over to the Old House at nine. Giddy's truck was sitting at the edge of the graveyard path, half pulled into the field. He was stamping around in the inch-high wheat, poking at the ground with a stick and muttering to himself. I stopped at the gap in the fence and he waved the stick at me.

"Are you looking for something?" I called.

"Blamed groundhog dens," he bellowed back. "Got more exits than a dog's got ticks."

"Did they get away?"

"Not one death. Mind you," Giddy said, coming closer to me and shaking the stick for emphasis, "I got four rats and a squirrel and somebody's cat lyin' out here stiff as boards. That's good stuff, that gas. But the groundhogs got out. Must be another hole out here somewhere. I got to get them before they go underground for the winter."

"Hope you can find the other hole," I said, insincerely. I walked on up to the Old House, bracing myself to face Granny Cora.

Granny was already eating bacon and fried eggs for breakfast. She said, "I got Attaway to fix me breakfast. To save you trouble."

"Thanks very much," I said.

"You're welcome." She sopped up some bacon fat with a piece of bread.

"How's Great-uncle Attaway doing?" I asked. I could hear

a hint of sarcasm in my voice, but Granny said, quite seriously, "Mad as a porcupine with the itch. He didn't have no will."

"Who?"

"Attaway told me this morning. Quintus didn't make a will. Spitting furious, Attaway was, although the farm goes back to him anyway."

"How much of the farm did Quintus own?"

"Half of it. Attaway deeded it to him a while back." Granny wiped up the last bit of grease on her plate and licked her fingers. "Anyhow, he tied it all up tight and legal, made Quintus sign a will leavin' the property back to his father should he die. And drew up a paper sayin' Quintus couldn't sell the land unless he got his daddy's permission. Got his Richmond lawyer to do it for him. Turns out Quintus went back up to the lawyer last week and got the will back and burned it."

"And he didn't make a new one?"

"If he did, it's hid fast away," Granny said. "Nobody can't find it. Attaway was up this morning frothin' about it. Doesn't make a huge matter, of course; like I said, Quintus's land goes back to Attaway anyway, but he's got to pay more tax on it since the boy died interstate."

"Intestate."

"Whatever." She hunched over her plate, staring out the window. I waited for the grilling to start, but Granny was preoccupied.

"Granny? What do you need me to do first?"

"I reckon you can clean off them old shelves in the basement. And when you're done, you can go on home early. You don't look so good."

"It's just a cold."

"A cold an' a funeral. You got on well with Quintus, didn't you?"

"Well enough to wish someone else in this family felt sorry that he's dead," I said, suddenly losing my temper.

I took myself down to the basement and banged around among the old canning jars. I was honest enough to realize that this was partly hypocritical. The shock of Quintus's death had passed. When I thought of him, I was shaken by sudden washes of pity and regret, but I had seen so little of Quintus that his absence left no hole in my life. His absence left no holes in anyone's life.

I went back up the rickety stairs when I'd finished. Granny was reading her *Daily Press* at the kitchen table.

"I'm going, then," I said.

"Mandy."

"Yes, ma'am?"

"I used to put flowers on Doris's grave, every week, for years and years. Did it till Quintus got big enough to take care of his own mama's grave. I reckon Miz Morris will watch after Quintus and Peggy. But you can take me down to Fowlerand Landing next week. I'm gonna put me some more flowers on Doris's grave."

I was making coffee the next morning when Thomas went out with a pan of scraps for the Saint Bernards. The door slammed. I heard his footsteps on the porch and the thumping sound of the dogs leaping up and down. His voice said, "Morning, Chelsea. Hi, Daphne. Yo, Roscoe."

When he came back in, I asked, "Who's Roscoe?"

"The deer. It's obviously going to be a permanent part of

the family, so I thought I'd name it."

I rushed to the back porch. The dogs were caked in mud, belly deep. The deer hide grimaced at me from the top step. It had lost an ear and was considerably worse for having been buried all night.

"How far do I have to drag it?" I demanded. Chelsea waved her tail happily at me, and Daphne sat on the hide's head.

"Ah, let 'em have it," Thomas said.

"But it's disgusting. I can take it down the road and dump it in the woods a couple of miles away."

"Not in my car you don't."

"I'll put it in a garbage bag."

I dug out my gloves and headed for the porch. Daphne and Chelsea watched in alarm as I wrestled the deer hide into a black plastic bag and dragged it towards the car.

The little hatchback was leaning to one side. I thought at first that it was sitting with one back tire in a hole. But the right rear tire was so flat that the hubcap was embedded in the dirt. I got down on my knees to examine it, pushing the slobbering muddy dogs away. A knife had been inserted into the sidewall and drawn upwards.

Thomas called the sheriff's department, then handed me the phone. The tire cut had a deliberate, unsettling coldness to it that we both disliked. A man in a rage might stab a tire over and over, but one smooth-edged cut seemed like a warning.

Helen Adkins answered the phone at the sheriff's office. I explained the situation. A long and thoughtful silence ensued.

"Okay," she said at last. "Someone'll come over."

She set the phone down, but before the receiver hit the cradle I heard her say to someone else, "Didn't that Humberston boy get out yester—"

The dial tone replaced the last word. I went back out in the yard, where Thomas was prowling restlessly around his car. The sheriff himself arrived a bare ten minutes later, in full uniform.

"You having a spot of trouble?" he called.

"Not that big a deal," Thomas said. "Just that someone slashed one tire on the car last night. And we thought, with everything that's been going on..."

"Mm," Jimmy White said. He crouched down to examine the tire. Thomas dragged the dogs away from him.

"Thanks," the sheriff said. He straightened up, looking around.

"Poverty Ridge Road the only way in and out?"

"Yes," I said. "That hill goes straight down to the river."

"How about that?" He pointed at a gap in the trees on the other side of the field that lay beyond the silos.

"That's an old trail that goes back through the woods around the edge of the farm. It comes out on Winneck Road about three miles down. But there's trees down all across it."

"You didn't hear anything during the night?"

"No," Thomas said.

"What about the dogs? Do they bark?"

"Usually they bark their heads off, but they spent all last night back in the woods. Digging up an old piece of deer."

"They will do that," Jimmy White said. He walked around the yard a couple of times, looking down the long dirt lane.

"Well, I'll tell you what," he said at last. "I can't go putting names on nothing like this, not before I do some work. But young Matt Humberston, he got out of MCV yesterday morning, got arraigned yesterday afternoon, and got freed on bail last night. Three hundred an' fifty thousand dollars. His dad put up the deed to his farm. So he was wandering around last night, that's all I'll say."

"Matthew Humberston is one of my deacons," Thomas said.

"Yes, I know it. I don't think young Matt's told his daddy all there is to tell about that night at the Fowlerand house. Not just yet, anyway." Sheriff White took one more turn around the yard and halted in front of the car.

"I checked before I left," he said. "That trial's been scheduled to start November 9. So you got about a month to wait. I'm going to send a deputy by here a couple times a week until then. And you might want to tie your dogs where they'll make a racket. Be better anyway if they don't roam around picking up things to eat. Man who'll slash a tire will poison a dog next. An' I don't want somethin' worse than your tire slashed, if you catch my meaning. Might send a deputy by the church on Sunday mornings too. You let me know if you have any other troubles. Helen'll put your calls straight through to me. You got a spare?"

"In the trunk."

"I'll give you a hand with it. I'm gonna take this one back with me, if you don't mind. I think," Jimmy White said, reflectively, "I'm goin' to have me a little talk with the judge 'bout young Matt's bail."

The two men set about changing the tire. I went back into the house to dress. When I came back out, Sheriff White was slamming his trunk over the slashed tire and Thomas was tying the muddy dogs to the back steps.

Jimmy White jerked his head at me, and I walked over to his car, buttoning my coat against the cold October wind. It struck me as I came up to him that I knew Jimmy White like I knew dozens of Little Croft residents; the planes of his face were as familiar to me as the Little Croft Church steps. I knew where he lived, I knew who his children were and where his wife went shopping. I had no idea what he believed, what angered him, why he had spent his life here.

"Amanda," he said. "I want to talk to you about Peggy Fowlerand."

"Yes?"

"I went over and talked to your grandma 'bout Peggy, and I talked to your great-uncle. Attaway Fowlerand was as helpful as a stone. Your grandmother spoke to me like I was a field hand. And your Uncle Giddy sat beside her and said he didn't know nothing about nothing, and none of them would look me in the eye."

Thomas was clucking to the dogs. Jimmy White leaned slightly towards me. "There ain't no way Peggy Fowlerand lost control of that car," he said. "I reckon she killed herself, drove into a tree on purpose. I wasn't goin' to say so, for Quintus's sake. Accident was all right with me. But I've still got some questions I want cleared up. Your grandma's got something on her conscience, Amanda."

"She thinks it was suicide. Like you."

"I thought it was suicide at first," the sheriff said. "So did her mama. She told us Peggy'd been wanting a baby ever since she got married, that she'd been tryin' to get pregnant for two years and had been to all sorts of doctors. She'd started to say that she'd never be a mama, and life wasn't worth living. It made sense." He lowered his voice. "She was seven weeks pregnant when she died. We found out at the autopsy. Why would she kill herself, then?"

"Maybe she didn't know," I said.

"She had one of them pregnancy sticks in her purse, with the little dot all turned blue. Zipped in an inside pocket."

"Did Quintus know?"

Jimmy White shook his head. "I asked him a whole list of questions. If she ever drank, if she ever had dizzy spells, was she pregnant, did she ever take tranquilizers. He never twitched an eye. Said no, no, no, no. Her mama didn't know either; she was mournin' for Peggy and all the things she'd never get to do."

"When you told Quintus she was expecting—"

"He never knew," the sheriff said. "The doctor didn't tell him, and Helen lost the stick out of Peggy's purse before Quintus came to pick up her things. There was no reason for him to weep twice, over something dead and gone."

I watched him get into the brown car. He leaned over to the open passenger side window.

"You think about that over the weekend, and then maybe you'll want to tell your grandmother about it," he said. "I think something's eating at her. Maybe it'll unseal her mouth if she knows a child died along with Peggy. And there's no reason not to tell now. They're all dead."

He drove away down Poverty Ridge Road. I walked over to the Old House with the words ringing round and round in my mind; a mournful refrain for the day's work.

I made a run to the grocery store in Mercysmith that evening while Thomas was walking the dogs. I put Roscoe the deer in the trunk of the little blue car and dumped him in a ditch four miles away. As I drove back into Little Croft, heading into the setting sun, I found myself behind a coffin. I was certain it was a coffin. It lay on the bed of a dark green pickup truck traveling at a careful thirty miles per hour, and dirt was crumbling off the edges. Two Fowlerand boys were perched up near the cab, their knees drawn up and their feet carefully not touching the long box. The back window was shaded, and I couldn't see the driver. But before I reached Poverty Ridge, the truck turned into Fowlerand Landing Road and drove towards the old Fowlerand graveyard.

Chapter Fifteen

I kept Peggy's secret over the weekend. Once I told Granny, I'd have to tell Thomas as well. I knew he was already wrestling with his obligations to the dead and to the living.

We were late getting up Saturday morning. I had woken at midnight and turned to Thomas in sudden need of reassurance. I wasn't used to keeping secrets from him, and I didn't like the sudden slight drift I felt between us. For three years, my marriage had been the center of my life; Thomas's tall broad-shouldered figure, the crinkles at the corners of his brown eyes, the strong line of his jaw and the way his skin smelled and the way he stood and sat and moved all sent the blood running warm beneath my skin. I loved him overwhelmingly. I wanted to see him happy. I wanted Attaway and Matthew and Matt and the rest of my family to go away so that he could do his work.

Thomas had answered my midnight panic without a moment of hesitation. We stayed in bed late Saturday morning; I was drifting in a pleasant pink doze when a fusillade of rifle shots went off just outside. I sat straight up in bed. Thomas put a pillow over his head and said, "Now what?"

"I'll go see," I said, groping for my clothes. Daphne and Chelsea were scrabbling and whining on the porch below. When I opened the back door, they darted in past me and dived behind the living room sofa.

I went out into the backyard. A four-wheeled vehicle like an oversized golf cart sat at the curve in Scarborough Road, fifty feet from the Tenant House. It was outfitted with rifle rests, gun racks, and a canopy. Two men were sitting in it. The backs of their heads were identical: square and thick-necked, bristly in short military haircuts. One was sighting a rifle with a scope the size of a summer zucchini toward the graveyard.

"Hey!" I said.

The rifle cracked, and the rifleman said, "Dang it!" A brown movement at the top of the graveyard hill caught my eye. The groundhogs were fleeing for cover.

"Hey!" I said, in a louder voice. The two men looked around. They both had dark eyes, strong jaws, prominent noses; the man with the rifle was long-chinned and lanky, the other rounder-faced and shorter.

"Mornin'," they said in chorus.

"What are you doing?"

"Shooting your groundhogs," the long-chinned man said. "Ronald Knox. This here's my brother Richard. Gideon Scarborough told us we could come up an' hunt."

"Did you have to start first thing on Saturday morning?"

"We got so little time," Ronald Knox said, apologetically. "We're up at Fort Eustis, see, and we gotta be back at six tonight. Mr. Scarborough said he had a couple stubborn old 'uns up at that graveyard. You tell him we've killed three already and spotted five more, and there's dens at the bottoms of all those telephone poles there. I reckon there's forty groundhogs in these four fields."

The poles ran through the middle of the corn, from the top of the hill all the way down to the blacktop. I eyed the rifle in Ronald Knox's hand.

"You're shooting towards the road," I said.

"Yes'm, but that's legal. Hundred fifty feet away, that's all we got to be."

"Doesn't that rifle carry farther than a hundred and fifty feet?"

"Oh, yes," Ronald Knox said, slightly shocked.

"Try not to shoot any of my relatives, okay?"

"Yes'm. We'll be careful. Don't worry, we do this all the time. Like a hobby for us, it is."

"Groundhog hunting?"

"Yep. We been all up and down Little Croft. Killed forty-two one day, out at the Humberston farm."

"What do you do with them afterwards?"

"Nothin'," Ronald Knox said. "The fun's in the shooting."

"I see."

"I c'n save a couple for those big old dogs of yours, if you want. Dogs love to chew on 'em."

"No thanks," I said.

I went back in the house. We ate breakfast while rifle shots popped away outside. In a sudden lull, Great-uncle Attaway's pickup truck came bumping over the hill. Instead of swinging past the Tenant House towards Granny's, Attaway pulled into our driveway. I heard his boots on the outside steps and a knock on the porch door.

Thomas disappeared to change his sweats for jeans. I went to answer the door. Attaway was wearing a blue shirt and a cream bow tie. He said, "Morning, Amanda. Clement here?"

"He'll be down in a minute."

"Right, then. Got a question for him." He sniffed and peered over the doorstep at me. He said abruptly, "You there, Amanda, when Matt shot my boy?"

"I was in the car when we went down, yes."

"Matt tell him anything? Say he did it? Say why?"

"Thomas doesn't tell me what's said to him in confidence, Uncle Attaway."

"Huh. Well, I'll find out soon enough, I reckon. Already been down to the courthouse a couple o' times, but the sheriff is full up of his own importance and won't tell me nothing. Jimmy White! Finally back off vacation an' acting like the king of the hill. I remember his daddy lyin' drunk out at the Cook's Hall corner all day when I was a boy, while I was working sunup to sundown in Daddy's fields."

He turned his head and spat, glanced down the road, and then back at me. There was an unmistakable tone of satisfaction in his voice.

"Won't get away with this one, Matt won't. Humberston can't buy everybody off this time. They were talking soft, down at the courthouse, but that's what it means."

I stepped back from the door, hearing Thomas's tread behind me. Attaway wasn't mourning for his son. He was purely rejoicing, polishing Matthew Humberston's shame and grief like a shining jewel.

Thomas went out, closing the porch door behind him. The two men stood in the yard, deep in conversation. I could hear them indistinctly; Attaway's drawling rumble, Thomas's answer. Eventually Attaway went back to his pickup truck. He drove past, heading back for the main road. Thomas came back up the steps, rubbing his unshaven chin. The rifle shots started up again.

"You're not going to believe this," he said.

"What?"

"He wants me to bury Quintus."

"Do another service, you mean?"

"No. Your Great-uncle Attaway dug him up. Moved him from the Morris plot to the family graveyard down at Fowlerand Landing. He wants me to go down this afternoon and help rebury him."

"Is that legal?"

"I have no idea."

"What did you tell him?"

"What could I say? He's got Quintus in a coffin on his back porch. I can't exactly refuse to put the poor man back in the ground, can I? My very first funeral in Little Croft and the body's already been buried once. Lemme go shave."

"Are you sure you ought to do it?"

"Listen," Thomas said, "everyone in this county has either Fowlerands or Humberstons in their family tree. If I end up in court, I'm going to make all the Humberston relations mad. I'm not going to alienate all the Fowlerands too. Anyway, Amanda, how can I leave Quintus unburied all weekend?"

I agreed, reluctantly. Thomas headed for the stairs. In a minute he put his head down over the banisters.

"Do me a favor, would you? Find the phone number of the Northend priest? I'd better make sure there's nobody on the way to arrest your great-uncle for desecrating holy ground or something like that."

The Northend priest, when reached, had just noticed the gaping hole in his graveyard. I could hear his deep indignant voice clearly from the receiver.

"...grave robbing...permission from the diocese...has to be authorized by the clerk of the court..."

Thomas said soothingly, "I'm sure Mr. Fowlerand did the proper paperwork—"

"I doubt it," I said.

Thomas scowled at me. The priest's voice went on. Thomas made reassuring noises. It promised to be a long conversation. I scraped the morning scraps into a pan and took them outside to feed the dogs. When I came back, Thomas was massaging his ear.

"Your relatives are insane," he said. "All of them. Apparently it's a felony to move a body without permission in Virginia. That's apart from the ecclesiastical problems. Anyway, I finally calmed him down. But he wants to come over and reconsecrate the body before it's buried."

"Great-uncle Attaway wants a good Protestant funeral," I reminded him.

"Great-uncle Attaway should have thought of that before the first funeral. Why didn't he just refuse to let the body be buried at Northend in the first place? I'd better call the clerk of the court. No, darn it, it's Saturday. First I'll do the funeral, and if Peggy's mother wants to dig him up and move him again, she can go file her own papers. Your great-uncle wants you to come, Amanda."

"I don't want to go!"

"He said he wanted family there, and Granny told him she was too old to go to the same funeral twice." Thomas knotted his tie. I waited for a moment for the other shoe to drop, but he was digging in the pockets of his funeral suit. He said nothing about wanting me along for moral support. I went upstairs and grumpily dug my dark dress out of the laundry hamper.

THOUGH THE DARKNESS HIDE THEE

~ ~ ~ ~ ~

We parked in front of the old Fowlerand house and walked around through the side yard. The front porch was scrubbed clean, but neither one of us wanted to walk across it. Short shadows of trees lay across the frosted grass in front of us. I could smell wood smoke.

"One," a voice said, around the corner of the house. "Two, three. Up!"

The thump of wood on metal was followed by a teeth-grinding scrape. We came around the edge of the house. Great-uncle Attaway was enthroned on the back steps. Roland, short and plumpish, was leaning against the tailgate of a pickup, mopping his forehead. Pierman, tall and stringy and weather-beaten, was lighting a cigarette. Quintus's coffin lay in the pickup bed. Dirt still clung to the corners.

Attaway pushed his feed cap back. "Boys," he said, "you remember Reverend Clement? He was at the funeral."

"Morning," Roland said, mournfully. Pierman nodded.

Thomas said, "Good morning. Mr. Fowlerand, did you know that before you dig someone up—"

A dark blue BMW shot past the house and slid to a stop. The Northend priest climbed out in a cloud of dust and strode towards the porch. Attaway felt in his pocket for a cigarette, his face impassive.

"Mr. Fowlerand!"

His name was Jarrow, Edward Jarrow. He was as tall as Thomas and heavier. He was full up with righteous anger, and uncomfortable with it.

"This breaks all the bounds of civilized behavior," he said. "You made no protest when Mrs. Morris made arrangements for Quintus's funeral. She is my spiritual responsibility, and this will cause her great distress. She wished to have her son-in-law buried next to her daughter."

"Well," Attaway said, "I'd a notion to bury him next to his mother. I imagine that's a better argument, Reverend." He tapped a cigarette from the pack.

"Quintus was a son of the Church."

"He was my son, and he's going into the ground here."

"To remove a body from consecrated ground, you must have the permission of the clerk of the court. And it would be courteous at the very least to discuss the matter with me as well."

Attaway put two fingers into the top pocket of his overalls and removed a stained piece of paper.

"This here," he said, "says I went down to the courthouse and paid for a permit to take Quintus out. And as for gettin' your permission, Reverend, I only got this to say. Fowlerands were buryin' here before the Cathlicks down at Northend first lit a candle. I'm not askin' permission from anyone to put my boy where he belongs."

He struck a match and lit the cigarette and drew in a deep lungful of smoke. Edward Jarrow threw up his hands.

"I've been at Northend ten years," he said. "I've never seen anything like this in my life. Are you Clement?"

"Yes," Thomas said.

"You're going to go through with this?"

"Maybe Mr. Fowlerand would allow you to come with me. That way you could tell Mrs. Morris that her son-in-law received a proper burial."

"My son," Attaway said again.

Jarrow hesitated, looking from face to face. Attaway blew a

puff of smoke into the air. Pierman was staring off into the distance. Roland dug dirt from around his fingernails. None of the Fowlerands showed the slightest tendency towards remorse.

He said at last, "Just a minute," and headed back towards his BMW. When he returned he held a prayer book in his hand.

"Good enough," Attaway said. "Pierman, you drive the truck on around. This way, Reverend Clement. Graveyard's on yonder hill."

Pierman dropped his cigarette and rubbed it into the ground with his toe. We followed the pickup's slow path up the rutted dirt road to the Fowlerand graveyard. Doris was buried here, behind a long row of leaning gray stones from the century before. Gideon Pierman Fowlerand, 1834–1836. THE DEAD IN CHRIST SHALL RISE. The Fowlerands had drifted far from that hope; Doris's stone read simply BELOVED MOTHER below a carved daffodil. Next to her grave, a neat hole waited for Quintus.

"Right, then," Attaway said. "Let's get him in."

Jarrow and Thomas looked at each other, but Quintus had been tall and his coffin was too heavy for Roland and Pierman to get into the hole alone. Attaway uncoiled two heavy yellow ropes from the pickup's passenger seat and threaded them through the coffin handles, one in the front and one in the back. The four men lowered Quintus into the hole silently, the quiet broken only by an occasional sharp direction. And then we all stood around it with our feet in the dirt and listened to Thomas read from 1 Corinthians. I fixed my eyes on the heap of dirt and listened to him. A hard crust had formed over the top of the dirt pile, and a dandelion was struggling for life in the turned-over red clay. How long did it take weeds to start growing again? Surely more than three or four days. I leaned forward, unobtrusively. The sides of the hole were perfectly straight. Someone with proper funeral-home equipment had dug that hole. And the clay was hard and dried. Attaway had prepared this hole well in advance; certainly before the Tuesday funeral at Northend. I looked sideways at the little cluster of Fowlerand men. Roland and Pierman had their eyes squeezed shut, pained expressions on their faces. Great-uncle Attaway was looking at his son's coffin. His light blue eyes were calculating, his eyebrows drawn together in thought. Thomas pronounced the amen and stepped back in deference to Edward Jarrow. Attaway made an impatient movement.

"Roland," he said, "get the shovels."

"Just a minute," Jarrow snapped.

"You do whatever you're gonna do while Roland gets the shovels. Go on, boy."

Roland shuffled towards the pickup. The priest cracked his prayer book open sharply. "Our brother," he began, "we commend your soul to the God who created you…"

Roland came back with the shovels and handed one to Pierman. He thrust the blade into the dirt heap. The dry top layer shifted away. Pierman hefted up a shovelful of damp red clay and tossed it onto the coffin. Edward Jarrow kept reading.

"Our Father, who art in heaven…" *Thump.* "Thy kingdom come, thy will be done on earth—" *Thump.* "—as it is in heaven."

Dirt spread across the coffin's brass plate. Quintus's name disappeared. I suddenly understood why Adkins Funeral Home had waited until the crowd departed to fill the Northend grave. I turned sharply away and walked back towards the Fowlerand place. The Chickahominy spread blue and glittering beyond the house. I went through the side yard, out to the little wooden dock, and sat there with my arms around my knees until Thomas called me.

I lay open-eyed for a long time that night, listening to the fall night: the rattle of a dead leaf on the tin roof, the distant sound of an owl, Thomas's uneven breathing beside me.

He said suddenly into the dark, "While you were down at the dock, when we were walking back from the graveyard, I got a look at that permit from the clerk of the court."

"Did it look official?"

"Yes, but it was dated the day of the funeral. By the time that funeral was over, it was past five and the offices were closed. Before Quintus ever went into the ground, Attaway was planning to dig him up and rebury him. And I helped him."

"You did the right thing. You couldn't leave him unburied."

He didn't answer. I curled over and put my head on his chest. Long after his breathing had slowed, I lay wide-eyed and awake. I thought: If I sleep, I might have another of those odd black-edged dreams. If the Tenant House ghosts were disturbed by the deeds of the living, today's funeral ought to stir them into a frenzy.

When I finally did fall asleep, I dreamed that Thomas had left me and gone to start a new life in California with some vaguely Eastern sect that required new believers to cut all ties with family; and that Quintus and I sat on the back porch in the summer heat and swapped our sorrows until the sun set and darkness drowned Poverty Ridge.

Chapter Sixteen

Sunday morning, a sheriff's car idled through Little Croft Church's parking lot just before the service began. In the daylight, the deputy Jimmy White had promised seemed like ridiculous overkill. Ambrose Scarborough watched him drive through in silent astonishment; John Whitworth's eyebrows winged upwards on his startled face.

But just before the benediction, I heard the scrape of tires in the parking lot. The muted roar of a truck engine cut suddenly into silence. When we opened the old wooden doors at the back of the building, Matthew Humberston stood at the foot of the outside stairs. He was straight as a pine and whipcord thin, as though he'd dropped ten pounds overnight. He was wearing his working clothes, a khaki coverall and boots. His head was bare, and his black hair brushed his collar behind. Under thick brows, his eyes were black fire.

The congregation filed past Thomas at the door and spread into a waiting silent pool out on the dirt of the parking lot. I put my arm through Thomas's. He squeezed my elbow hard against his side, and we walked out onto the porch together.

Matthew had to tilt his head upwards to where we stood at the top of the church steps. John and Ambrose were shuffling their feet on the bricks behind us.

"Morning, Matthew," Thomas said.

"Clement," Matthew said, and jerked his head at me. "Morning, Amanda. I've got a word to say to you, Reverend.

You're here in the sun, this morning. My boy's sitting back over in a courthouse cell. One day of freedom, and they've got him back behind bars."

The Little Croft churchgoers were listening, eager and open-eyed.

"I'm sorry," Thomas said steadily.

"Don't you send him back there to stay with your words."

"I haven't been subpoenaed yet, Matthew."

Matthew looked around, but no one was budging. He climbed the steps so that his face was eight inches from Thomas's. "Please, Reverend. Whatever he did was done in youth and in anger, not with hate. Don't you tell no jury otherwise."

"I have to tell the truth."

Matthew Humberston stepped backwards. He turned his head and spat into the shrubs that bordered the old brick steps.

"Whose truth?" he said. His eyes held Thomas's for a long minute, until he turned and walked away. His walk was light-footed and springy, as though the bitter energy that drove him would break out at any moment. He slammed his truck door and spun his tires on the dust.

The waiting crowd shuffled its feet. As nothing else seemed likely to happen, it eventually dispersed and the waiting cars began to pull out of the lot, one by one, in a slow disappointed parade.

"Don't you worry," Ambrose said on his way past, and John Whitworth grunted in agreement.

Thomas worried. He took the dogs out for another long walk Sunday afternoon and came back in tired and covered with bits of weeds. I'd finally gotten the chimney swept, and I lit a fire against the October night. Thomas sat in front of the flames, picking sheep burs and beggar-ticks off his thick socks and tossing them into the grate one by one. I brought in tea and gingerbread and we ate at the hearth in silence.

"I went to see a lawyer last week," Thomas said abruptly.

I looked at him over the top of my cup, surprised. "When did you go?"

"Wednesday morning, after you went over to the Old House. I made an appointment right after the murder. Ambrose gave me a name in Williamsburg."

I nibbled the edge off a gingerbread square. I felt slightly hurt that he'd kept the secret this long, but I told myself sternly not be inconsistent. I was still concealing Peggy's pregnancy.

"What did he say?"

"He said that a priest or pastor can treat confessions as privileged information, even in court. So I don't have to tell them what Quintus said to me about Matt intending to kill him."

"How about Matt's saying 'Good!' when he heard Quintus was dead?"

"That doesn't qualify. But it isn't as damaging as Quintus's indirect testimony."

"So you could keep quiet, in other words?"

"Yes."

It was a way out. I could hear in Thomas's voice that he wouldn't take it.

"I've been trying to convince myself that I would be a good pastor if I kept my mouth shut," he said. "And every time I do I feel this huge surge of relief, so I know that's the wrong answer. I'm afraid, that's what it is." He pitched another sheep bur into the fire and watched it flare scarlet, then crumple into ash. "When we came back, your family was so different than what I expected; and I kept telling myself it didn't matter, the church was my real family, and now I'm afraid of ruining the church as well…"

His voice trailed off. He shrugged uncomfortably, ducking his head down. I watched the red light flicker against his face: the deep-set eyes and elegant line of jaw and cheek.

I said, "I wish I could have brought you a flock of Northeast relatives and connections to a city pulpit in a civilized Boston suburb."

Thomas grinned. "It's going to cost us a hundred bucks," he said.

"Oh, well."

"And I don't know what'll happen, once I do testify. Folks at Little Croft Church like Matthew. I like him. They don't like your great-uncle. I'll sound like I'm backing Attaway up against Matthew. I don't want to be seen as Attaway's man. Just the rumor that Attaway had some say in Little Croft Church ruined my whole visitation program down in the Winneck slums. But I have to tell the truth about what I heard…no matter what happens. Even if Matthew or Matt sets out for revenge. Even if I get picked off in the church parking lot by some Little Croft hired goon."

"Hired goons are for soft city folk," I said. "Down here, we do our dirty work ourselves."

The subpoena arrived Monday morning. I was up early, reading one of the God-has-deserted-me psalms and watching the sun rise. A brown sheriff's car appeared at the little hill in

Poverty Ridge Road. Twin puffs of dust followed it. I wished it around the curve, towards Granny's house, but it pulled past the Tenant House and disappeared. Tires scraped on the dirt of the backyard. The dogs set up a welcoming chorus.

"Who's that?" Thomas said from the upstairs hallway.

"Looks like the sheriff's department."

He came down the steps and opened the back door. A sheriff's deputy was emerging from the car. He was a young black man, Thomas's height, and he held a white envelope.

"Thomas Clement?" he said.

"Yes?"

"Subpoena for you, Reverend Clement."

Thomas took the envelope. The deputy nodded politely at me and climbed back into his car. Thomas opened the subpoena as the deputy pulled away, the dogs yelping at the strange car from their safe haven beneath the porch.

"November 9," he said.

I could imagine it. *Mr. Clement, could you repeat for us your conversation with the accused?* Thomas, in his wedding and funeral suit: *He said, Matt said he'd kill me. Told me yesterday he'd kill me. Tonight, said he'd been meanin' to kill me all his life and now he had the chance.* The prosecution: *And what did Mr. Humberston say?* Thomas's answer, avoiding Matthew Humberston's furious eyes: *He asked me if Quintus was dead. I said he was. He said, 'Good!'*

Thomas tucked the subpoena into his back pocket. "Can you come with me tonight to visit the Kinderleys? The family with the little girls? They were in church again Sunday. I should have gone to see them last week, but Quintus's funeral messed up my schedule."

"Yes, of course."

"I'm going door to door this morning just to let people know we're here. I haven't knocked on any doors since that day no one would speak to me down in Attaway's slums. It's time I got back to it." He turned around and went back into the house.

I poured a bowl of cereal, ate it standing up, and headed over to the Old House. I arrived at three minutes after nine. Granny was eating herrings and fried bread for her breakfast: pure salt and grease. She said instantly, "You were late and I had to fix my own breakfast."

"Huh," I said.

"An' you can start out this mornin' by pinning the batting on the back of my quilt. I'm gonna finish my breakfast and read the paper."

I looked at her narrowly, but she wouldn't meet my eyes. The quilt was stretched on a frame in the small back bedroom at the other end of the house. I went off to isolation and pinned cotton batting onto the back of Granny's log cabin quilt, biding my time. The sun came up on the other side of the house, so the little room was cold and shadowed. Granny hid in the kitchen, sitting in the bars of morning light and reading the *Daily Press*.

I tried a few conversational shouts, hoping we could warm up to the subject of Peggy's death.

"How's Uncle Attaway doing, Granny?"

Little pause. "What say?"

"Attaway! How's he doing, now that Quintus is buried for good?"

"Can't hear you," Granny bellowed. I pinned batting all along the far end of the quilt before I tried again.

"So how much extra tax is Uncle Attaway going to pay?" I shouted down the hallway.

"Not tacks. Pins. They're on the edge of the sewin' machine."

"I mean the inheritance tax. Is Uncle Attaway going to lose much because Quintus didn't leave a will?"

"Ain't got enough breath to yell at you all morning, Amanda, so do your work and hush up."

It was only ten in the morning, and unless she planned to deprive me of lunch, she couldn't keep me in that back bedroom all day. I devoted myself to pinning as fast as possible. By eleven-thirty, the shadows outside the little brick-framed window had shortened into nothing and the quilt was ready to be sewn. I headed into the kitchen and started to pull out lunch stuff before Granny could tell me to go polish jars in the far corners of the basement.

"Lettuce and tomato and cheese?" I asked.

"And bacon."

"You've had enough salt to last you a week." I sliced tomatoes onto the white bread and set out her plate and her glass of iced tea. She sat down with a grunt.

"You're worse than your mama ever was," she complained.

"Thank you. Want me to pray?"

"I'm not givin' thanks for that unless you put some bacon on it."

"Nope."

"Suit yourself. Gimme the *TV Guide* to take my mind off m' food."

I ate my own sandwich standing up at the counter. Granny read the soap opera listings. When she was finished she pushed her chair back and said, "Thought you could clean the rest of those canning jars out of the basement this afternoon while I watch my story."

"Granny," I said, "did you know that Peggy was pregnant when she died?"

Granny held her *TV Guide* with both hands, close to her chest. I watched the side of her face. A hundred tiny wrinkles, furrowing her cheeks and puckering her mouth, masked any change in the muscles beneath the skin. Her blue eyes were fixed on the distant line of pines at the edge of the front field.

"Go on down to the basement," she said at last.

I headed for the basement door, but before I reached it the creaking voice stopped me.

"No. I've thought of somethin' else for you to do. I got a whole drawer full of old pictures like those I gave you. All curlin' up at the edges and turning brown. You get them out and put them in picture books for me."

I came back to the kitchen. "Where are the books?"

"Haven't got any yet. But you c'n sort them out for me. They're in that dresser there." She pointed through the glass doors that led from kitchen to living room. A walnut sideboard stood against one wall, across from a red velvet sofa and a cabinet piano. I went into the chill smell of dust and furniture polish and opened the sideboard's long top drawer. It stuck, halfway out, crammed to the top with old photos that sprang up at me.

"I got too many pictures anyhow," Granny said.

I worked my hand along the drawer's track. A wad of glossy paper was jammed between the far corner of the drawer and the front of the sideboard. I managed to hook it with my index finger and ease it out, but the folds dragged and tore. The drawer popped open the rest of the way. I scooped up an armload of old photos and brought them to the kitchen table.

Granny limped to her chair and turned on the television.

Her afternoon soap poured into the room, and I sorted out the quiet dead faces. I piled the relatives I'd never met in one stack and put it to the side. The other pictures—Granny and my grandfather, Attaway and Doris, Attaway with his brother-in-law, Quintus and Matt—I laid out in a tiled checkerboard in front of me. The earliest picture was of Granny Cora in her late twenties, wearing a hat and a little veil and white gloves, standing with her hand on her husband's arm in front of the Old House. Nathaniel Scarborough stared defiantly into the camera. His blond hair was white against the dark-shadowed boards of the house. Here was a series of Thanksgiving dinners: Attaway dark and glowering with a towheaded baby on his knee, Granny at forty in a checked apron, my teenaged mother in front of turkey and dressing. Another picture showed four handsome blond children on the grass with a catch of river fish: my mother, Giddy with a rare grin, my aunt Winnie who lived in Raleigh and never came home. I didn't recognize the fourth. Stephen? No, the children in the picture were older, and Stephen had died at six.

I got up for a glass of water. The movement dislodged the torn wad of paper from my lap. I caught it as it fell and noticed a colored corner. Granny watched on, oblivious to my sortings. Outside the kitchen window the harvesters moved silently across the brown cornfields, traveling back and forth between the pines at the farm's east border and the line of scarlet gum trees on the west. I unfolded the picture. A jagged rip extended across its face, running almost down to the bottom. The fuzzy color was late seventies in vintage. My grandfather Nathaniel, old and thin and stooped, was standing at the top of the Chickahominy River hill, both hands on a stick he had jabbed into the dirt. A hunting dog sat at his heel. Great-uncle

Attaway stood beside him, twenty years younger and fifteen pounds lighter. Quintus sat at the far side of the picture with his hands knotted underneath the collars of two other dogs. The picture had a dark unidentifiable border at the bottom and a strange delicate tracing across its surface. I walked to the cabinet for a glass, considering the scene, and as I turned on the faucet I glanced idly out the window above the sink and recognized the setting. Someone had taken that photo out of the kitchen window, through the screen. The windowsill had blocked the bottom of the lens. My grandfather, Nathaniel Scarborough; Attaway, his wife's brother; Quintus, Attaway's child. Nathaniel Scarborough's Nordic features stood out in profile, the small straight nose and thin-lipped mouth. Quintus on the grass had turned his head to look down the hill, and against the background of sky and tree his nose and mouth repeated my grandfather's face.

I opened my mouth to say, "Ever notice how much Quintus looked like Papa Nat?" when a sudden thought silenced me. I thought of the note I'd found, in the house where Doris had lived.

I went back to the table where I'd left the other photos. The four fair-haired children grinned up at me from the grass. Nathaniel Scarborough's children: my mother, my uncle, my aunt. And Quintus Fowlerand, a catfish dangling from his hand and the triumphant Scarborough smile splitting his small face. I thought of Granny Cora, who had borne Nathaniel Scarborough four children and never, never spoke of her dead husband; and I thought of Attaway Fowlerand, looking down at his child and naming him Quintus. Quintus, the fifth child of Nathaniel Scarborough. Attaway had known.

I said nothing to Granny. Twenty years ago she had seen that fleeting moment of likeness and had recorded it; her husband and her brother's child, creator and image. And yet she had never acknowledged it. I had the symbols in my hand, but the labyrinthine truths that wound away behind them still eluded me.

Chapter Seventeen

I remembered, on my way back to the Tenant House, that Thomas wanted me to pay a pastoral call with him. I hurried in and showered and put on a pastor's-wife skirt, and we drove over to the Kinderley house in the early dark.

The images from the photographs clung to my mind like a grimy slick after rain. If Quintus had been my grandfather's son, and my grandmother had suspected it, what chill had risen between the two of them? I remembered the photograph marked 1955, where Cora Scarborough strained away from her husband's hand. Yet Quintus had been born some years after that picture. And Granny Cora had always shown a marked preference for Quintus. She had protected him from Attaway's sneers, and Quintus had been up and down the stairs of the Old House a dozen times a week, running errands for his aunt. I corrected myself. Not his aunt, if Attaway hadn't fathered him. No blood relation at all. And Attaway was childless.

I stared at my indistinct reflection in the dark window of the car and saw with sudden clarity the Tenant House, thirty-four years ago. It was cut away like a doll's house. Cold morning light crept over its rooms and halls. Attaway lay on the living room sofa, his boots tipped over on the rug and his arms flung up over his head. Around him sprawled the tired bodies of his hunting partners, young Giddy and the two solid Humberstons, snoring beneath quilts and blankets.

In the shabby bedroom above him, a motionless body lay

underneath a comforter, curtains drawn against the encroaching light. Across the narrow hallway, a toddler stood upright in his crib, screaming. His wails pierced the still air until the man on the sofa grunted and turned and sat up, irritably; but the mother's still form never moved.

"Hello?" Thomas said.

I jerked my head away from the dark car window and looked over at him. "What?"

"What color is the sky in your universe?"

"Sorry."

"This is Riverside Farm." He slowed and turned off the road onto a long dirt lane. The Kinderley family lived over on the other side of Route 5, in a gracious white colonial house that had once been attached to a plantation estate.

"You seem to be visiting both ends of the social scene at once," I said. "First the Winneck Road slums, and now this."

Thomas parked our battered little car next to a gleaming Lexus and squinted up at the dormered house. He said, "Well, I thought Christ would be more likely to visit the Winneck slums first. But even Christ didn't spend his time with the unwilling."

"How was the door-to-door visiting today?"

"No one actually shot at me."

"That good?"

We walked up the flagstone path between trimmed hedges and rang the bell. The sweet smell of boxwood and spruce drifted across the steps. The door opened on a wood-paneled hall warmly lit by shaded lamps.

Tim Kinderley put out his hand. He filled the door; a solid prosperous man in khakis and an oxford shirt, his shining blond hair brushed flat down on his head. His face was unpleasantly heavy, but his blue eyes were friendly and his voice was warm.

"Come on in, Reverend Clement," he said. "Mrs. Clement, welcome. Amy and Kristen were just on their way to bed. Say good night, girls."

The little girls were clean-faced, in Disney pajamas, with fair hair neatly brushed. They wished us good night in shy voices and scampered up the banistered stairs. A woman's voice called, "I'll be down in a minute, soon as I get the girls in bed. Tim, the coffee's in the living room."

Tim Kinderley led us into the living room, where a small fire burned against the slight fall chill. He settled into a cream linen-covered chair, motioning us to the sofa. The bright pillows on the light furniture matched an antique patchwork quilt that hung on the wall. A tray on the table in front of the fire held four china cups and saucers, a carafe of coffee, cream and sugar, and shining silver spoons. It was miles away from Winneck Road; or Granny Cora's kitchen, for that matter. Thomas poured us both coffee while Tim chattered. He was a software engineer working in Richmond. His wife stayed home with the two little girls and grew roses. The sheer normality of the pretty warm room was immensely reassuring. Thomas was telling Tim Kinderley about our move from Philadelphia, his voice relaxed and cheerful, when Mrs. Kinderley came into the room.

"My wife Eileen," Tim said.

She murmured a greeting and sat down. Tim lifted his empty cup, not looking at her, and she leaped up to fill it. I coughed over my mouthful of coffee. Thomas shot me a warning glance.

"So," Tim said, receiving his coffee cup from his wife without a word of thanks, "we've enjoyed our visits, these last two

Sundays. I was glad to see the church filled with children of Adam."

I was preoccupied with Eileen Kinderley, sitting on the edge of her chair with her anxious attention on her husband. The oddity of this phrase caught up with me a second later. Children of Adam? What had he expected to find, a blessing of the animals?

Thomas said, cautiously, "Well, we're all children of Adam together, aren't we? We try to welcome all sinners."

"We've tried several churches in the area," Tim said, "but we've been disappointed to find that they don't honor God's separation of the races. Little Croft Church seems to have kept its purity."

"Ah. Racial purity, you mean?"

"Exactly," Tim said.

"Because no blacks attend?"

"Right. I'd like you to read something…it explains the original Hebrew of Genesis, and why God never intended us to intermarry with the *esh.*" He produced a thin gray-covered booklet. We bent our heads together over the scabrous object. The writer explained with confidence that the Hebrew of Genesis proved Caucasians to be the only true creations of God.

I said at last, "You must be kidding."

Thomas put his hand on my knee. "Mr. Kinderley," he said patiently, "I read Hebrew. So does Amanda. This is just plain wrong."

Tim Kinderley's blue eyes hardened. "Then why does Genesis use two different words for man?"

"Because—" Thomas began. His eyes traveled from corner to corner of that graceful welcoming room. "Mr. Kinderley, if I

170

could prove to you beyond a shadow of doubt that this man's Hebrew is lousy, would you change your mind about black people?"

Tim Kinderley rattled his coffee cup on the table beside him. His wife's eyes were fixed on him anxiously. He looked up at the ceiling, and his heavy face stretched into set and inflexible folds.

"No," he said.

Thomas set down his own cup. "Thank you for the coffee," he said, "and we'll be going." He stood up and headed for the door. I lingered, looking at Eileen, but Thomas grabbed my hand.

"Come on," he said, and stalked down the stairs.

I went with him. I'd been thinking, not of Tim Kinderley and his racist proof texting, but of the two little blond girls asleep upstairs. Thomas started the car and spun a bit of unregenerate gravel on his way down the drive.

"Two sets of visitors so far," he said. "White supremacists and King James fanatics. Doesn't that strike you as a mighty high percentage of nut cases?"

"Mm," I said.

"What's been bothering you all evening?"

"Something Granny told me. In a way."

"What is it?"

"I don't know whether or not it was in confidence, Thomas."

Thomas nodded, his eyes on the road. I watched the side of his face. The moon had come out, and the cold white light turned his strong features into a map of hills and shadows. The fair eyebrows, winging out slightly at the corners, were drawn down over his eyes, and his strong hands were tight on the wheel. I didn't want to say, Here's another secret in your new family: I think my grandfather fathered the child of his brother-in-law's wife.

We turned onto Poverty Ridge Road. The lights of the Old House shone dim and tiny across the vast expanse of field. Suddenly another piece of the puzzle clicked, unasked, into place. Quintus wasn't even Attaway's son. Quintus destroyed his will before he died. Quintus's closest relative wasn't Attaway at all. The heirs to that huge chunk of farmland were likely to be his unacknowledged siblings: my mother and Giddy and Aunt Winnie.

And his uncle, his mother's brother. Matthew Humberston.

Granny offered me chitterlings again for lunch on Tuesday, so I went home to make myself a bowl of pasta. Thomas was eating a sandwich at the sink. He was humming to himself between bites. I said, surprised, "What have you been up to?"

"I went visiting again this morning, and I found a door that didn't slam in my face. I spent all morning with this guy I met around the Loop. Eddie Winn. He lives in that old trailer just before you get to Matthew Humberston's lane."

I shook Parmesan cheese onto my pasta. I knew Eddie Winn; he was a dark man of forty-odd who'd spent ten years staggering through a Jack Daniels fog. He never worked, but he appeared at Winn's Grocery every two weeks with a wad of cash and left with one bag of groceries and two of bottles.

"Was he sober?"

"Yes," Thomas said, "and shaking like a leaf. He was sitting on his back porch with a pistol in his hand, popping at cans he had set up at the edge of the woods. I swore I was going to visit four new houses this morning if it killed me, so I went up through the yard and told him who I was. He looked at me with these red watery eyes and finally held the pistol out and said, 'You better take this, Reverend. I was gonna use it on me, when all the cans were down.' He was three cans from the end of the line. I sat down with him on the back porch, and we didn't move for the rest of the morning. I gave him the message of the gospel from start to finish. And when I was done he went inside and came back out with a whole armful of bottles and dumped them in my lap. He said, 'I've either got to change or die, Reverend, and you'd best help me.'"

Thomas's voice thrummed with energy; Eddie's response had heartened him, like a hot meal in the stomach of a famished man. He finished the sandwich and wiped his hands vigorously on a nearby dish towel. "I'm going to make some calls and see if I can't get him in a dry-out program somewhere, and meanwhile I thought he could have a few meals over here, with us? I don't think he ought to spend all his time alone in that dingy old trailer. Can he come over tonight?"

"Sure. I'll cook if you'll clean the bathroom."

"Is Granny done with you for the day?"

"No, I was taking a lunch break. She tried to feed me chitterlings."

"What are chitterlings?"

"Pig intestines."

"I can't believe your relatives eat spare pieces of pig."

"So do yours. Scrapple's made out of pig bits and pieces."

"No!" Thomas said, as though he'd just heard the truth about Santa Claus.

"Snouts and ears, boiled up." I went out and dug through

the freezer for a pot roast, and wrapped it in foil so that it could cook all afternoon. I was so pleased to hear enthusiasm in Thomas's voice again that I'd have had a repentant Charles Manson for dinner.

When I came home that evening, a battered unfamiliar truck was parked next to the little blue hatchback. Inside, the house was bright and smelled of window cleaner. Eddie Winn was sitting in the kitchen, drinking a cup of coffee and listening to Thomas talk as he scrubbed the stove. He stood up when I walked in.

"My wife, Amanda," Thomas said. "Eddie Winn."

"I was Amanda Hunt," I said, shaking his hand.

"I remember your mama," Eddie said. His hand was dry and shaking. He sat back down quickly, his coffee mug rattling on the tabletop. Eddie's mother had been to school with my mother, and I'd seen him off and on through my teens. He had been a handsome solid man, almost Thomas's height; but now he was stooped and painfully thin, his knuckles almost breaking the skin. The arched English nose common to so many Little Croft residents jutted out between red-shot eyes. He wiped his nose continually on his sleeve.

"I told him to come over and talk to me while I cleaned up," Thomas said. "What's in the oven? Smells great."

"Pot roast," I said. "Sorry I'm late." Granny Cora had gone silent and sulky, after the revelations of the day before, and nothing had suited her all day. I was forty minutes later than usual.

"Kin I use your bathroom?" Eddie asked. "I need to wash m' hands."

"Top of the stairs, second door," Thomas said. Eddie walked carefully away. We heard the bathroom door close.

"I can start an AA group at the church," Thomas said quietly, wiping his hands on a towel, "but that guy ought to have residential treatment somewhere. He's shaking like Jell-O and I think his liver's probably going to fall out onto the floor. But he doesn't have insurance, or a job, or anything apart from that beat-up old truck. What's he live on, anyway?"

"No one really knows," I said. "Food stamps, I guess."

"If I can't get him into a program, do you mind if he spends some time over here?"

I pulled lettuce and tomatoes out of the refrigerator, thinking. "No," I said finally, "as long as you're here whenever he is."

"Why? You think he's going to steal the spoons?"

"No, I don't like the way he looks at me."

Thomas picked up the plates I'd set out. "I know he's shabby, Amanda, but he's just starting on a new life."

"Yes, but…" Until he'd drunk his looks away, Eddie'd had a reputation for chasing women. And even in the throes of D.T.s, he'd found time for a quick up-and-down glance that raised the hair on the back of my neck.

"He wants to change," Thomas said. "Amanda, I think God is in this."

"Okay," I said. "Then it's fine with me."

I didn't sleep well that night; I dreamed of Peggy's car sliding across the great curve of Winneck Road and crumpling into a solid tree trunk, over and over again. I pulled myself out of the weary circle of dreams at six and staggered downstairs to put the coffee on. Gray light was just starting to trickle over the sill of the kitchen window. I didn't have the energy to go dress while the coffee brewed, so I hung over the coffeemaker, waiting for a cupful to drip into the pot. Slowly I became aware of a mournful pair of eyes staring at me over the windowsill.

"Aighh!" I shouted and bolted backwards. The eyes blinked. They were surmounted by an orange feed cap. A hand came up to adjust the hat.

"Morning," a voice said sadly on the other side of the glass. I leaned forward and pushed the window up.

"Roland," I said, "what are you doing on the grass?"

"Uncle Attaway told me to come check around every once in a while an' make sure old Humberston ain't bothering you none."

I suddenly realized I was wearing my usual sleeping clothes—Thomas's big old Maryland T-shirt and not much else. Roland gazed up at me, a lugubrious doughboy in farming overalls. I said, "Wait a minute," slammed the window down, and hurried upstairs. Thomas was in the shower. I found my jeans, pulled them on, and went back outside.

Roland had traveled around to the far side of the house and was prodding at a hole in the ground with his toe. The dogs were hiding; I could see their leads snaking away from the steps around the corner of the little toolshed in the backyard. Daphne's tail stuck out, thumping a slow satisfied rhythm on the grass. I walked around the shed to see what they were up to. A big dead groundhog lay between them. Daphne was chewing happily on one hind leg, and Chelsea was licking its snout with tender affection. Roland joined me as I stood looking down at them.

"One o' the groundhogs the Knox boys shot," he said. "Picked it up for your dogs. Didn't want 'em to bark at me, see. Thought they might like somethin' to chew on, since you're tying them up."

"Thanks," I said.

"Sure enough."

"Why'd Great-uncle Attaway send you to poke through the yard, Roland?"

"Oh, sheriff's been up to see him. Told him 'bout your tire. Uncle Attaway's up in arms, protecting the family from Humberstons. Said we should keep an eye on things."

I suppressed a groan. I didn't blame Jimmy White; he was operating under good standard Little Croft procedure, roping in friends and relatives to keep the peace and saving his own spread-thin deputies to cope with crimes already committed. But Thomas would look more than ever like Attaway's protégé.

"Thanks," I said, "but we're fine. Honestly."

"Your mailbox's down. Aunt Cora's too. Somebody swiped at 'em."

"Well, that happens pretty often, actually."

"We'll keep coming by," Roland said. "'Tain't no trouble. Them Humberstons are crooked as a dog's hind leg. We won't let you come to no harm. Might want to get you a new mail-box, though. Well, guess I'll be on my way. Lots of work to be done, with Quintus gone."

He gave me a dismal smile and waddled away towards his pickup, parked out on Granny Cora's lane. I watched him drive towards the Old House, and thought to myself that if Attaway's property traveled through Quintus to the Fowlerands and the Scarboroughs, Roland and Pierman—Attaway's partners on the farm and his heirs apparent—would suffer for it. Roland and Pierman were the long and short of trifling, but violent passions might bubble even under Roland's puffy unlined surface and Pierman's vacant stringiness.

I whistled to the dogs and took an energetic stroll down to the blacktop. At the end of the dirt road, the Tenant House and Old House mailboxes lay toppled sideways. Most of the mailboxes on Little Croft road were battered and misshapen; whacking mailboxes with baseball bats was a favorite midnight stress-releaser for the local teenage boys. But the posts themselves were half out of the ground. The wide dirt shoulder showed a row of tire marks. Someone had swerved off the narrow blacktop road, put a right-hand tire in the ditch, and simply mowed the boxes down. A little farther down the road, a mark showed where the driver had pulled back out of the ditch just in time to avoid the next mailbox down. I nudged the nearest post with my toe and wondered whether Matt Humberston was out of his courthouse cell once more.

Chapter Eighteen

Giddy propped the mailbox posts back up, and the days until Sunday ticked away. Eddie came over three nights out of the four remaining in the week, growing visibly more comfortable with his new profession. Thomas threw himself into his visitation and sermon preparation with renewed energy. He and Ida Scarborough were busy organizing a fall party for all the prospective preschoolers and their parents. John and Ambrose formed a joint delegation to assure Thomas that Matthew Humberston's hostility wouldn't affect his job. "The man's hurtin'," Ambrose said. "Don't make no difference to Little Croft Church. You don't concern yourself with it. We know you ain't supposed to go talk to him. That's just fine. John here's the chairman of the finance committee, so you ain't got nothing to worry about."

"That's right," John said solemnly. "Nothin' at all."

Attaway called the sheriff about the mailboxes, with the result that another deputy showed up Sunday morning and sat in the parking lot, watching the Little Croft congregation file in. He was an Adkins, one of the white Adkinses who lived just down from Winnville, not a black Adkins from the other side of Route 5. He was a big-bellied, red-faced man, bored with his Sunday morning assignment, and he amused himself by chain-smoking three packs of Marlboro Lights and listening to the police-band radio.

This was not the best atmosphere for a worship service, especially since the weather had turned suddenly warm. We cracked the church windows to the Indian summer, and all through Thomas's sermon we could hear the crackle of Deputy Adkins's radio.

"…was headed down Winneck Road towards that big ol' turn and went right over sideways. Overloaded…"

"As Jesus began his journey towards Jerusalem, he sent scouts ahead to a Samaritan village with the intention of ministering and staying there. But the Samaritans, who have received Jesus before, won't show him hospitality now. He's headed towards Jerusalem."

"…send an ambulance?"

"Nah. Driver's fine. Corn everywhere, though. There's gonna be a great crop in the ditch…"

"James and John were incensed by the snub of the Samaritans. And seeing them as rejected half-breeds anyway, they wanted to call down fire from heaven in judgment over them. But Jesus' answer to them is both a rebuke and a diagnosis of their spiritual condition. They didn't understand their job: They were to rescue men, not judge and destroy them."

"…issue a summons. Open beer can on the seat…"

Thomas preached doggedly on, but between the static-filled voices outside and Eddie Winn in the pew just ahead of me, I missed four out of his five points.

Eddie had arrived just before the service began. He had taken great care with his clothes; his hair was damp and clean, and he had shaved meticulously along his jawbone. But heads turned and voices whispered when he crept along the side aisle and slid into an empty pew. He clasped his thin hands in his lap and kept his eyes on Thomas, but waves of small tremors broke over him continually. I felt my revulsion fade away in pity.

He came to shake hands with Thomas after the sermon, last in the line filing by, walking as though the boards shifted beneath his feet. This time there was no mistaking the appraising glance he shot at me.

I excused myself abruptly and walked outside. Deputy Adkins was leaning against his car, watching the parking lot empty. I crossed over to exchange afternoons with him.

"Everything go all right?" he asked.

"Yes, thanks. You might have wasted a morning."

"Oh, I don't think so. Matthew Humberston drove into your lot halfway through the service. Him and his son together. But they saw me sitting here and pulled right back out again. If I were you, I'd keep right on locking my doors. You tell the reverend I said so." He nodded politely and climbed into his brown car.

Thomas was walking down the brick walk towards me, bouncing very slightly on the balls of his feet, overflowing with energy. Eddie's battered green truck crept out of the lot. Thomas put his arm around my shoulder.

"Deputy see anything?" he asked.

"He says Matthew was here. Matt too."

"Eddie has been five days without a drink. He's actually been eating, putting on a little weight. I wish I could do something more to help him."

"You're giving him your time."

"Yes, but if I could only do more. Eddie is real pastoral work. He's the first glimmer I've seen that God might be working here in Little Croft." His voice was strong and enthusiastic, and so I suppressed my misgivings and said nothing.

~ ~ ~ ~ ~

Monday morning, I woke up and thought: It'll all be over in a couple of weeks. Matt's trial loomed up in my mind, cutting off my mental horizon. I wasn't even thinking of the verdict, merely of Thomas's testimony. Once the words came from his mouth, that constant pressure that was distorting our lives would disappear.

Thomas was pulling out of the yard, on his way over to the church, when I remembered something I'd meant to ask him. I ran out after him and yelled, "Thomas!"

He put his head out the window of the car. "Yeah?"

"What was the name of the lawyer you talked to, about whether you had to testify at Matt's trial?"

"The lawyer?"

"Yes."

"Why?"

"I want to talk to him about Granny's arrangements, that's all."

"Oh," Thomas said, losing interest. "His name's Timothy Whitehead, and his number's in the kitchen Rolodex."

He waved and drove off down the road. I went into the kitchen and found the number under the *W*s. It was a Williamsburg number, which surprised me slightly; I thought Thomas had gone to Richmond.

At lunchtime, I came home from Granny's and dialed Timothy Whitehead's number. His secretary informed me that I had just caught him on his way out, but that he could spare me a moment or two. She put me on hold and I listened to Neil Diamond and made myself a peanut butter sandwich. Eventually Neil Diamond went unlamented away, and a strong male voice with a hint of Iowa in it said, "Timothy White-head."

"Mr. Whitehead, my name's Amanda Clement. My husband came to see you—"

"Oh, yes. The pastor and the grand jury. What did he do?"

"The trial's not till next week," I said.

"Ah. And is he still undecided?" It was a round fruity sort of voice, and I pictured a large wide-shouldered man in an expensive suit, leaning back in an expensive chair. A distant creak suggested that he had done just that.

"Not exactly. The situation's complicated—"

"They always are."

"And I wanted to ask a related question. But I wasn't trying to get free advice. You can send me a bill."

"I shall not fail to do so. Go ahead, Mrs. Clement."

"If a man dies intestate, and his only living relatives are an uncle and three half siblings, what happens?"

"A big mess," Timothy Whitehead said cheerfully.

"Really?"

"What size estate are we talking about?"

"I'm not sure of dollar amounts, but probably eight hundred acres of land or so."

"A huge mess. No way anyone's going to let that size of an inheritance go unchallenged. I can't predict exactly how it would come out, of course, but I expect the estate would be divided in four equal parts between the three siblings and the uncle. They're not full siblings?"

"No."

"A full sibling would take priority over an uncle, but half siblings and an uncle would probably be considered equal in terms of an inheritance. No parents are involved?"

"There's a father, but he turns out not to have been the father after all. I mean, we all thought he was—is this in confidence?"

"Of course."

"No one else knows that he isn't the father. Except for the father's sister, who won't say so."

There was a thoughtful silence. "The deceased wasn't aware that his father was not, in fact, a blood relation?"

"I don't think so, no."

"So he didn't know that he had half siblings?"

"No."

"If the deceased died intestate, but died with the confidence that his supposed father would inherit, the putative father could well go to court and get at least part of the inheritance back. On the grounds that the deceased believed the property would go back to him anyway."

"He had a will leaving the property to his father, and he destroyed it two weeks before he died."

"Was he on good terms with the uncle?"

"Er…well, the uncle's son murdered him."

Another silence. "Mrs. Clement," Timothy Whitehead said finally, "what you have here is a big, nasty, three-way lawsuit. Maybe a five-way lawsuit, if the half siblings are on bad terms with each other. You say no one else knows that the father—who would otherwise inherit—is not in fact the father?"

"Right."

"And you're not absolutely sure?"

"Well," I said, "as sure as I can be without a DNA test."

"Which is exactly what the court will require."

"He's already been dug up once."

"By whom?"

"His—what d'you call him? The putative father."

"Why?"

"I think he wanted to make sure that no one would question the blood relationship, so he made a huge countywide song and dance about getting his son buried on the family plot instead of his wife's plot."

"You're assuming that the putative father knew no blood relationship existed?"

"Yes."

"Did it work?"

"Apparently."

"But you saw through it?"

"The putative father's sister is my grandmother."

"Just a minute. I'm diagramming this on the back of my next client's will."

"The putative father is my great-uncle."

"Mm. So he is. Mrs. Clement, you have brightened an otherwise dull morning of estate planning. The giving of pleasure outweighs any monetary considerations...but I'm still going to bill you. You're asking me what will happen to the deceased's property if you blow the whistle on your great-uncle?"

"Well...yes."

"And do you benefit personally?"

"I don't get any of the property, if that's what you mean. No, I take that back. My mother is one of the half siblings."

Timothy Whitehead's pencil scratched in the distance. "This would mean that the blood father would have to be your..."

"Grandfather."

"Grandfather. Dare I hope that the grandfather in question is the husband of the putative father's sister?"

"Er…" I had to untangle this one in my head. "Yes. My grandfather had a fling with his wife's brother's wife."

"I'm sorry," Timothy Whitehead said, smothering a chuckle. "It's not funny, I know." He cleared his throat. "Mrs. Clement, my advice is that you be extremely careful about opening this can of snakes."

"Don't lawyers thrive on this sort of thing?"

"Your mother's not going to hire me, is she?"

"I doubt it."

"Then it's no skin off my nose to tell you to leave it alone. Mrs. Clement, I have practiced family law for twenty years. Granted, I was in the Midwest for fifteen of those years, and Midwest family tangles, while they produce just as much heartburn as southern family tangles, do not tend to be quite as inbred. No offense intended."

"None taken."

"But I've seen a plethora of families battle it out in court over property. And it doesn't take much to rip every blood tie to shreds. I once saw an entire clan from Norfolk break up over a set of china dishes made in occupied Japan. No replacements, you see, because all the factories had been bombed. Valuable, but not all that valuable. You're talking about eight hundred acres of farmland—"

"Waterfront farmland and old timber."

"The mind boggles."

I sighed. He must have heard the sound, because he said quite kindly, "Abstract justice is a very noble aim, Mrs. Clement. I'm telling you that you won't get abstract justice if you cut through this particular Gordian knot. The cut ends will spring out and cause open wounds, that's all."

"I wasn't thinking about justice," I said. "I just want my family to stop ruining my husband's job." I was about to launch into an explanation of Matthew Humberston's hatred and Great-uncle Attaway's treatment of his wife and son and Thomas's unhappy place in the middle, but I remembered that Timothy Whitehead's meter was ticking. I thanked him, gave him my phone number for his files, and hung up.

Tuesday was Halloween, a day when all country dwellers take down farm signs, lock up sheds, and park cars close to the house. Thomas left in old clothes, promising to be back early; he was due to help Ida Scarborough with her preschool party, but we had been invited to Joe and Jenny Morehead's for dinner and Halloween games.

I walked down to fetch Granny's paper for her midmorning. Roland and Pierman were at the end of Poverty Ridge Road with two shovels and a wheelbarrow full of gray lumpy soup. The mailboxes lay on their sides in the dirt once more.

"Hey," I said. "What are you guys doing?"

"Mornin'," Roland said, puffing slightly. "We're settin' these here new posts in concrete."

"What new posts?"

"There." He pointed at two steel pipes that lay half-invisible in the red dirt. "Uncle Attaway says Giddy just did a white-trash repair job on them posts, so he sent us over to do it right. Before it gets dark. Thought this was a likely night for you to lose your boxes again."

"Where's Granny's paper?"

"On the front seat of my truck."

"Thanks," I said.

Roland started to shovel the lumpy concrete into the hole. Pierman, smoking a cigarette with his right hand, hoisted up one of the pipes with his left and set it into the gray soup. I took the paper and headed back up the road. The Indian summer was fading; I could feel cold striking up from the dirt, and wisps of white cloud coiled around the dim sun.

By the time Thomas and I were home, changing for the party, the temperature had dropped fifteen degrees. We debated what to do with the dogs, and finally I suggested it might be better if they were near the back door of the Tenant House. So we left them there, tied to the pump house.

Joe and Jenny lived up near Route 5, in a new two-story house with grass still thin against red clay. Jenny's living room looked like a *Good Housekeeping* illustration; I looked at her Laura Ashley patterns and hardwood floor with envy. They had invited two other young couples from their neighborhood; and we stayed later than we intended, eating candy and listening to Joe's CD collection. Frost rimmed the sides of the road as we drove home. Now and then, a truckload full of whooping boys sped past. Toilet paper decorated the hedge at Cooks' Hall, and the speed limit sign just before Poverty Ridge was full of shotgun holes. The mailboxes were still upright, although Granny's was listing slightly.

We turned onto the dirt road. As we drove up the little hill, Thomas's headlights picked out two wisps of brown forms, sliding across the dim road and into the graveyard field.

"What's that?" Thomas asked.

"Foxes. Looks like they've moved into the groundhog dens."

"Your uncle is definitely losing the battle. What's that noise?"

A low sobbing moan vibrated through the dark air. He slammed on the brakes and accidentally killed the motor. We sat in the sandy curve just in front of the Tenant House. The lights were all off; the sound came from the pitch-black shadows behind the house. I grabbed at Thomas's hand and felt the hairs on his arm standing straight up. Quintus was in my mind, choking in blood on the Fowlerand front porch. The moan rose again into the cold breeze and broke at the end into a strangled howl.

"The dogs," Thomas said. His voice quavered. "It's just the dogs—Amanda!" He threw the door open and ran for the house. I scrambled after him. The backyard was a patchwork of moon and shadow, and half in a pool of darkness the dogs lay in a heap. The tangled tethers wound around them. Chelsea was moaning and pushing at Daphne with her nose. Daphne was stretched on her side, her massive furry head straining backwards unnaturally.

"There's a vet on Route 5," I said urgently.

Thomas was already unclipping the lead from her collar. I shoved Chelsea away. Chelsea whined, scrabbling on her belly after us. We wrestled Daphne towards the car. As we braced ourselves to lift her into the backseat, she went into a shuddering convulsion and stopped breathing.

"Thomas!" I said.

He was still trying to maneuver her front end through the door. In the moonlight, I could see only the outline of his head and his straining shoulders. He had his knee jammed under Daphne's body. Chelsea strained at the end of her leash, flat on her belly and keeping up a high constant whine.

I said again, "Thomas."

"Okay. Put her down." His voice was harsh.

We lowered Daphne to the ground. Thomas sat down on the ground beside her. He still had his hand on her motionless head. I wiped the back of my hand across my face.

"I'll call the sheriff," I said at last.

He nodded, almost invisible in the dark. I went in and dialed the sheriff's number, which I now knew by heart. An unfamiliar voice told me without haste that Sheriff White would receive my message as soon as possible.

I went back out and sat next to Thomas in the cold dirt. He was stroking Daphne's head. He put his other arm around me. We stayed there in the dark, while the Milky Way slowly emerged over our heads and an owl called from the riverbank.

Chapter Nineteen

We covered Daphne with a blanket and brought Chelsea up onto the back porch. Thomas, still silent, went into the dark kitchen and came back out with a pound of hamburger I had planned to cook for the next day's dinner. Chelsea nosed at it but wouldn't eat. She huddled against his legs, and finally we took her inside and shut her in the bathroom.

We turned on the lights, blinking in the sudden glare. Thomas's face was carved with deep unfamiliar lines. His eyes were dry and angry. He said, "We can't leave her out there all night."

"The sheriff will want to see her."

Thomas walked to the window and looked out. The glass was a flat sheet of black; the car and Daphne's blanket-covered body were invisible.

He said, after a long somber moment, "I'll work on my sermon."

"I'll stay up with you."

So I made a pot of coffee and built a fire, and we kept a vigil over Daphne. Thomas spread out his Bible and his commentaries on the kitchen table and hunched over a pad of yellow paper. I got out my Hebrew Bible and submerged myself in the calming details of grammar and vocabulary. I was working my way through Exodus. The old glorious phrases of the faith had always lifted my eyes from the shadowlands to the sunlit reality of the unseen. Tonight, though, the shadow was solid and black, and the descent of God in fire to his people seemed a distant fairy tale.

Around three in the morning, weariness came over me in a sudden staggering wave. I went upstairs and lay down across the bed and went instantly to sleep. Darkness covered me in a roaring stream and divided and piled up into two towering walls of black. Quintus stood between them with a baby in his arms. The grim lines had left his face; he was blue-eyed and bright-haired, and his head was bent down over the child. The baby's head was turned into his chest. A pillar of smoke and fire receded from him, away down the avenue of dark. The ground shook. Something was coming down the dark avenue between the watery boundaries, something invisible in the shadows that lay beyond the light. The noise of its approach grew louder.

I yelled out in warning and sat up. The windows were bright with morning. The telephone was ringing in the kitchen downstairs. I stumbled down to answer it, hearing Thomas's footsteps on the porch outside.

Helen Adkins's voice said, "Amanda?"

"Morning."

"Jimmy White told me to call and tell you he'd be out in about an hour. He wants to take a look at your dog."

"Okay, Helen. Thanks."

"Sorry to hear you're having troubles."

"Yeah," I said and hung up.

Thomas came in from the porch. His short hair was ruffled up, and his eyes were red. Chelsea whined from behind the closed bathroom door.

"Are you all right?" he said.

"Yeah, why?"

"I heard you yelling, just before the phone rang."

"I keep having nightmares."

"I'm not surprised."

"Let's take Chelsea for a walk down to the mailbox," I suggested. I had to be at Granny's by nine. She would want her *Daily Press,* and I needed a pick-me-up, but I'd drunk coffee until my tongue was sore.

"Yes, all right. I could use some air myself."

I went for Chelsea's leash, and by unspoken agreement we went out the front door and headed down the dirt road towards the mailboxes. Away from Daphne's body, Chelsea put her ears up and looked reassured. Every once in a while, she would flatten her tail between her legs and look nervously around, but our voices seemed to comfort her. She even strained sideways as we passed the graveyard, sniffing at the road where the foxes had crossed the night before. We climbed the little hill in Poverty Ridge Road and walked down the other side, towards the blacktop road.

I thought at first that Granny's mailbox was leaning because Roland and Pierman had set it in crooked. Thomas crouched down to look at the pipe. Chelsea licked his ear happily. He pushed her head away.

"Someone's hit this again," he said after a minute. "See the tracks? And the concrete's just a little bit cracked. A truck drove right into it and then had to back up."

"Bet he's got a dent in his grill."

A black pickup rounded the far curve of Little Croft Road and drove towards us. Thomas straightened up. From the other direction, a second pickup appeared over a little rise. The two trucks converged on Scarborough Lane, slowing to a stop right where we stood in front of the Tenant House mailbox.

The driver of the second pickup pulled it to the side and climbed slowly out: Attaway Fowlerand in gray shirt and yellow bow tie, his white hair hidden under a green John Deere cap and his narrow blue eyes bright with anger.

The window of the black pickup descended. Matthew Humberston gazed out at us. I hadn't seen Matthew since his warning to Thomas after church two Sundays ago. His thick dark eyebrows stood out against skin drained of blood. When he spoke his voice was a rough cover over fire.

"Come to check on your boy, Fowlerand?"

Attaway spat. "Come to check on my sister. Seems a snake's been slitherin' round these parts."

"Them snakes'll bite if you don't take some care."

"I don't take care," Attaway said. "I take a corn cutter to 'em." He made a quick graphic gesture with his left hand; his right held tight to his cane, thrust into the red dirt of the lane.

"I know that," Matthew said. "You're a regular terror to evil, Fowlerand. I've seen that for years. Judge, jury, and—"

"See your truck's been beat up some," Attaway growled.

"Hit a deer."

The hood of Matthew's truck was buckled, and the grill was dented in a straight vertical line right up the middle. Attaway gave a disgusted snort. I could hear Thomas breathing raggedly beside me. Chelsea was sitting on his feet, her tongue hanging out the side of her mouth.

"Mr. Humberston!" Thomas said.

Matthew turned his head slightly. I saw for the first time that Matt was slumped in the passenger seat beyond him. I couldn't see his face in the dim interior of the pickup.

"My dog's been poisoned. You know anything about that?"

Thomas's voice thrummed with anger. Matthew let his

eyes move over the two of us and shrugged, the tiny movement barely visible.

"I got better things to do," he said.

Attaway snapped, "Too busy hangin' around Jimmy White's office, tellin' him how your boy's been misunderstood?"

"I ain't the one been spreading rumors," Matthew said. "I'm surprised you even had the time to talk to everybody in Reverend Clement's church, what with moving Quintus here and there in all your spare time."

"You laughing at my grief?" Attaway spat back at him. His face was swelling into purple, and his breath was coming short and hard. Matthew jerked the door of the pickup open and vaulted out. Thomas and I both stepped backwards. Attaway braced his shoulders, leaning on his stick and shaking with anger.

"Your grief?" Matthew said. "The only time you felt grief in your life was when I bought the land you wanted, down by the landing. And maybe when Nathaniel Scarborough rooked you out of the Brickyard fields for a song and a promise. You didn't mourn when Quintus died. You were glad—glad to see my boy in jail, glad to see Doris's boy dead. Grief? I watched you at her funeral, Attaway. You was dry-eyed and hard-faced, and you never looked at her or at Quintus, cryin' for his mommy. You looked at Nathaniel Scarborough and you smiled. You worried about justice now? Where was your worryin' for justice when my sister died, alone with you in the house?"

"I wasn't in the house that day," Attaway bellowed at him. The end of the cane came up off the dirt. He shook the stick at his brother-in-law. "I ain't going through this with you again,

Matthew Humberston. You been telling that story on me for twenty years. She killed herself, your sister did, because she was a whorin' woman thrown over by somebody she thought she loved."

"She never strayed one inch from you. She wouldn't have dared. She loved you even though you treated her like one of your hounds, throwin' her a crumb now and then and kicking her when it suited you."

"You don't know nothin'."

"You go talk to your sister one of these days, Attaway. You hear what she's got to say."

"Cora? What's Cora got to do with it?"

"Oh, she's a Fowlerand, right enough," Matthew sneered. "She sits on those secrets like all of you—like you and Giddy—smilin' and white on the surface and with her very bones rotten underneath."

He came a step nearer. Attaway thrust the point of the cane towards him, but Matthew stepped sideways and put his face up to the old man's.

"You think I don't care that Quintus died?" he said, low and strong. "She was like my mother, Doris was. She raised me. Got me dressed for school and saw I was fed and warm when my mama didn't get out of bed for days at a time. Nobody ever spoke nice to her. She never had a minute's happiness till she married you, and I reckon that joy ended the night after the wedding."

Attaway's breath was coming hard, and his lips were blue with effort. Matthew's mouth was at his ear, but we could hear the angry sibilant words with perfect clarity.

"I could hear her when Quintus talked. He'd laugh and turn his head a bit and I could see Doris smilin' at me. And my boy killed him. You think I want Matt to get off because Quintus didn't mean nothing to me? You're a fool, Attaway Fowlerand; a fool and a murderer, messin' about with cement under your mailboxes while all your family's tearin' itself to bits around you. And you," he added, turning around to Thomas with such ferocity that we both rocked back on our heels. "You got nothing better to do than weep over a dead dog? I thought you were here to act like a Christian and show the rest of us how. You ain't thought twice about my boy. You never even visited him when he was in that cell."

I looked past Matthew's shoulder to where Matt sat slumped in the pickup's cab. He had inched forward into Matthew's seat and was watching us, his shoulders hunched. His dark hair was stringy beneath his cap, and a straggly beard hid his profile. Under the bill of the cap his eyes were dark and wretched. When he saw me watching him, he pushed himself back into the passenger seat. His hands were shaking.

Attaway hissed, "I'll have you up for slander, Matthew Humberston."

"Suit yourself," Matthew said. "Then I'll say it to the judge. That what you want?"

"You don't know nothin'," Attaway said again.

"I knew Doris. She loved me like a mother, and she loved Quintus even more. She wouldn't never have left him to your care, Attaway. She wouldn't never have killed herself with her little boy there. But that wouldn't matter to you. You treated Quintus like a dog, and he died like a dog, scrabbling at your door, an' you were glad. If God always does right, like Clement here preaches, you'll burn in hell till time ends."

He climbed back into the driver's seat and started the engine, and spun the tires on the blacktop. Matt hunched against the far window. The black pickup roared away. As it disappeared over the little hill, the sheriff's car came nosing around the far curve. It drew up beside Attaway, and Jimmy White got out and stretched his arms. He looked from our stunned faces to Attaway, shaking and purple with rage.

"Morning," he said. "You been having some Halloween trouble?"

Sheriff White wanted an autopsy on Daphne's body. He walked around the backyard, inspected the tethers where the dogs had been tied since the previous Friday, bent over the dog food still in the dish. He said at last, "If she was tied up here all night, somebody musta come up into the yard."

"We were both gone last night," Thomas said.

"Was anyone at the Old House?"

"Amanda's grandmother."

"Would she have seen anyone come up the road?"

Thomas blinked at him. He seemed to be having difficulty focusing his thoughts.

"She'd have seen a fly walk up over that hill," I said. "She sits in her front room and watches the lane." And all the movement up and down Poverty Ridge Road today would have her in a tizzy of curiosity. I'd already heard the phone ring twice inside the house, but I hadn't bothered to go in and answer it.

"Well, I don't like this much," Jimmy White said. "Somebody poisons a dog that's tied up, means they sneak up into your yard. That's mighty deliberate, and it's a grade more serious than slashin' your tire. But we can't swear the dog's been poisoned unless we have an autopsy done. I could send her up to the state medical examiner's office—"

"You send dogs up there?" I asked, surprised.

"Well, to the Department of Animal Health. They'll check her out and tell us what's inside her."

I knew, half a second in advance, that Thomas would shake his head. "No," he said. "It's not worth it."

"Your call," Jimmy White said. "But if it was my yard, my dog, an' my wife sleeping in there, I'd sure want to know what was going on."

"I know what's going on."

"You might be surprised," the sheriff said.

"What would you do if you found out she'd been poisoned for sure?"

"Well, not much. I'll go up and have a word with your grandma, Amanda, but if she didn't see nobody come up the road, we can't really go slingin' accusations around. And it was Halloween, after all. Any number of no-goods 'round here could've gotten the urge to pull a trick on you." His solid competent face was lined with frustration. "I'll keep sendin' those deputies by, but it hasn't done much good so far, has it? All right. You let me know, anything else happens. I'll go up and see Miz Scarborough now."

Thomas and I carried Daphne down to the little clearing behind the pigpen, buried her, and piled stones on the grave. Thomas crouched beside it, rubbing absently at the dirt on his hands. Sun fell through the branches and striped the ground; the woods smelled of fern and clean leaves. His fingers were trembling. I thought he was distressed, but when he lifted his head I saw lines of rage around his mouth. His brown eyes were dark with fury.

"How dare he," he said. "He knows that I couldn't visit Matt, not until after the trial. Ever since Quintus died he's been tormenting us. What does he think I'm going to do? Roll over and say, 'Oh, sorry, Matthew, I'm afraid you might poison my other dog, so now I won't say anything'? Or 'I'm afraid people will leave the church, so I'll just keep my mouth closed'?" He picked up a lump of hard forest dirt, straightened, and threw it as hard as he could against the trunk of a nearby tree. A crow rose protesting from the top limb.

"I wanted a family," Thomas said, "not a civil war." He thrust his hands in his pockets and tramped away through the woods, his head down.

I sat by the grave with my arms clasped around my knees until I heard Jimmy White's car drive away down the lane; and then I got up and walked back to the house to change. The telephone was ringing. This time I answered it. Granny Cora's old, old voice said, "Amanda? I'm goin' to bed. Don't come up today."

"Don't you want me to help you get back to bed?"

"Nope."

"What about your lunch?"

"Giddy'll make me a sandwich when he comes in. I don't feel so good and I'm goin' to bed."

"Want me to call Dr. Jones-Boston?"

"Nope. I want to be left alone. Giddy can fix me my dinner too. You can come over tomorrow mornin' and curl my hair for me."

She hung up before I could answer. I looked down the road at the puff of dust behind Sheriff White's car and wondered what he had said to her.

Chapter Twenty

Granny called Thursday morning and told me she was staying in bed again, and that Louella Watkins was going to come by and visit, so I might as well stay home. I cleaned the kitchen from top to bottom and read a chapter of Hebrew.

Friday morning the solid gray sky opened and dumped water down in cold sopping sheets. The temperature hovered just above freezing. The phone rang again, but I didn't answer it; I was beginning to worry about Granny, and I didn't want her to tell me to stay home one more day.

Thomas gave me a ride up to the Old House. He was due to meet with Ambrose and John, early, about the church pantry budget. Anger still lay just beneath the surface, but he had smoothed it over with his church face. He dropped me off at Granny's steps, and I knocked on the screen door and went straight in. By nine in the morning, Granny was usually up and sitting in her chair watching the morning news. I could smell coffee, but the chair was empty.

"Granny?"

"I'm in here."

I followed the sound down to Granny's bedroom. She was still in bed, submerged in pink chenille bedspread and crumpled sections of newspaper. The room smelled of newsprint and stale air and hound. I bent down and said sharply, "Come out, Dog-dog!"

Dog-dog slunk out from under the bed and wrinkled his lip at me.

"Scraps on the table," Granny said from behind the sports page. "And you can bring me some more coffee. Giddy put it on to perk this mornin'."

"Aren't you getting up?"

"Nope," Granny said, shaking the paper in front of her face.

I prodded Dog-dog down the hall and put him out on the steps with the greasy bowl of scraps. The coffee had perked itself black and thick. I poured it and took it in to her, and she put the paper down.

I hadn't seen Granny since Tuesday evening. In three days she had shrunk visibly; she seemed to huddle inside her skin. She had brushed her own hair, and white bits stuck out from her scalp. The steel blue eyes were sunk underneath puffy lids. Her hands shook as she reached for the cup. I held onto it and said, "Don't burn yourself, Granny—"

"Oh, go on, girl," she said, with a flash of the usual irritation. "Give me the cup. I'm not so old I can't feed myself."

I relinquished it and sat down on the edge of the bed to watch her drink. The expression of her mouth and eyes didn't suit her strong bitter face, but I'd seen those lines before. I sorted through a heap of mental images and finally found its twin: the preoccupied eyes and close-folded mouth of an old, ill woman at All Saints. She had been dying of cancer, her mind and body slaves of the thing eating at her from the inside.

"Are you going to get up today?" I said, when she had tipped the last drops of coffee from the bottom of the cup.

"Might get up, later."

"Granny, if you stay in bed too long you won't be able to

get up at all. You lose muscle strength if you don't get up and move around."

Granny Cora sniffed. "I'll mind my own strength, thank you. You go scrub off my kitchen floor for me. Giddy's been cookin' for me, and he flings food around like he's feeding a flock of hens. And I spilled a glass o' milk yesterday and didn't want to get down on m' knees to mop it up."

"Lovely," I said, taking the cup. "Want me to call Dr. Jones-Boston?"

"Nope, I ain't sick."

"No, I know. I thought she might start looking for a nursing home bed, since you're not planning on getting up anymore. You're too heavy for me to lift."

Granny sniffed again, but with less contempt. "You go scrub and quit tryin' to scare me. I'll get up in my own good time."

"Suit yourself. There's some nice broth in the fridge. I'll bring you some for lunch if you're still in bed. It's good invalid food. Won't give you much strength, but then you don't need any if you're going to stay here all day."

I went back to the kitchen and dug out the pail and sponge. Uncle Giddy had indeed spattered his cooking around the floor. I found the rubber gloves, armored myself to the elbows, and scrubbed the green-and-white linoleum until it glowed.

I'd almost finished when I heard the bed creak. Granny's uncertain feet padded across the pine floor of her bedroom to the closet. A hanger rattled.

"Amanda!"

"Yes?"

"You can get my curlers and do my hair for me. I look like

an ol' cottonhead. An' fix me some breakfast."

"You going to wash your hair first?"

"I reckon so." She came hobbling out of the bedroom, peeling off her nightgown as she went. I squinted modestly until her backside had disappeared into the bathroom, and then took off the gloves and put some Cream of Wheat on the stove.

Granny said, "Huh!" over the Cream of Wheat, but I'd put an inch of brown sugar on top, so she ate half of it while I pinned her damp white hair into coils.

"Granny," I said, rolling a coil, "you remember Miss Bonnie, down the road?"

Granny Cora craned her neck around and looked at me aslant. "Why?"

"Her brother shot himself going across a barbed-wire fence with a loaded shotgun, remember? And everyone thought it was an accident? I forget his name."

"Edwin," Granny said.

"Edwin, that's it. And Miss Bonnie went for fifteen years saying what a good brother he was, and never telling anyone that he used to punch her in the face and then go into crying jags for days on end and swear he'd kill himself and he wasn't fit to live. And no one knew that until she died and they found her old diary in the bottom of her drawer."

"Yes," Granny said, her voice growing suspicious.

"She was a quiet little lady, Miss Bonnie was. No taller than I was, even when I was ten."

"Dried-up little bit of string. No nerve, Bonnie hadn't. Shrunk up like a dried apple, and just as much flavor."

"She never did anything useful the rest of her life," I said. "It took all her energy to keep that secret from breaking out. It sucked every bit of life out of her." I pinned up a curl at the back of her head. "I felt sorry for her when it all came out. But I guess everyone pitied Miss Bonnie, wasting her life keeping someone else's secret."

"Get that bit of hair over my ear," Granny Cora said. She sat impassively while I twisted the last bit of white hair up and around a curler. When I'd finished she got up and plumped herself down in her chair. The old face had hardened into its usual lines.

"You can run an errand for me sometime soon," she said. "I got to send some preserves over to Miz Whitworth."

"The deacon's wife?"

"The same one. Tongue like an ever-running saw blade an' a soul like lemon juice. But I been promising her some cherry jam, and you can take it as soon as she's home. An' the recipe. Then she won't trouble me for it no more. Drive my car over."

"Granny—"

"And today you can sort out those jam jars in the basement. An' do my laundry. I told Giddy to put a load in, but he won't touch my underwear an' I got it piled all over the closet floor."

I reflected that a good psychiatrist could probably get three or four published articles out of Uncle Giddy. I tramped down to the basement, resigning myself to failure. That old Fowlerand secret was locked inside Granny; it could batter her, trying to get out, but she would never open her lips over it. Upstairs I heard the scrape of Granny's chair, shifting on the floor as she scooted it towards the telephone. A pause, and then her voice.

"Amelia? Cora Scarborough here. Thought I might send you some jam." Pause. "What you mean, you got enough?"

Pause. "Well, this is from those cherry trees out back, the ones like John said he was going to plant. Don't you want to see what kinda jam they make?" Pause. "Oh, you can't never have too much jam. You goin' to be home this afternoon? How 'bout tomorrow? Where you off to then?" Another, longer pause. "Okay, then. I'll send Amanda over on Monday afternoon, and you can give her a cup o' tea."

The receiver clicked down. I went on dusting jars, thoughtfully, until Granny yelled, "Ain't you ever going to fix lunch, Amanda?"

We let Chelsea stay off the leash. The tether hadn't protected Daphne, and Chelsea was inclined to stick close to home. She dragged the dead groundhog up onto the back porch and lay curled up on it, gnawing it contentedly. Even I didn't have the heart to take it away.

But the dead-animal smell clung to her, and Thomas insisted that she sleep at the foot of the bed. So every evening I hauled her into the bathtub and held her, while Thomas scrubbed her off with Pert shampoo. The result was mixed. Her coat was plenty shiny, but when she trotted through the house, an olfactory swirl of dog and dead groundhog and perfumed conditioner trailed along behind her like an invisible genie.

Saturday morning I woke up to the combined smells of shampoo and Saint Bernard and coffee. Thomas was coming in the door with a tray of bagels and coffee. I sat up, stretching in sheer comfort. He'd toasted the bagels just the way I liked them: in a very hot oven for a short time, so that the bottom was warm and soft and the top crunchy and buttery. The coffee was strong and hot. The branches of the old maple tree in the side yard slapped against the window frame; Friday's rain had given way to an unsteady cold wind under dry skies. I heard a whistling current of air curl its way around the gables. A loose piece of tin roofing started to bang somewhere overhead.

"I have a proposal," Thomas said after a moment.

I licked my fingers. "What is it?"

"Listen to me all the way through before you say anything."

"What?" I said, growing suspicious.

"Because I think it's important."

"Thomas—"

"I want Eddie to move in with us for a couple of months."

I ate another mouthful of bagel. Saturday mornings were our time alone together; the Tenant House was a small circle of refuge in the surrounding noise of wind.

"Where?" I said at last.

"In the second bedroom. We're not using it for anything but storage right now anyway."

I imagined Eddie in the Tenant House, lurking in the hallway while we drank our morning coffee in bed, sitting between us at the kitchen table while we ate.

Thomas said, "I tried to get him in a dry-out program, Amanda, but he's broke and he doesn't have any insurance. Every day he stays in that trailer alone is a day he might give in, hating himself all the while. Here." He took my empty cup, bounced off the bed, and disappeared down the stairs.

I listened to the maple tree tap insistently against the house. When Thomas reappeared, steam rising from the cup and that reassuring energy infusing his steps and his hands and his face, I said, "Do you really think this is the right thing to do?"

"I think that I don't quite know what I'm supposed to be doing here," Thomas said, "or how, or why; except for this one small duty. What I ought to do for Eddie seems clear as light to me. The rest is all…fog." He gave me the coffee cup and went to pull up the shade. The morning light crawled in through the glass, gray and dim and shadowy. He cracked the window at the top. A thread of cool air twined through the warm room.

"I haven't been much of a pastor here. Not so far," he said eventually. His back was to me, and I couldn't see his face.

"All right," I said.

"Really?"

"Yes."

He came back and sat on the bed and kissed me, careful not to upset the coffee cup.

"I love you," he said.

"I love you too."

"Can I talk to him about it on Monday?"

"Sure."

"Want some more coffee?"

I agreed to fresh coffee. The screen outside the window had begun to creak its way loose. I got up and opened the window and pulled it back into place. I could hear Thomas in the kitchen, humming "Bind Us Together, Lord" as he energetically made a second pot of coffee.

Chelsea woke me up early Sunday morning. The windows were still charcoal. A severe November wind whistled around the corners of the Tenant House. Thomas was already gone.

I let Chelsea out the back door. I put my hand out into the dark air, and I could feel an occasional drop of rain hit my hand like a solid ball of ice. The big oak back behind the pig-pen was moaning softly; lightning had struck it in the spring, and a huge branch at the top moved and spoke in high winds. Chelsea tucked her tail between her legs and scooted off into the dark.

I made coffee and pulled out sugar and flour and milk for a coffee cake. Usually I devoted Sunday mornings to spiritual reading—François Fénelon, or the psalms, or one of the Puritan writers I loved for their robust common sense. The wind and the spattering drops and the ceaseless moan from the dark woods behind the house unsettled me. I didn't want to sit down and listen to the morning. I clattered pans, so loudly that I almost missed Chelsea's whining at the back door. I let her in, and she shot through the kitchen into the little living room and hid behind the sofa.

Dawn was horribly slow in coming. A thick layer of gray clouds coated the expanse of sky, with a single thin rim of light around the edge, like a giant metal bowl turned over us and held just above the surface. The winter wheat stirred under the pewter clouds. I drank three cups of coffee. The coffee cake browned, and I took it out.

Eventually I forced myself to sit down and read, but the spiritual checklists of the Puritans grated on my nerves. We'd done all the right things, so far as I could tell, and we were still surrounded by chaos. Thomas's *Imitation of Christ* lay on top of his Bible, in front of me. I flipped through the Gospels and pictured Christ in my mind: God on earth, smoothing out tangles, healing, bringing light and sight and understanding; clearing up messes and sweeping away chaos.

~ ~ ~ ~ ~

The back pews were still empty when Thomas stood up to preach. The crowd had dwindled slightly. Joe and Jenny were among the listeners, and Eddie in the corner of a far pew, and Ambrose and Ida, John and Amelia. But other faces I'd grown familiar with were missing. A tall cadaverous turf farmer and his wisp-thin wife were absent; the worried woman with the three sulky teenage boys had disappeared from the second pew to the front; the square doughy family from up the county was gone. I sat and worried it over while Thomas worked his way through the story of the shepherds in the field. I'd thought Daphne's poisoning and the slit tire to be the sum total of Matthew Humberston's malice. But perhaps it had only been an outward sign of gathering hatred, working its way through the congregation like yeast through dough. Gossip was as clinging and destructive as any phosphorous fire.

Thomas had been quiet since we buried Daphne, and I had not pried. He was working through some knot in his own mind. I had learned, early on, that my prodding only drove him backwards; so when he disappeared into the intricacies of a problem, I generally gritted my teeth and waited for him to come back. It had been easier, this time. I was preoccupied. I seemed to hear Matthew Humberston's words at odd moments. *Oh, she's a Fowlerand, right enough. She sits on those secrets like all of you, smilin' and white on the surface and with her very bones rotten underneath.* I nursed my own secrets and said nothing.

Whatever tangle possessed Thomas's mind had not affected his preaching. The sermon pulled me away from my own scattered thoughts with the story of God's shining glory, breaking through to the ragged and helpless. When he bent his head for the final prayer, I could hear inheld breath expelled all throughout the sanctuary.

"Almighty Father—"

Before he could finish the first sentence of the prayer, someone stumbled past me. Eddie Winn went down on his knees at the front of the church. He was sobbing; not hysterically, but deep and unashamed. I could hear a rustle of murmurs as the congregation craned their necks forward. Little Croft had never been a rambunctious church; if the Holy Spirit was determined to descend, he was welcome to do so unobtrusively, and the Little Croft congregants would all celebrate the event with a decorous hymn.

John Whitworth had woken up. I could see, from the side of his face, that curiosity and indignation were struggling for the upper hand. But Thomas came down from the pulpit. He knelt beside Eddie, his hand on the man's shaking back, and spoke quietly to him. The little old organist was wringing her hands over her postlude, away in her corner. Thomas was oblivious to the stir, but I wondered how Eddie felt with thirty-five pairs of curious eyes fixed on his kneeling form.

Across the aisle from me, Ambrose Scarborough bounced to his feet. "Bring them in, bring them in, bring them in from the fields of sin!" he caroled. For a little fat man, he had a stirring baritone. "'Bring them in, bring them in, bring the wandering ones to Jesus!'"

A voice near me picked up the verse.

"'Hark! 'tis the Shepherd's voice I hear, out in the desert, dark and drear!'"

Voices chimed in from the front and back.

"'Calling the sheep who've gone astray, far from the Shepherd's fold away!'"

The little old organist stopped wringing her hands. She stomped the pedal and plunged in. The whole church—barring John Whitworth and his wife—was on its feet now, singing.

Bring them in, bring them in,
Bring them in from the fields of sin!
Bring them in, bring them in,
Bring the wandering ones to Jesus!

The second verse got Amelia Whitworth off her bottom halfway through; and by the third verse, John was standing as well. Under Thomas's urging, Eddie stood up and turned, reluctantly, to face the congregation. His eyes were wet and red. But his face had lost the furtive, scuttling expression of an unwelcome intruder. He looked relieved, as though some bloody inner battle had finally concluded. In him, I could see the ghost of the strong handsome man he had once been.

Out in the desert hear their cry,
Out on the mountains wild and high!
Hark! 'tis the Master speaks to thee,
"Go find my sheep where'er they be!"

In the echo of the final chorus, Thomas raised his hand.
"We welcome Eddie Winn to the kingdom of God," he said, his voice strong and triumphant. "I ask you to come forward and show your love for this new brother as we close. Now may the God of peace, who brought up our Lord Jesus from the dead, that great Shepherd of the sheep, through the blood of the everlasting covenant, make you complete in every good

work to do his will, working in you what is well pleasing in his sight, through Jesus Christ, to whom be glory forever and ever. Amen!"

"Amen!" the congregation responded, in great good humor, and surged forward to welcome Eddie to the family of God.

I let myself be carried up with them, meeting Thomas's glance over the crowd. His eyes were damp as well. I went past, shook Eddie's hand, and took my place at Thomas's side.

I couldn't doubt Eddie's sincerity or the reality of what had just happened here. But I wished, with all my heart, that I liked the man.

Chapter Twenty-one

Monday morning, Thomas went off to talk to Eddie about moving in. I trudged down to the Old House, got Granny up and fixed her breakfast and carried a couple of jars of cherry jam out to her old car. Amelia Whitworth, Granny Cora informed me, was waiting anxiously for her jam.

John and Amelia Whitworth lived in an old brick house across Route 5, on a corner of a century-old forest that belonged to one of the plantations. The house was small and the brick had begun to crumble, but the fanlight over the door drew the eye up to graceful dormers, and English boxwood lined the old walk.

Amelia Whitworth opened the door: small and thin in an immaculate apron, brown hair drawn back into a tight-pinned bun, and her glasses on a chain around her neck. The hallway behind her was narrow and dark, but she led me through it into a windowed kitchen with herbs in pots on the sills and a checked cloth on the table. She took the two jars of jam from me with an impatient shake of her head.

"I got three shelves full of jam in my closet," she said, "but when your grandma gets something on her mind the angel Gabriel can't shift her. Sit down and have a muffin, Amanda."

She bustled off with the jam. I sat in a walnut chair and looked around. The kitchen windows were dark with shadow, but the sun lay on the lawn in back. Not a pine needle marred its brown clipped surface. The glass shone like crystal, and the canisters on the kitchen counter were spaced with perfect symmetry. Next to the refrigerator, a pyramid of apples rose in mathematical precision from a square basket. Blueberry muffins steamed on a platter in the middle of the table.

Amelia Whitworth reappeared a moment later, whisked butter from the refrigerator, and poured tea and sat down and folded her hands.

"Jam?" she said. "Lord knows I got enough."

"No, thank you, Mrs. Whitworth." I buttered a muffin. They were good muffins, tender and sweet with big plump blueberries.

"So is it true that you're letting that no-good hound dog of a Winn move in with you?"

"Thomas is helping Eddie kick his drinking, Mrs. Whitworth."

"You'd best be sure he kicks more than that," Amelia Whitworth said, her sharp little eyes creased into serious lines. "If that trifling man ever finds himself a spine, won't be because a whole church o' hardworking people slobbered all over him once on a Sunday. We going to have any more outbursts like that?"

"If the Spirit moves," I said, unable to resist.

Amelia snorted. "I reckon he's got more important folks than Winns to occupy him. How's your mother?"

"She's fine. She likes Montana."

"Dry air. She'll age faster out there. You remember coming down here trick-or-treating when you were little? You were dressed like the Statue of Liberty, and your brother was a robot, an' you'd both made your costumes yourselves."

I remembered; she had towered in the doorway and distributed neat square-edged packages of Rice Krispies marshmallow bars, unsmiling. She had one Halloween decoration, a monster head in the middle of the door with eyes that really glowed. We all begged Mom not to take us back.

"You never came but that one time," Amelia Whitworth said. "I always wondered what you came up with next, after the Statue of Liberty. Well, you and Reverend Clement been here since August, and John and I haven't had you over yet for supper. Not out of meanness, you understand, but we've been busy as a one-handed paperhanger with hives. Our grandchildren been staying with us most of the summer and fall, did you know? They just left, beginning of this week. Have another muffin."

I took a muffin. "Did they come with you on Sundays? I never saw them."

"No. No, they didn't. I wanted to bring them, but their mother—my daughter—she used to come pick them up on Fridays and bring 'em back on Sunday nights. My daughter... Amy...she can't—she's a sweet girl, but she can't take care of two little children like that, not properly."

"How old are they?"

"Four and two. Boys, both of them. Still babies." Her tone was brisk and cheerful, but the sharp little eyes were looking past me, into the empty hallway.

"I remember Amy," I said, at a venture. I wasn't sure why Granny Cora had suddenly sent me over here, but I heard an edge of something fathoms deep underneath the matter-of-fact voice. "She came to my eighth birthday party."

"She's older 'n you," Amelia said doubtfully.

"By a few years. She came to help my mother out with all the eight-year-olds and their little brothers and sisters. She looks like you, doesn't she?"

"Like me in most ways. Terrible determined to do what she wanted, no matter what. But prettier than I ever was."

I remembered a slight, brown-haired girl, outwardly compliant, her small eyes dark and implacable. Amy Whitworth had drifted around the edges of Little Croft all through my teens, and then had pulled herself together and set off for a job, somewhere in northern Virginia.

"She got married before we knew it," Mrs. Whitworth said, brushing specks of transparent dust from the checked tablecloth. "John kept saying, 'At least she's married, Melia. At least she's married.' He always worried about Amy, John did. But she—he—sometimes she needed to send the children here. So they could get away. She—she stays with him. She says he's really a good man. He wanted the boys back, not to stay with us anymore. Well, they're his boys." Her nervous fingers twitched over the napkin in front of her, straightening the fringe. "You two settling into Little Croft all right? Matthew Humberston came by to talk to John one night an' sounded right unhappy about Reverend Clement. They went out on the porch, though. All John would say after he left was, 'It'll be all right, Melia.'" She peered over at me, curiosity struggling with lingering distress.

"Matthew doesn't want Thomas to testify at Matt's trial."

"Then he shoulda taught the boy not to go around shootin' folk."

"Yes, well, that's what Thomas says."

"More tea?"

I accepted. The basement dust had dried my throat. She poured tea into my cup, her mouth pursed thoughtfully.

"Matt's not much more than an arm of his father's rage," she said. "Matthew's filled him so full of the Fowlerand misdeeds, he's been boiling like a kettle for years. Mind you, I reckon Attaway brought this on his own family. If you don't mind me talkin' so about your great-uncle."

"Not at all," I said.

"When he touched Doris, he was marking the apple of Matthew's eye. Storing up the whirlwind for himself. Matthew saw Doris change from a sweet loving girl to a woman who drank a glass of whisky before dinner to nerve herself up for Attaway's coming home, and half a bottle afterwards to forget what he'd done to her. Muffin?"

I shook my head.

"You sure you don't mind me talking about Attaway this way?"

"I've been away from Little Croft for years," I said. "I always wanted to come back home, Mrs. Whitworth. But now I'm finding a mess. Too many secrets, tucked away and kept in the family."

"Your grandma could tell you what went on between Attaway and Doris."

"She won't, though."

"No. I don't know that I blame her."

"For keeping secrets?"

"For wanting Attaway on her side. How old is your grandma, Amanda? Eighty?"

"Eighty-one."

"And still in good health, I know. But how much longer? She's startin' to slow down now. If she got bedrid, who'd take care of her? Not your Uncle Giddy. I daresay he likes his mama well enough, but he's not going to wait on her hand and foot for ten years if she breaks a bone and never gets up no more. Your mama might, but she's out in Montana, and Winnie's so taken up with all her men and children and their children and their ex-wives, she hasn't got the time or energy to worry about Cora. And you're going to have babies o' your own and look after your own house and maybe move away. We all know that Little Croft Church ain't a final resting place for a young preacher like Reverend Clement. If it weren't for Attaway and his money, Cora'd have nothing to fall back on. She has trouble making her ends meet now, I reckon. Your grandpa left her some investments, but Giddy told John she goes into her capital every few months just to pay her bills."

She broke a sugared edge off the muffin in front of her and ate it. I sloshed tea around in the bottom of my cup. Granny had lived in that little brick house at the top of the Chickahominy hill for my entire life. I'd never considered what she might do when she couldn't live alone anymore.

"Say what you will about the Fowlerands—and there's plenty to say—they're family-loyal." Amelia Whitworth said, "Attaway won't ever see Cora put in a nursing home, and I reckon even if he dies first and leaves his money to Roland and Pierman, he'll have made some arrangements for her. She isn't going to go telling tales on her brother, not in this life."

"No one wants to tell tales on Great-uncle Attaway."

"No. He sits where he likes, and always did. We used to live down there, you know. Down in Winnville, afore John got on his feet good. We was like everyone else, Amanda. We never said anything to Attaway about…well, about Doris. I didn't— we didn't—" She broke off and ate another bit of muffin. Her eyes were shadowed and unreadable, but the muscles around her lips were twitching. I waited, silently.

Amelia Whitworth said in a sudden burst, "I reckon, if I knew then what I know now, I'd have spoken up and let him kick us out. But that was a long time ago. We didn't talk about our husbands in those days. Doris used to come over and let Quintus play with Amy, and she'd wear long sleeves in the summer. Sometimes Quintus'd have a bruise over his eye, or a red lump on his head. And we never said nothing. We sat and drank coffee and talked about our gardens, and I never said a word to her until the day she died. I thought she'd leave him if it got bad enough. I didn't know why she'd stay with a man who did that to her. I never did understand why, until...until the last couple of years. She wouldn't never have left him. It half killed her, that he wouldn't love her, but she kept tryin'."

She got up suddenly. "I got pictures of Amy and her boys. Want to see them?"

"Yes, I would. Very much. Mrs. Whitworth, a few days ago Great-uncle Attaway and Matthew Humberston had a big screaming match out in the middle of the road, and Matthew called Attaway a murderer. Is that what he meant, that Attaway made Doris so miserable she didn't want to live?"

"No," Amelia said, "I reckon Matthew meant just what he said. I reckon he thinks Attaway killed her."

Eddie Winn arrived at the Tenant House early Tuesday morning. He carried a battered tote bag stuffed with clothes and two boxes of junk: old books, a couple of pots and pans, a .22 pistol, and a stack of magazines. When he knocked, I was in the kitchen, eating my cereal and toast standing up.

"Thomas," I called. There was no answer. Eddie knocked again. I put my toast down and jogged up the stairs, but the upstairs rooms were empty. I figured he must have gone out the front door to take Chelsea for a walk. The knock came once more, short and insistent. I went down and opened the door and smiled at Eddie with all the grace I could muster.

"Morning," I said. "Come on in."

"I do appreciate this, Miz Clement." Eddie had a soft ingratiating voice. He was looking more respectable every day; his color was back, his wavy dark hair was neatly cut, and he had shaved for the occasion. He was standing straighter too.

"We're glad to have you," I said.

Eddie hauled his box and tote bag in. Another box sat at the top of the porch steps. I propped open the door and brought it in for him. The boxes smelled of mildew. I made a mental note to go over Eddie's belongings with Lysol one day when he was out. He stood in the middle of the kitchen. His shoulders were squared, but as he shifted his grip on his bag I could see that his hands still trembled.

"Come on upstairs," I said. "I'll carry your other box for you."

I led him up the stairs, conscious of his footsteps behind me. I pushed open the door of the little spare bedroom and was unpleasantly aware, all at once, of how close he was and how small the little landing seemed. I set his box down in the doorway.

"Take your time unpacking," I said. "There's cereal on top of the fridge and bread in the basket on the counter."

I went back downstairs to finish my bowl of cereal, now soggy on the counter. Chelsea's claws clicked on the porch, and a moment later I heard Thomas on the steps. The kitchen door creaked, and he came in on a gust of clean November air.

"Thought you'd already gone to your grandmother's," he said.

"I'm moving slow this morning."

"Eddie here already?" His voice was pleased.

"He's unpacking."

"Great. I'm going to start studying Romans with him. We can do an hour of work before I head over to church. Did you check his boxes?"

"For what?"

"A bottle."

"No, I didn't want to poke through his stuff."

"I'll run up and do it."

I left my cereal and intercepted him at the doorway. He wrapped his arms around me. His body was lean and warm and strong, and I burrowed my arms underneath his jacket and buried my face in his chest.

"What's the matter?"

"Oh…nothing. I'm tired, and Granny's hard to get along with."

Thomas kissed the top of my head. His jacket smelled of fall and leaves, and where it had been unzipped, his shirt was slightly damp with morning air. We stood together for a long moment, until the old stairway to the second floor squeaked under Eddie's feet. Thomas unwrapped his arms.

"I love you," he said.

"I love you too. Can we go have a picnic next Saturday?"

"In November?"

"We'll wrap up. We can take Chelsea and walk down to the dam and take cheese and crackers and that half-bottle of wine…"

"I dumped it out," Thomas said. "Didn't want to have it in the house with—" He motioned with his head towards the door.

"Right," I said. "Well, we could walk down to the dam with a thermos of coffee, then."

Thomas smiled down at me. Eddie reappeared in the doorway just then, so I headed outside. Chelsea was contentedly gnawing on her groundhog in a corner of the back porch. She thumped her tail at me without getting up.

"Enjoy your visit yesterday with Miz Whitworth?" Granny asked from behind her paper.

I went on stirring her oatmeal. A lone sausage patty sputtered on the back burner. I hoped the single piece would lull her into acceptance of the oatmeal. I'd gone straight home Monday afternoon, without coming back to Granny's house.

"She gave me very good muffins," I said at last.

"Oh, Amelia was always a good cook. Folks say that's why John puts up with her bossy ways."

"Is she bossy?"

"Treats him like she was a broody hen with one sick chick."

"Maybe he likes it."

"Huh."

"Or maybe she just has that reputation because she won't let him push her around." I slid the sausage onto a plate and poured oatmeal into a bowl.

"She won't let him do nothing," Granny said, putting her newspaper down and eyeing the dishes I put in front of her. "If you want me to eat that stuff, you better put more sugar on it so I can't taste it."

I shoveled brown sugar in a thick layer over the oatmeal.

"That's all right," Granny said, satisfied. She picked up her spoon. "John and Giddy went out an' got drunk one night, 'bout fifteen years ago. Giddy came back laughing. He wasn't so bad off, but John Whitworth was blind drunk and happy as a pig in slops. Only time the man's had any fun in twenty-four years of bein' married to Amelia. She took one look at him and got a fryin' pan and started chasin' him around the porch with it. Giddy said he scooted from one side to th'other with his arms over his head, squealing, 'Don't hit me, Melia! Don't hit me again, Melia!' Far as I know, he's never had a drink again, poor man."

"He looks happy enough."

"Oh," Granny said, poking at the oatmeal, "fair to middling."

"You think he'd be happier if he could smack her whenever he felt like it?"

"Don't sass me. Did you find that pork fat for Dog-dog?"

"He's out on the steps eating it. Granny…"

"What?"

"I don't remember Papa Scarborough very well. I was only nine when he died." I remembered a tall gaunt man with big-knuckled hands and a sharp loud voice, quick moving and quick tempered. He'd had a heart attack when I was six and spent three years as an invalid, sinking deeper and deeper into an early senility.

"He took a long time dyin'," Granny said, rather shortly.

"Can I ask you a personal question?"

"Anybody washes my underwear's seen all there is to see, Amanda."

"Were you ever afraid of him?"

I thought for a moment she would push the plate away and get up, head for the bathroom or her bedroom to lock herself away. But she caught herself and sat still, folding her old hands in her lap. She turned her head and looked out the window, over the wide fields with the morning clouds drifting above them and the sheen of winter wheat rising above the corn stubble.

"No," she said at last. "No. Nat wouldn't never raise a hand to a woman. That wasn't his way."

I was disappointed. I'd assembled all the players on the stage: Cora Scarborough, too terrorized by a violent husband to rescue her sister-in-law; Attaway and Nathaniel Scarborough, explosive and hard-drinking and feuding. Granny caught the expression on my face.

"How old are you?" she said. "Twenty-six? Twenty-seven? You think a fist is the only way a man can hurt his wife? You don't know nothing yet, Amanda. Nat Scarborough could suck all the life out of a woman and leave her dry. See those pictures?" She pointed at the far end of the table, where I'd stacked the old photos into neat sorted piles. "See him smilin', with life just shining out of his eyes? He got that from women. He fed on them, took all the breath right out of them and went on an' left them behind. I never knew how many there were. I was glad when that man died. I'd-a sung at his funeral if I hadn't been afraid of shockin' all those hens down at Little Croft Church. They stood around weeping for my loss, and I reckon there weren't but three or four that he hadn't romanced. Only good thing Nat Scarborough ever did in his life was build Poverty Ridge up from that little mess of small fields and pig farms that was here when my daddy was alive. I wasn't afraid of Nat Scarborough. I hated him."

She pushed herself up on the edge of the table. "Now I'm goin' to the bathroom, and you can go out and pull the grass out of my mums. You happy, now that you got your secrets?"

She hobbled off to the bathroom and slammed the door. I cleared her dishes and put the half-eaten oatmeal out for Dog-

dog, who would have eaten cardboard if brown sugar was sprinkled on it, and then I went out to weed the rest of the perennial bed. Some of the chrysanthemums came up as I worked; the wire grass had twined itself so securely into the roots that I could no longer separate flowers from weeds.

Chapter Twenty-two

B y Thursday, the November weather turned out-and-out cold. It was in the twenties when I got up, windows iced over, a hard killing frost coating the fields, the tops of the pines motionless against a pale blue sky. Thursday, November 9: the first day of Matt Humberston's trial.

Eddie's door was still closed. I let Chelsea out and made coffee, wondering where Thomas was. I heard his voice a few minutes later. He was calling to the dog, somewhere around the front of the house.

I peered out the window of the fireplace room. He was sitting out on the little-used front porch, next to the front door that we never opened, in Miss Clunie's old rocker. He was wearing his wedding and funeral suit and a dark tie. Chelsea had flopped happily down at his feet. Thomas was leaning forward, his hands clasped between his thighs, staring down Poverty Ridge Road. His breath clouded the air in uneven puffs.

I went out and stood beside him. Cold stung at my eyes. I said gently, "Can I do anything for you before I go?"

He shook his head. "I meant to do it. Tell them what Quintus said, for his sake. But I'm so caught between anger at your great-uncle and anger at Matthew that I don't trust myself to speak anything for the right reason."

I stroked the back of his head. "Do you want me to come today?"

"No." He turned his lips briefly against my palm. "Just pray for me. I sat down this morning to pray, and I started out 'Almighty Father' and heard myself…such an impersonal phrase, but I always start that way. The truth is that God's a distant father to me; he's like my own father, the one who left us to cope on our own. I've been chasing a family on earth all this time, so I could feel some kind of belonging, but I don't think I'll find it here."

He sat with my hand against his face for a long moment. "I want to," he said. "I want to be like Christ, surrounded by brothers, a mother, the disciples who were more than family. People all around him. I don't know how long I can struggle on by myself."

I walked over to Granny's with my mind repeating once more: *Lord, have mercy. Christ, have mercy.* Granny handed me the keys to her old navy blue Granada as soon as I stepped into her living room.

"Courthouse," she said. "That Humberston trial's this morning. I want to hear it."

"Oh, Granny—"

"You hush. Matt's the nephew of my dead sister-in-law, an' he killed her son. I got a duty to find out what happens to him."

This, I thought, was a particularly bad excuse for plain old cat-whiskered curiosity.

"Can't we wait till afternoon? They won't get to anything interesting much before lunch."

"No matter. I don't want to miss seein' Matthew's face from the start. Reckon they'll call him up?"

"I wouldn't think so. He wasn't there."

"Good thing," Granny said. "That man could lie the soda out of a biscuit without touchin' the crust, and no oath on God's green earth would make a difference. Let's go. Put Dog-dog in the basement first. I got a nice deer shank for him."

So I herded Dog-dog down the steep basement steps, drove Granny down Route 5 under the arched branches of the old trees, and walked her up Courthouse Hill to the little brick building perched on top. Thomas's hatchback was already parked in the lot.

The Little Croft courthouse was a tiny, ancient, dark-roomed building, unaltered since the early part of the century. The courtroom itself was dark walnut, with pews like a church and the Little Croft seal all gold and red above the judge's bench. It smelled like Little Croft Church: old wood and carpet and furniture polish. Thomas was already sitting at the far end of a front bench. His fair head was bent; he had his elbows on his knees, his long fingers locked behind the back of his neck.

Little Croft folk were trickling steadily in through the door. Attaway was absent; his nephew Roland, pudgy and glum, slumped on a bench near the front. We sat ourselves in a back bench, a bare minute before the deputy sheriff at the front called out "All rise!" and the judge came into the room. Judge Ryland Banks was a distant cousin of some sort, although I'd have had to diagram the family on a big piece of paper to find out exactly where our blood mingled. He was tall and blond, fading to gray, which probably meant the relation-ship was somewhere on Granny's fair side of the family.

He sat down and eyed the front bench for a long moment. Matthew Humberston was looking thoughtfully into the empty jury box.

"Morning," Judge Banks said at last. "Let's get this jury seated."

The jury selection was dull, lengthy, and devoid of incident. Granny Cora kept up a running stream of whispered commentary as juror after juror was seated or turned away. Very few Little Croft citizens, it appeared, led stainless lives. The twelve citizens who ended up on the front benches were almost evenly black and white, mostly male: a blameless-looking crew. According to Granny, they included two thieves, one wife beater, three drunks, and one enterprising marijuana grower.

When they were seated, Judge Banks looked at his watch. "It's almost one," he said. "Let's break for lunch before we get moving on this matter."

The clerk of the court duly called a lunch break. The spectators around us started to shift and chatter. Granny announced, "I want me a ham sandwich."

"Too much sodium," I said, pulling myself out of a reverie. Matthew Humberston sat motionless in the corner of the front bench. Thomas had not shifted.

"You won't let me eat anythin' I want," Granny said loudly.

"Let's go on home. I'll fix you a nice lunch."

"Nope. I want to hear the testimony. Go get me a sandwich."

"If you eat all that salt, your ankles will swell up."

"They never do. I've had fat legs all m' life, that's all. Go get me a ham sandwich from Winn's and quit quoting that blamed doctor."

Winn's Grocery sat at the bottom of Courthouse Hill, at the curve of the narrow blacktop road. The two elderly Winn brothers made sandwiches at the meat counter in the back: egg salad, bacon and egg, thick salty ham and mayonnaise on Wonder Bread. I trudged down the hill and stood in line, hearing flicks and tails of other conversations. The store was dark and close, the windows half blocked by display cases.

"Matthew's got a black grudge against that preacher," an old voice ahead of me croaked. "Seen him glaring?"

"That's no news," someone answered.

"Where's Attaway today?"

"Sulkin' at home," a younger voice said.

"He must be wishin' Quintus had died before that land deed was signed. How much'll he have to pay, you reckon?"

The first voice said, "None at all, if all had their rights."

And then my presence must have been noted, because the thick Little Croft accents died away, and ancient Charlie Winn said, "What can I get you then, Amanda?"

"Granny wants a ham sandwich," I said. I waited while he slapped the white slices over the pink slabs of ham and wrapped it up in waxed paper. The line behind me had gone silent. When I turned around, no one was looking at me.

I stepped out of the screen door. Across Route 5, the old woods were full of late reds and browns. Courthouse Hill rose up above me. The centuries-old oak behind the courthouse stretched thick huge branches up into the blue sky, and a hawk hung motionless over it. It swayed and darted, and the wild keening came down to me on the November breeze. I stood with my feet on the pavement and loathed the Fowlerands and the Scarboroughs and the Humberstons with all my strength.

The courthouse's little back porch was empty, but the air was thick with cigarette smoke. Back inside, the spectators were rustling and settling themselves. I made my way to Granny's side and handed her the wax-wrapped square.

"Look at that gristle," Granny said. "Charlie Winn's gettin' stingy. Ain't you going to go speak to Reverend Clement?"

"No. He's thinking." Thomas hadn't moved from his seat, and his profile had that shuttered look I'd learned to leave alone. Matthew sat in the corner of his bench, still as stone. The jury began to file back. The watchers in the courtroom quieted. The air was silent; a foot shuffled, a cough sounded.

"The Commonwealth of Virginia versus Matthew Humberston Jr.," announced the clerk of the court.

A rustle went through the shifting courtroom. Thomas sat up. He was looking uncommonly grim. The door on the left side of the courtroom opened, and Matt Humberston came into the room with his expensive lawyer. He was neatly brushed and wearing a suit. No longer grubby and morose, he had been washed and shaved and polished up, and he shone like a young dark angel. His hair, like his father's, touched his collar in the back in heartbreaking waves, and his profile was clean and heroic.

The commonwealth was charging Matt Humberston with first-degree murder, largely on the weight (I thought) of Quintus's final words. The prosecuting attorney, Jeremiah Adkins, called the state trooper who had arrived first that night. He recited the facts: Quintus Fowlerand had been dead when they arrived; Matt Humberston had been badly beaten about the head and shoulders and had been taken by ambulance to MCV.

A Fowlerand cousin, his voice tight with hatred, testified that the two men had been drinking and arguing until well into the night. Another Fowlerand had seen them shouting obscenities at each other at the entrance to Fowlerand Lane. Quintus was empty-handed; Matt's shotgun hung broken open over his arm.

"Had they been hunting?" the prosecutor asked. Jeremiah Adkins was a well-spoken black man in his forties, a longtime Little Croft resident.

"Too dark," the Fowlerand said.

"I mean, earlier in the day?"

"Sure. Rabbit hunting, over on the Humberston farm."

Without Thomas's evidence, I thought, the jury could indict for second-degree murder, or even manslaughter. With any luck, Matt could spend a year or less in jail. The Fowlerand cousin sat down.

"The prosecution calls Thomas Clement," Jeremiah Adkins announced.

Thomas rose and went forward. He seated himself and fixed his eyes on the public prosecutor, ignoring Matthew's steady black stare.

"You arrived at the residence of Attaway Fowlerand at 2:00 A.M. on Saturday morning the fourteenth of October?"

"Yes," Thomas said.

"Will you describe what you saw and heard?"

"There was a circle of pickup trucks at the front of the house with their headlights on. Mr. Fowlerand was lying on his stomach on the porch. Mr. Humberston was on his back, with his head on the top steps, all bloody. He was going in and out of a daze. I went up on the porch to see Mr. Fowlerand, because he'd asked for a priest. He was alive, but he was breathing blood and it was hard for him to talk. He said, 'Matt said he'd kill me. Told me yesterday he'd kill me. Tonight, said he'd been meanin' to kill me all his life and now he had the chance.'"

Alone on the front pew, Matthew Humberston straightened up and started to search through his pockets, one by one.

He discovered a handkerchief in the fourth pocket and shook it out over his knee to examine it. The jury's eyes were riveted on him. I remembered him at the funeral, dropping his sunglasses under the chair and rooting for them while the entire gathered crowd watched him instead of the priest.

"Did he say anything else, Reverend Clement?"

"The rest was confidential," Thomas said. "It had to do with his spiritual state."

"What happened then?"

"I turned around to the guy on the steps—"

"That would be Matthew Humberston Jr.?"

"Yes. He was yelling, 'Is he dead? Is he dead?' I said, 'Yes, he's dead and you killed him.'" He paused. The words hung on the thick polish-scented air.

"And how did Mr. Humberston react?"

"He said, 'Good!' and passed out."

Matthew Humberston coughed shortly. The prosecutor said, "Thank you, Reverend Clement."

Matt's defense lawyer stood up.

"Reverend Clement, if you were to characterize the mental states of Mr. Fowlerand and Mr. Humberston—"

The state prosecutor snapped, "Objection! Witness isn't an expert."

"Yes, but if we're going to rely on this secondhand account, I'm entitled to ask—"

"Overruled," Judge Banks said. "Get on with it."

"Reverend Clement?"

"Mr. Fowlerand was in a great deal of pain, but he was lucid," Thomas said. "Mr. Humberston was conscious at the moment he said 'Good,' and he appeared to know what was going on. That's all I can say."

"Reverend Clement, how many deathbeds have you attended?"

"Excuse me?"

"How many people have you seen die?"

"In my pastoral role?"

"Yes, that's right."

"One."

"Ah. How many violent deaths?"

"None. Till now."

"So you have practically no experience in dying confessions? No way to evaluate the lucidity of these two men? No yardstick to measure their last statements against?"

"Perhaps Mr. Hall would save his closing statement for the close?" the state prosecutor inquired.

"I think you've made your point, Mr. Hall," the judge said. "Any other questions?"

"No, Your Honor." The defense lawyer returned to his seat.

Thomas stood up. His eyes, traveling vaguely over the packed courtroom, landed on me. I made an apologetic gesture at Granny Cora. He gave a tiny shrug, stepped down past Matthew, and went out the side door. Judge Banks pressed the heels of his hands against his eyes. His shoulders were hunched forward as though his stomach hurt.

"Gentlemen," he said, "it's almost five. May I suggest that we wait for our next witness until tomorrow morning? Who are you calling next, Mr. Adkins?"

"Attaway Fowlerand, Your Honor. Father of the deceased. I have no objection to waiting."

"Nor do I," Matt's lawyer said from his chair.

Judge Banks smiled dryly. "How agreeable." He rapped

once with his gavel and rose, grimacing. "Then we'll adjourn until tomorrow morning."

"Man's got an ulcer," Granny said loudly. "But then if I was married to Lelia Banks, I'd most likely have an ulcer too."

Thomas was waiting for me in the kitchen when I came back from Granny's. As soon as I came through the door, he said, "Let's go to Williamsburg for dinner."

"What about Eddie?"

"He's gone to clear some stuff out of his trailer. Said he'd be back late."

"Okay," I said. "Let me change." I kissed him in passing and felt the tension that strung his tall body through from head to toe.

We went into Williamsburg and ate sandwiches and cheesecake at one of the college delis. We were surrounded by crowds of cheerful students, and the Terrapins and Cavaliers were playing silently on the TV screens above the bar. We watched the game and talked about everything under the sun except for Quintus and Matthew and Matt and Attaway. I waited for him to mention the trial, but he didn't bring it up.

We drove home on Route 5, crossed the Chickahominy at Barrett's Ferry Bridge, and turned off onto the winding narrow roads that led into Little Croft's heart. I leaned my head onto Thomas's shoulder. He put his arm around me, and suddenly stiffened and slammed on his brakes. I caught myself on the dashboard and pushed myself upright. In the headlights, the church sign hung splintered from one bracket. Pieces of smashed wood littered the grass beneath it.

Thomas pulled to the side of the road and got out. I followed him, shivering as the icy air crept through my layers of coat and sweatshirt. He crouched down and swept splinters together with his hands.

"I'll call Ambrose tomorrow," he said, half under his breath. "Maybe we can get a new sign before Sunday. Then no one will have to know…"

"Aren't you going to call the sheriff?"

Thomas shook his head. He straightened up, dusting his hands.

"Why not?"

"I deserved that," he said. "I was angry, today. I didn't decide to speak because I wanted justice. I was just plain mad."

Chapter Twenty-three

"Your Winn's looking better these days," Granny said over breakfast.

"Yes, he's put on some weight."

"Used to be a terror for the ladies, Eddie Winn did."

"So I've heard."

"Where is he this mornin'?"

"Out looking for work, Granny."

"Well, I do hope so."

"What does that mean?"

"Nothin'," Granny said. "What's that you're cutting up?"

I plopped a grapefruit in front of her. "If you eat that, I'll fix you a piece of bacon."

"I ain't eating that. It's sour."

"It's very sweet, and I've cut all the chewy parts away. See?"

Granny poked at the grapefruit suspiciously with the tip of her spoon.

"Are we making pies this morning?" I asked.

"Nope. Going back to the Humberston trial."

"I don't want to go back to the Humberston trial."

"Well, I do. Attaway's speaking out. I ain't heard him say much about Quintus's murder yet, not even to me." She took a bite of grapefruit and made a dreadful face.

"It isn't that bad."

"Yep, it is. And Dog-dog was sick right behind the washer there, just before you came in. You want to wash it up afore we get going?"

"I'm assuming that's a rhetorical question," I said. I put Dog-dog out on the porch with a bowl of dry dog food and cleaned up the mess. I was still down on my knees, half behind the washing machine, scrubbing at the cracks in the green linoleum when I heard a truck pull up to the house. The motor cut off; the door slammed; heavy feet plodded down the little cement walk, accompanied by the tapping of a stick. The screen door opened and crashed closed. Great-uncle Attaway's voice said without preamble, "What's that Winn boy doing in the Tenant House?"

"Good mornin' to you," Granny Cora said. "Amanda's rescuing his soul. Aren't you, Amanda?"

"No," I said from behind the washing machine. "Thomas's helping him get sober."

"He don't have no business there," Attaway growled. The vibrations in his voice were belly deep.

I leaned back on my heels to see his face. He was scarlet, standing in the middle of the floor with his knobby hands white over the head of the cane. He was dressed for the courtroom in a white shirt and navy bow tie, gray trousers belted tightly around his massive waist.

"What's your liver in a knot for?" Granny said. "Sit down and have some breakfast. If Reverend Clement wants a trifling no-good Winn in his house, that's his business, ain't it?"

"I don't want him in there, Cora. You see he gets out."

Granny's old shoulders stiffened, very slightly. "That's my house, Attaway. You keep your eyes on your own land."

Great-uncle Attaway thrust his head forward like an old bear weaving towards the attack. His light blue eyes glittered and his breath rasped in his thick throat. "Get—that—man—out."

He turned around and stamped out. The door banged behind him. Dog-dog yelped on the steps outside. The truck motor roared up again. Granny sat perfectly still, watching the pickup travel down the long dirt road. When Great-uncle Attaway had vanished onto the hardtop road, she stirred.

"Go see where Dog-dog is," she said.

I stripped off the gloves and went outside. Dog-dog was hiding underneath the front steps. A muddy boot print marked the fur on his side, and he scrambled away from me with alacrity.

"He's all right," I said, coming back in. "Granny, I'd be glad to have Eddie move out."

"No!"

"But if Uncle Attaway doesn't want—"

"That's my house. Nat left it to me. Attaway thinks somebody died and made him God. But he can't tell me what to do here on my own land. I ain't going to talk about it no more, Amanda, so never you mind. Get m' billfold and see if I've got enough money for lunch."

"I'll pack you lunch. A nice low-salt sandwich with tomato on it. I bought you some tomatoes at the grocery because I know you like them and yours are all gone."

"I seen 'em. Somebody took those poor little things away from their mothers too soon. I'll get me another sandwich at Winn's, thank you."

We drove up to the courthouse, parked under the bare oak tree, and walked across the little lawn to the brick courthouse steps. Granny gripped my arm tight, her feet uncertain on the slippery carpet of leaves. She kept hold when we gained the solid porch and went through the doors into the little court-room. I helped her into one of the long wooden seats at the back. Judge Ryland Banks was just seating himself at the bench. Granny's hand stayed on my arm, and when Attaway appeared at the front of the room, the bony tips of her fingers clutched painfully at me.

"So help me God," Attaway said, and sat down. His face was still pink with lingering anger.

"Mr. Fowlerand," the prosecutor said, "my sympathies on the death of your son."

"Humph," Attaway growled. His eyes were narrow under thick white brows.

I craned my neck; from the back, I could only see the back of Matt Humberston's head. He'd been shaved again and washed and dressed in his nice blue suit. Matthew was sitting on the front bench directly behind his son.

The prosecutor, thrown off balance, turned back to his papers. "Mr. Fowlerand, did you see your son the night before he died?"

"Yep."

"And did he tell you that he was going down to the Humberston farm?"

"Objection," said Matt's lawyer. "Leading question."

Judge Banks said crossly, "Gracious sakes, Mr. Hall, I know you're anxious to justify your fees, but what possible difference does it make? Mr. Adkins, kindly make Mr. Hall happy and refrain from leading questions. Let's get on with it."

Jeremiah Adkins rubbed his nose. Attaway scowled down at him from the witness box; no black lawyer, even the com-monwealth's attorney, was going to get much cooperation from my great-uncle. Mr. Adkins amended his question to, "What did your son say to you when you saw him on Thursday?"

"Saw him at lunch. He told me he was goin' rabbit hunt-ing down on the Humberston place, Friday just before sun-down. I told him to be careful."

"And why was that, Mr. Fowlerand?"

"'Cause them Humberstons hated my boy—"

"Objection!"

"Overruled," said Judge Banks.

"—and I didn't know any good reason why Matthew should ask him to come hunt rabbits all of a sudden like."

"And did you speak to him after that?"

"Nope. He went out an' shot a couple of groundhogs for me, an' then got in his truck and drove off without comin' back. Never saw him again."

"Thank you, Mr. Fowlerand." Jeremiah Adkins's voice was discontented. I guessed that Attaway's matter-of-fact tones had disappointed him; he had not exactly presented himself to the jury as a bereaved and grief-stricken father. The jury looked over at the judge. Their middle-aged faces were studiously blank.

"Cross-examine?" Judge Banks inquired.

"Yes," Matt's lawyer said, popping to his feet. "Mr. Fowler-and, you say you never saw your son again?"

"That's what I said."

"So what would you say if a witness saw you speaking to your son in the lot in front of—" the lawyer glanced down at a paper in front of him—"in front of Little Croft Church, at nine-thirty Friday night?"

"Huh." Attaway lowered his head, bull-like. "Ain't nobody saw me, 'cause I didn't talk to him."

"Objection!" Jeremiah Adkins announced.

"Mr. Hall," Judge Banks said, fumbling for an antacid tablet, "I assume you have this witness somewhere and will produce him or her at the proper time?"

"Yes, Your Honor."

"Then we'll just let that stand, Mr. Adkins."

"I have no further questions at this time," Matt's lawyer said.

"I expect you'll want this witness back later?" Judge Banks inquired wearily.

"Yes, Your Honor."

"Very well. Let's take a break." Judge Banks stood with a grimace.

Attaway hoisted himself up and balanced on the head of his cane, scowling over at the Richmond lawyer. I felt Granny pulling on my arm.

"Let's go," she whispered.

"But we've only been here an hour."

"Let's go, Amanda. I'm done. I don't want to hear no more."

Attaway was hobbling from the witness box. It suddenly occurred to me that she didn't want her brother to see her, so I helped her out of the pew and out the door under cover of the milling spectators. We walked back across the slick brown leaves to the car. I drove us back out to Route 5. Granny sat beside me, her hands knotted quietly in her lap. Her old lips were moving. As we turned into Poverty Ridge Road, I caught part of a sentence.

"...alone with Peggy before..."

She looked shaken, drawn down with worry, and fragile. When I had gotten her back into the house, I said, "Would you like to go to bed?"

"Yep," Granny said.

"I can bring you your lunch on a tray."

"Okay."

She hadn't moved from her chair. "Do you want some help?" I asked.

"Yes," Granny said, whispering.

I crouched down beside her and said, "Granny, what is it?"

"I cain't say."

"Yes, you can. Granny, if you know anything, you can tell me and then we can decide what to do."

"No. Amanda, you told me Thomas was like a doctor, right? That if I tell him somethin', he don't ever have to say what it was?"

"That's right. Do you want him to come over?"

Granny sat, looking down at her blotched hands. "Get me my nightgown an' get me in bed. I want to eat my sandwich and have me a nap before my story comes on."

"Do you want Thomas to—"

"Well, if I do, I can pick up the phone and call him, can't I? Go get me my nightgown. An' don't you put no green tomato on my sandwich neither."

I half expected her to call that evening, but the phone stayed silent. I woke up Saturday morning to bright fall sunshine and the smell of coffee, and no obligation to run off to Little Croft Courthouse. I felt pleasantly languorous; I turned over and hugged the pillow and half dozed, waiting for Thomas to bring the coffee and bagels. I could hear him moving, distantly, in the kitchen below. The smell of toast drifted up. I woke up by degrees. When I was wide awake and hungry and slightly cranky, I realized that Thomas wasn't bringing me breakfast in bed. I could hear his voice down in the kitchen, talking to Eddie.

I got up, pulled on my clothes, decided I didn't want to appear in front of Eddie ungroomed, and trailed grumpily down to the shower. I remembered halfway down the hall that I couldn't exactly skip from the shower back to my bedroom in a towel as I usually did. I went back to our room and collected a stack of clothes so that I could dress in the bathroom. Our bathroom was small, and Eddie had left shaving stuff all over the shelf above the bathtub. I piled my clothes precariously on the edge of the sink, showered, and dressed while still damp.

I stumbled down to the kitchen, irritated and headachy. Thomas gave me a companionable smile and a cup of coffee. I sat down at the table to drink it, looking out at the morning sun on the corn stubble and not paying much attention to Eddie.

"We were just talking about grace," Thomas said, drawing me into the conversation.

"Oh?" I said politely.

"Eddie was saying he sat up last night and craved a drink so badly he'd almost have killed for it. He was asking me why he wants to get his life together and craves something destructive at the same time."

I sighed and pulled my eyes away from the brown and green of the field. This was Saturday. I wanted to drink coffee and be quiet. Thomas looked at me expectantly. I resigned myself to talking about sin first thing in the morning. There was no more coffee; my cup had drained the pot.

And so we talked about sin. I thought that Eddie would never stop rephrasing the same question in different words.

Long, long afterwards, he pushed his chair back and got up.

"Well," he said, "I guess I'm starting to understand. I sure am grateful to you folks for taking me in."

"That's why we're here," Thomas said.

"Anything I can do for you, you just tell me. I'm right handy around the house. Something breaks, I'll fix it for you an' you won't have to bother Mr. Fowlerand."

"Thanks, Eddie."

"You know, my friends were down drinkin' at Joe's, down the road, the other night. They came by and asked me to go with 'em. I knew I was comin' down here, and I didn't dare go get drunk and then face you the next mornin'."

"That's the way pastoring is supposed to work."

"Yeah. Thought they were off to have a good time," Eddie said, a hint of scorn creeping into his voice. "They didn't have a clue that they were ruinin' their lives. Guess I'll go get ready for my day."

"When you're done, come back down and we'll do our morning's study," Thomas called after him.

I said in a low voice, "Are we still walking down to the dam for a picnic?"

Thomas hesitated. "I don't want him to feel left out. I was about to bring you coffee when he came down this morning, but I was afraid he'd feel snubbed if we stayed in our bedroom."

"I know," I said. "But we still have to have our time alone."

"Just give him a few days to settle in first, that's all. We could do our picnic next Saturday."

I swirled cold coffee around in the bottom of my cup. "Okay. But Thomas, I was thinking…I don't want you to go off to the church and leave me here alone with Eddie."

"Why's that?"

"I just don't think it looks right."

Eddie's feet creaked overhead. Thomas leaned forward and pitched his voice low. "He's got a pistol in his stuff," he said.

"Yeah. I saw it on the top of his box."

"Should we worry about that?"

I blinked at him. Eddie set off lots of caution bells in my head, but the pistol had passed my eyes without alarm. Everyone in Little Croft had guns while I was growing up. Even my father, a physician who painted watercolors on weekends and never hunted, had owned a closetful of shotguns and rifles and handguns.

"It's just a target pistol," I said.

"It is?"

"I expect he shoots tin cans and the occasional rabbit."

Thomas gave me the skeptical stare of a suburbanite.

"Don't worry about the gun," I said. "No one with murderous intent is going to bother with a .22. I'm not scared of Eddie, I just don't want people gossiping about the preacher's wife. And if you want to worry over something, you might suggest to him that it's a bit early to start getting self-righteous. Is there any more coffee?"

Thomas interpreted this, rightly, as a wish that he would get up and make more. He pushed his chair back, opened the cabinet over the sink, and pulled out the box of coffee filters; and then he muttered something and ground into the floor with his heel.

"What is it?"

"Don't know. Some disgusting bug." He bent over and examined the corpse. I got up and peered over his shoulder.

"It's a cockroach!"

"I didn't know we had cockroaches."

"We didn't. Giddy had the place fumigated before we moved in. Don't tell me that Eddie—"

"He brought some groceries from his house with him. Cake mixes and flour and stuff like that. I told him to put the food in our cabinets."

"They'll be in all his stuff!"

"Well, don't panic," Thomas said. "It's just one."

"One cockroach seen means twenty under the floorboards."

"Is that what your grandmother says?"

"Yes, and she's right. You take Eddie over to the church for your morning study and I'll go up and do his room with bug spray."

"If you coat his room with that stuff that smells like a melting chemical factory, he's going to notice it when he gets back."

"I don't care if he does. I'm not having cockroaches in my house."

I never did get the second cup of coffee. Thomas took Eddie over to the church, and I went up and ripped his room apart, tipped all his stuff out of the cardboard boxes and sprayed the bottoms with Raid, which was all I had in the house. I remembered seeing an old package of cockroach motels at the back of Granny's cleaning cupboard, so I walked up the dirt road to the Old House and dug around for them, enduring her running commentary on Winns. Granny had recovered some form since Friday's flight to her bed.

"Just seems fitting somehow," she said while I shook motels out of the plastic wrapper. "Cockroaches always skitterin' in the dark and puttin' their dirty little feet where they ought not to be. Seems right that Eddie Winn should be carryin' them around with him."

"You think he's likely to put his feet where they're not supposed to be?" I said.

"I ain't worried about his feet."

I bit my tongue. "Want me to stay and fix lunch for you? There's some lovely cabbage in the bottom of the refrigerator. I could fix you some stir fry with that low-salt sauce. And lots of carrots."

"I don't have to eat rabbit food on weekends," Granny said, sniffing.

"Then I'll go catch my cockroaches."

"An' don't forget to feed the big one." Granny was still chuckling to herself when I left.

I trudged back to the Tenant House, installed roach motels in all the closets, and went back into Eddie's room to run all his clothes through a hot bleach wash. His drawers smelled powerfully of smoke. When I shook out the sweatshirt at the bottom of the last drawer, something heavy fell from inside it and clunked into the back of the drawer. A bottle, I thought, and got down on my knees to pull it out. But my hand touched metal. Eddie had rolled a .357 magnum and a box of hollow points into his sweatshirt.

I sat back on my heels and stared. After a moment I rolled the gun and ammunition back up and stuffed the sweatshirt back into the drawer. I refolded the other clothes and replaced them as well. I wasn't frightened of Eddie. His tongue was malicious, but I felt no violence in him. But I wondered what terror had caused him to hide that powerful handgun in his clothes, out here at the end of quiet Poverty Ridge Road.

Chapter Twenty-four

Eddie made a very good show at Sunday's service. He was clean and neatly dressed, and the tremor in his hands had lessened. He settled himself in the end of the Whitworth pew; Amelia Whitworth, small and straight-backed, shot continual wary sideways glances at him, as though she expected him to bolt to his feet and shout "Hallelujah!" without warning. But she was occupied with keeping John awake, and Eddie behaved himself.

Ida had a chest cold and had stayed in bed, so I took her place at the back door and handed out bulletins. As the service began, I slipped into a back pew. I could see that the crowd had shrunk again. I couldn't quite identify the missing faces, but there was no doubt about it. The pews were emptier than they had been the Sunday before.

On the other hand, a new face had appeared, a thin, tired, straw-haired woman with two small children. She was listening with rapt attention, her mouth hanging open slightly. I had shaken her hand at the door, and she'd told me in a weary whisper that her name was Tammy Watts, and she lived down near Winnville. The children, clinging to her legs, had refused to go off to children's church. They sat very still, holding hands; a little boy and a younger girl, perhaps three and two.

Thomas had reached the eighth chapter of Luke. He was telling the story of the demon-possessed Gadarene, the naked man who lived among the tombs, tormented by inner voices and gashing himself with stones.

"And then Christ came," Thomas went on, "and in his presence, evil screamed out in fear—"

A shriek split the somnolent air. I dropped the bulletins I still held in my hand. Heads swiveled. The thin straw-colored woman had bolted to her feet. Her head was flung back. The two preschoolers huddled in the pew, staring at their mother in terror. I couldn't make out any words, but the long high sound was full of syllables. Thomas stopped with his mouth half open over his next phrase.

I left the bulletins on the mat and ran to scoop up the toddlers. They were light, all bones and big eyes. Their little bodies smelled of unwashed clothes, and they clung to me like a pair of frightened tree frogs. Tammy Watts went on screaming. I could distinguish a word or two now, bobbing up in the stream of noise. She was shouting out names of Satan: Lucifer, Beelzebub, Lord of the Flies.

Thomas had left the pulpit and was walking purposefully towards us, but I could see from his face that he didn't have a clue as to what he'd do once he arrived. The little old organist chose that moment to launch into a hymn, as though the music would smooth things over. I was having difficulty thinking with the double din of screams punctuated by organ chords beating against my ears. I'd never seen anyone demon possessed, but that was the only category I could think of at the moment.

Thomas arrived and tried to take her hands. I attempted to get my mouth somewhat near his ear and bellowed, "Her name's Tammy Watts."

"Mrs. Watts?" Thomas said, grabbing for a waving wrist. "Mrs. Watts, can you sit down?"

She wasn't going to sit down. Her legs were stiff as posts.

He hissed at me sideways, "You try!"

"Tammy!" I said. She went on screaming. I heard a little voice, down near my shoulder, speaking words I couldn't understand. I stooped my head down. The three-year-old was speaking.

"Mommy," he said.

"What is it, sweetie?" I asked.

"Mommy doesn't like Satan."

I looked over at Thomas. He grimaced slightly.

"Okay," he said. And then, mostly under his breath, "Satan, I command you to leave her in the name of the Lord Jesus Christ!"

Tammy Watts went on yelling.

"She didn't hear you," I said.

"Yeah, well, I wasn't talking to her."

"Better try again."

Thomas looked around. All of Little Croft Church was hanging breathlessly on his next words in any case. He said, in a loud and sheepish voice, "Satan, I command you to be silent in the name of the Lord Jesus Christ!"

The scream cut off in midstream, like a kettle suddenly taken off the burner. Tammy Watts collapsed sideways into the pew and started to sob gently. Thomas crouched down in front of her.

"Mrs. Watts," he said, "are you all right?"

"Yes…yes," Tammy Watts wept.

"Can you sit up?"

She struggled up to a sitting position and wiped at her eyes.

"Sorry," she gasped. "I'm sorry. I can't—whenever I hear it—that name—I can't help myself."

By now practically everyone was either standing in the aisle or climbing up on pews to get a good look. Thomas straightened up and patted her on the shoulder and leaned over to me. He murmured, "If she's going to start yelling like that every time I say the name of Satan, you'd better take her back to my office for the rest of the sermon. There's a hot plate and a teapot in there, and a package of cookies."

"Right," I said.

Amelia Whitworth's sharp curious face bobbed into view beyond Thomas's shoulder. I saw her, and Amy's two little boys came to my mind with a curious surge of relief.

"Mrs. Whitworth," I said, "will you take the children back to the Sunday school rooms and give them a snack and some juice?"

The two little faces showed a sudden lighting of interest. Amelia Whitworth held her arms out. "Of course," she said. "We got chocolate cookies and grape juice in the back."

They transferred their little bodies to her at once. She walked away towards the back door with them, and I helped Tammy Watts to her feet.

"Come on," I said gently. "I'll help you get your face washed and we'll get you a drink."

She came along with me, sniffling and stumbling. The organist was still playing gamely, but I could see her craning her neck for a view of the action. Thomas went back towards the pulpit. The Little Croft congregants hurried for their seats.

I took Tammy Watts back to the little pastor's office and shut the door behind us, decreasing the sound of Thomas's voice to a vague and distant echo. I made her a strong cup of tea and made her eat three cookies. She swallowed the tea and then put her arms on the desk and slumped her head into them and sat perfectly still.

I sat and watched her quietly. When a faint tap came on the door, she didn't move. I got up and went to the door. Amelia Whitworth peered at me through the crack. I slipped out and closed the door gently behind me.

"Are the children all right?"

"Eating like they'd skipped a week's meals, poor things. What brought all that on? Reverend Clement's little sermon?"

"Maybe she's demon possessed," I said, doubtfully.

"Huh! Demon possessed! That's little Tammy Watts from down in Winnville. She ain't got demons; she's got bills and a no-good husband and female troubles. That's plenty enough. Satan won't bother with her as long as Tom Watts is around. A paycheck and a bottle of aspirin and a good night's sleep would do that girl more good than a hundred deliverance services."

"Could we get her to a doctor?"

"You can deliver her and doctor her tomorrow. Today, she needs a good square meal and a cup of coffee and a shoulder to cry on."

"We can take her home with us," I said, mentally going over the contents of the refrigerator.

"You don't worry about it. I'll get John to come back with me when Reverend Clement's done talking about the devil, and we'll take her home with us for lunch. I got a chicken in the oven and lots of toys that Amy's boys play with when they come. You've got enough to do with that Winn person to take care of. He don't have no business around a poor starved girl like Tammy Watts. She'd love a stump if it spoke to her nice. Talk about the devil bein' an opportunist! You ain't seen nothing till you've seen a Winn in action."

"Mrs. Whitworth," I said, "did you know you're a minister, just as much as Thomas?"

Amelia Whitworth's face grew pink around the ears. "No such thing. If I can't feed my own girl, I'll feed someone else's. You keep her drinking tea, and we'll be back and get her whenever the reverend's done preaching."

She started down the hall. Just before she reached the door, she turned around and said with her customary tartness, "One of these days soon, can we have a Sunday morning without any screamin' or sobbin' or collapsin' in tears in it?"

"I'll be sure to ask Thomas," I said.

We went home stupefied, holding our tongues, aware of Eddie's pricked ears. He wanted to talk about demon possession all during lunch. In his voice I heard the same smugness that had jarred me on the day he moved in: the suggestion that he was now one of the enlightened, looking down on the wretched mistaken masses.

"See," he said, slathering ketchup onto his hamburger, "the way I figure it, if you start gettin' into that satanist stuff, you're just asking for it. Me, even at my worst, I never looked at black magic. Wouldn't do it."

He rattled on. Thomas ate at the other side of the table, preoccupied. I could tell from the occasional twitch of his eyebrows upwards that he was holding an involved conversation with Tammy Watts inside his mind. I wondered if he was having any success. Exorcisms had not been included in his reasonable Presbyterian education.

Eddie finally finished eating. He wiped his mouth, stretched, yawned, and looked from me to Thomas. We gazed back at him silently. He'd held forth all through lunch without much response from either of us.

Eddie snagged two cookies from the box on the counter. "Guess I'll go have me a nap," he said, finally giving up.

"Good idea," Thomas said.

Eddie shuffled regretfully off. We waited until the upstairs door closed behind him.

Thomas said immediately, "Do you think she was demon possessed?"

"I don't think it's likely, but I don't want to discount it either."

"Yes, that's how I feel. I'm supposed to go visit her tomorrow."

"Take someone with you," I said.

"Can you come?"

"I will if Granny will let me off."

"I'd like to get it done first thing in the morning."

"Amelia Whitworth would go with you," I suggested.

"The deacon's wife?"

"She might surprise you."

"She would surprise me."

"What are you going to do once you get there?"

"Pray for her. Find out what's going on with her family. Set up a doctor's appointment for her, maybe."

"What did she say to you on the way out?" I had shepherded Tammy Watts back into the sanctuary after the sermon, but she had broken from me and hurried away, scooping up her children and pausing briefly to speak to Thomas at the door.

Thomas said slowly, "She said, 'I want you to help me, Preacher. Satan's after my soul, and he's gonna get it. But if anybody can help me, you can. Matthew Humberston told me so.'"

We sat silently, looking at each other. The telephone rang. I got up and answered it. A woman's voice on the other end said, "Amanda?"

"Yes?"

"This is Jenny. Jenny Morehead, from church." Her voice was cheerful and refreshingly normal. She said, "We wondered if you wanted to come over for ice cream tonight, after the evening service. And games. Joe's not real quick at games, but he likes hearts and Uno, so we could play that."

"Oh, Jenny, we'd love to. It's been such a weird day. Wait and let me check it with Thomas." I covered the phone and said, "Joe and Jenny want us to come over for ice cream and games after the six o'clock service."

"Great. Let's go. Wait a minute, what about Eddie?"

"We don't have to take him everywhere with us, Thomas!"

Thomas made frantic shushing noises. I lowered my voice. "I'm glad you're helping Eddie," I said. "I'm thrilled that he's making progress. But he can't attach himself to every part of our lives!"

"Sometimes that's what ministry is. I've left Eddie alone a lot this week, and weekend nights are when he's most tempted to drink."

"Thomas, we're both under a lot of pressure. We have to have time alone."

"This isn't time alone. It's social time. Listen, Amanda, I don't know what I'm doing in any part of this job except for Eddie. I don't have the faintest idea what to do tomorrow when I go see this woman who thinks Satan's trying to snatch her soul. What I said today, I heard on TV once, and I have no idea why it worked. When I preach they all stare at me like I'm speaking Greek. They come out past me and say, 'Wonderful sermon, Reverend.' They'd say that if I preached on the latest Tom Clancy novel. I've got no one to tell me what to do or how to do it. We don't have any money. The church is shrinking. I've just put a deacon's son in jail for life because I was mad at his father. All I know is that Eddie is starting a new life, and I don't want to jeopardize that."

"Thomas, you can't make Eddie into the family you haven't found here. He isn't your brother."

"He's my brother in Christ." Thomas didn't meet my eyes. I turned my back on him. I stared at the telephone until I thought I could control my voice.

"Jenny?" I said. "I hate to ask you this, but we've got this guy staying with us—Eddie Winn—yes, that's him. Would you mind if he came too? Thomas doesn't want him to feel left out. Are you sure? Thanks."

I hung up. She had sounded surprised, but not unwilling, and she'd known at once who I meant. I could hear Eddie's feet creaking on the floor above.

"I'll take Chelsea for a walk," I said. I went out the door without looking back at him, and walked Chelsea all the way down to the dam. I sat and looked out over the water while she covered herself with strong-smelling mud. The cold November wind blew in my face. Across the river, a child was flying a red-and-white kite. I watched the water shine underneath the low fall sun and fell into a comfort of dreaming; our visits to Little Croft when we were engaged and first married, long drives down Route 5 under the tunnel of leaves and branches, fall afternoons with picnics, the patterned and satisfying dance of two like minds.

The kite dipped towards the water. A tiny figure came out onto the dock and called the child; he turned and dashed in, trailing the kite behind him. I felt suddenly desolate. I wanted to go home.

I called Chelsea and we trudged back towards the Tenant House. The kitchen was empty; Thomas had gone out. I sat on the sofa with a book and waited for evening.

Chapter Twenty-five

We drove over to Joe and Jenny's with a bag of M&Ms and a bottle of caramel sauce and Eddie, folded into the backseat of the little car. We played Uno and Dutch Blitz and Spoons, loudly and energetically, and talked about everything under the sun, and ate ice cream. Jenny was quick; Joe was well-intentioned but slow, and eventually I took pity on him and teamed with him against Thomas and Jenny and Eddie.

Eddie repeated his thanks again and again; his face was full of enjoyment, and his black eyes practically shone. We went home late, full of conversation and sugar.

Thomas hadn't looked directly at me all evening. He disappeared into the bathroom and closed the door. I went down to the kitchen and cleaned up all the leftover lunch dishes. I scrubbed the counters and the sink and opened the cabinet to put the chips away. As I did, a cockroach fell out and scurried away into the darkness.

I got up early Monday, while Thomas slept, and lit a fire so that I could do my Hebrew in front of the flames. Here they were, the ragged Israelites, finally free. Coming home at last, and full of misery, because the salvation they had waited for all their lives had turned dark and sour. Looking for the presence of God in the land and finding nothing but soil and rocks.

By the time I got over to Granny's, she was already dressed

and enthroned on her TV-watching chair. I banged around her kitchen, fixing breakfast and dropping everything that came to hand. When I put the tray on the table she hauled herself up and hobbled over and settled herself with a grunt.

"You gonna eat?"

"No, Granny. I'm not hungry."

"Well, sit down anyway. You'll break something if you keep bouncing round my kitchen like a cat in fits."

I sat down obediently and folded my hands. "Want me to say the blessing?"

"You fry this egg in lard?"

"No. Fat-free cooking spray."

"Well then. No blessing." She forked up a piece of egg.

"Granny," I said, "would it be all right if I went to visit someone with Thomas this morning?"

"Can't he do his own work?"

"Yes, of course, but—"

"I need you to drive me back to the trial this mornin'. An' don't tell me you don't want to. The other side's going to talk today."

"The defense?"

"Yep. I want to hear the defense."

I got up. She said at once, "Where you off to?"

"The bathroom."

"Ain't you going to fuss about the trial?"

"You just told me not to." I headed towards the bathroom, and then backtracked and swiped the saltshaker off the table. "And you can't cover that egg with salt while I'm gone."

"Tastes like water," Granny complained. "Least you could do is make it salt water."

When we arrived at the courthouse, the parking lot under the oak tree was almost full. I inched the old car into a narrow spot at one edge while Granny issued a stream of warnings. Her door would only open halfway, and while she squeezed and grumbled her way out I stood patiently at the back bumper and waited. I glanced idly around the lot and spotted a familiar truck, half hidden behind the building. A green pickup with a long diagonal scratch across the tailgate; it looked like Eddie's but he was supposed to be job hunting this morning.

The defense lawyer was already on his feet when I maneuvered Granny through the courtroom door and into a back bench. She wriggled around until she was mostly hidden behind a large man in a checked shirt. Five rows ahead of us, Attaway's sweep of white hair rose above the spectators. He was hunched forward, his head thrust towards the witness box.

I listened carefully, trying to piece the defense's argument together. Mr. Hall, hampered by five Fowlerand eyewitnesses to the slaying and Matt's own drunken confession, could hardly plead his client's uninvolvement, but he was working hard to make Quintus a threatening figure: devious and eaten up with envy and hatred, luring young Matt Humberston down a long deserted road peppered with other Fowlerands and trapping him at its end. Quintus's gun had been found beside the porch, where he had flung it in a dying convulsion. It was loaded, with the safety off. An emergency room physician from MCV agreed that Matt's injuries were the result of a brutal beating at the hands of the Fowlerands.

Andrew Hall was worth his fees. The tale was vivid and believable, and I could almost see Matt, frightened and threatened by an approaching ring of Fowlerand cousins, jerking his gun up and firing wildly at his tormenter. When he stopped and drew a breath, though, I couldn't reconcile that taunting figure with Quintus, gentle and defeated. Quintus had always spoken wistfully of the mother he could not remember, and he had early rejected the Fowlerand hatred of all things Humberston.

The lawyer dismissed the ER doctor, gathered the threats of his story up into one final knot, and turned to the judge.

"The defense calls Eddie Winn," he said.

Ahead of us, Attaway rose half to his feet. Every head in the courtroom turned towards him. He settled back into his seat, his thick neck flushed red and his hands tight on the pew in front of him.

Eddie shambled from a side door up into the witness stand. His healthy color had drained away, and his body held some of the shrinking furtiveness that had disappeared over the last weeks. His voice was low and uncertain. I watched, fascinated, as Great-uncle Attaway's hands squeezed the wood in front of him until his knuckles turned white.

"Would you state your name for the record, please?" the defense lawyer began.

"Eddie Winn."

"And where do you live, Mr. Winn?"

Eddie said hoarsely, "Right now I live with m' pastor. Thomas Clement."

"But at the time of Quintus Fowlerand's death, you lived elsewhere?"

"That's right. Lived in a trailer round the Loop."

"This is the road directly across from Fowlerand Landing Road?"

"That's right."

"Can you describe to the court what you saw on the evening of Friday, October 14?"

"Sure," Eddie said. "I was drivin' back from Williamsburg, about eight in the evening. Sun was down, and the lights in front of the church were on."

"You're referring to Little Croft Church, which sits near the entrance to Fowlerand Landing Road?"

"That's right. I could see a pickup sitting at the corner of the church, so I slowed down. Thought someone might be breakin' in. Then I saw it was Attaway Fowlerand's truck, and parked right beside it was Quintus Fowlerand's truck. The two of them were arguin'. They didn't see me, so I slowed up and just kind of edged off the road into the grass. My windows were open, see. It was a nice night."

"And what did you hear?"

"I heard Attaway yellin' at his son." Eddie's voice was gaining strength. "Told him he'd failed at everything he ever did. Said he couldn't father a child on his wife, couldn't even make his wife happy, that Peggy killed herself 'cause Quintus couldn't satisfy her. Said even a Humberston could farm better than Quintus. Said Matt deserved the land he'd deeded to Quintus. Said he was a nameless bastard and the son of a whore."

My eyes were stinging. In my mind I saw Quintus, shaking under his father's onslaught, going to his death with those harsh names ringing in his soul.

"And then what happened, Mr. Winn?"

"He left."

"Who did?"

"Quintus Fowlerand. Kind of staggered over to his truck, half sprawled on the seat, and threw it into gear. Drove off, and ol' Attaway stood there with his hands on the top of his cane lookin' satisfied—"

"Objection!" Jeremiah Adkins bellowed.

At the same time, Attaway rose to his feet like a puppet pulled on a string and yelled, "You lyin' son of—"

"Mr. Fowlerand!" Judge Banks shouted.

"He's lyin', the sneaking drunk snake of a Winn! All he ever did in this county was steal and prop up the likker sales down at Winn's Grocery, and he sits there and says—"

"Mr. Fowlerand, you may control yourself or leave the courtroom! Which is it?"

"Hah!" Attaway said. He shuffled his feet and sat back down and blew his nose.

Eddie hunched his shoulders defensively, looking away.

"Now," Judge Banks said, "where were we?"

"I was objecting, Your Honor."

"Right. Sustained. Strike that. Mr. Winn, tell us what you saw, not what you think you know."

Eddie opened and closed his mouth several times before sorting this out. "Well then," he said at last, "Attaway stood there for a while an' finally got in his truck and drove away."

"Thank you, Mr. Winn."

The defense lawyer yielded the floor to his colleague. The prosecutor paced back and forth for a moment, his face visibly perplexed. I shook my head slightly. Like Jeremiah Adkins, I didn't see the point. Attaway had given Quintus a tongue-lashing the day of his death and had lied about doing so, but that was understandable enough; even Attaway might blanch at inform-ing a courtroom full of Little Crofters what his last words to his son had been.

"Mr. Winn," Jeremiah Adkins began, finally, "what had

you been doing in Williamsburg?"

"Objection!" Matt's lawyer said, without much energy.

"Goes to witness's credibility, Your Honor."

"Oh, all right," Judge Banks said.

"Mr. Winn?"

"Been to visit my niece," Eddie said.

"And why exactly did you stop to listen to the Fowlerands arguing? Didn't you see that they were having a private discussion?"

"They was yelling," Eddie said. "I had m' windows open. Sounded like trouble to me. I thought they might start fighting, and maybe if someone else was there it would keep the peace."

Granny mumbled, "Like a Winn ever cared 'bout peace in his life."

Jeremiah Adkins said, "Yet you stayed out of sight?"

"Well, didn't want to butt in 'less they needed me."

"Huh," the prosecutor said.

"Objection!"

"To *huh?*" Judge Banks inquired. "Forget it. Go on, Mr. Adkins, but give us some relevance, would you?"

"So you drove up to Little Croft Church, Mr. Winn, yet they didn't hear you?"

"They was shouting."

"Loud enough to drown out the sound of your pickup truck?"

"Well," Eddie said, "I'd parked on the side of the road, like."

"And why was that?"

Eddie cleared his throat and mumbled something.

"Why, Mr. Winn?"

"Had to take a—"

"Please," Matt's lawyer said, "how long do we need to sit through this?"

Jeremiah Adkins said, "So you were actually in the bushes around the Little Croft parking lot, relieving yourself?"

"Well—"

"Where did you say you were living, Mr. Winn?"

"With my pastor. Thomas Clement an' his wife."

"This is the same Thomas Clement who testified at the beginning of this trial?"

"That's right."

"And why did you move in with Reverend Clement?"

"I was broke," Eddie muttered.

"Was that the only reason?"

"An' I needed to…needed to stop drinking."

"You needed to dry out, Mr. Winn?"

"That's what I said."

"You're an alcoholic, Mr. Winn?"

"Yeah, I reckon."

"Ever had hallucinations?"

"Had what?"

"Seen things that weren't there? Heard voices?"

"Well, maybe every once in a long while. When I'd been drinking. But not that night. I was driving, see? Not drinking."

"You don't drink and drive?"

"Nope," Eddie said promptly.

"Ever gotten a ticket?"

Eddie cleared his throat and said something indistinct.

"I beg your pardon? Were you not cited for drunken driving on—" Jeremiah Adkins crossed back to his table and checked his notes—"January 5 of this year, again on March 10, again on July 11—"

"I forgot those," Eddie said, thickly.

"Remember them now?"

"Yeah, I reckon so."

"So you admit that you sometimes have hallucinations when you drink? And that you sometimes drink when you drive?"

Eddie shrank down into himself. "Yeah," he mumbled.

"You weren't drinking and driving that night, yet you couldn't wait ten more minutes to return home in order to use the restroom there?"

"Yeah."

"That's all." Jeremiah Adkins walked back to his table and sat down.

Eddie was turning green under Attaway's steady scornful gaze. He made a sudden retching noise, clapped his hand over his mouth, scrambled down from the witness stand, and ran through the side door. Judge Banks peered after him.

"I reckon the witness can step down," he said mildly. "Mr. Hall?"

"Yes, Your Honor. The defense calls Matthew Humberston Jr. to the stand."

Judge Banks scowled down at the defense lawyer. "Counsel will approach the bench."

The two lawyers went up to the front and held a vigorous whispered debate, while the spectators shifted and looked at each other.

Judge Banks leaned back. "Okay," he said. "Let's get on with it then. Mr. Humberston?"

The two lawyers returned to their seats. Matt walked to the stand and settled himself, facing the courtroom crowd. I was struck, suddenly, by how very young he looked. He had his father's strong arched nose and dark coloring, but the heavy eyebrows cut oddly across the undeveloped face, and the high cheekbones were obscured by childish roundness. He kept his eyes on Andrew Hall, waiting for his cue.

"Mr. Humberston," the defense lawyer began, "will you tell us in your own words what happened on the night of Friday, October 13, and the early morning of Saturday, October 14?"

"Okay," Matt said. His voice was shaking. He steadied it and said, "Friday night I went down huntin' rabbits on my dad's place. They were eatin' his late garden down to nothing."

"This is Humberston Farm, on the Loop Road?"

"Yeah, that's right. I was huntin' and Attaway Fowlerand drove up. I was right surprised, 'cause Attaway ain't spoke to us since my aunt died, a long time ago. He mistreated her some-thing awful, and now—"

Attaway lurched to his feet again, his neck scarlet and his hands outstretched.

"Mr. Fowlerand," Judge Banks snapped, "you are excused from this courtroom!"

Attaway said hoarsely, "Want to hear what he says about m' wife."

"Mr. Fowlerand, if you don't go outside and sit down, I will hold you in contempt of court. Deputy Adkins will take you outside."

Helen Adkins had walked quietly up the side aisle. She said in a low voice, "Come on, Mr. Fowlerand. I'll get you a drink and find you a quiet place to sit. Let's go outside."

Attaway's hands were shaking. He grasped his cane with both hands. The end of the stick rattled against the floor. He stumped towards the front side door. I felt Granny relax beside me as the door closed behind Helen's uniformed figure.

"Now then," Judge Banks said.

The prosecutor was standing. "Your Honor, I object to this whole line of testimony. It's hardly relevant what the defendant thought about Mr. Fowlerand's treatment of Mrs. Fowlerand back in 1970, and whatever the defendant says is gossip and hearsay. He wasn't even born until 1975."

"Your Honor," Andrew Hall countered, "my client is on trial for murder. His state of mind towards the entire Fowlerand family is relevant and vital to his defense."

"I'm going to allow this," Judge Banks said, "but let's make it quick, all right? And we'll break for lunch before cross-examination."

"Yes, Your Honor. What were you saying, Mr. Humberston?"

Matt's voice was shaking again. He said, "Old Attaway, he used to beat my aunt."

"How do you know that?"

"My father told me so. Told me Attaway beat his sister, and killed her spirit, and finally killed her. Told me never to trust a Fowlerand, that the Fowlerands would look for every chance to do me wrong, might even kill me if they thought they could get away with it. So I'm hunting rabbits," Matt said, recalling the train of his story, "and up comes Attaway and gets out of his truck, and leans on his cane, and watches me. I've got my rabbit gun, so I feel safe. I say, 'What do you want?' and he says, 'I came to tell you something. Came to tell you I ain't got a son. All that land in Quintus's name ought not to belong to him. He ain't my flesh and blood at all. I told him that. I told him I ought to leave it to my nieces and my nephews, not to him, and now he's ragin' around sayin' no Humberston'll take his land away from him. I thought you ought to know.'"

"Couldn't stand it no more," Granny murmured.

"What?" I whispered.

"Couldn't stand to think of Quintus gettin' that land. I knowed Attaway wouldn't be able to live with that will he made. Been eatin' at him ever since he signed it."

Matt's lawyer said, "And how did you feel when Mr. Fowlerand told you that?"

"I reckoned I better watch my back. Quintus, he came by later. Said he wanted to talk to me 'bout something."

"Did he seem angry?"

"Nope. Seemed stunned, like. Real quiet and—and sad. He waren't raging around at all. But I loaded my shotgun anyway. Thought he might be faking it. He wanted to go sit and talk, so we took a couple of six-packs and went and sat on the church steps. See, that wasn't on my land, nor on his. Reckon he felt safer on the church property."

"And did you talk to him?"

"Well, mostly he talked to me. Said he'd had some bad news, but never could bring himself to say what it was. Talked all around it for hours. Then he started weeping."

"What was the cause of the final quarrel between you, Mr. Humberston?"

"I don't remember," Matt said.

"Were you shouting obscenities at each other, as other witnesses suggest?"

"I don't know. I don't remember anything after Quintus started cryin'. Doctor says I got some kind of memory loss."

"What?" bellowed Jeremiah Adkins.

"Amnesia?" Mr. Hall said, paying no attention.

"Yeah, from bein' beat on the head."

"Mr. Hall," Judge Banks said, "I'm assuming you have a

medical expert to testify to this point?"

"Yes, Your Honor. Mr. Humberston has seen a psychiatrist and a neurosurgeon. I have a deposition—"

"Objection!" shouted Jeremiah Adkins. "That was never entered into evidence."

"We just received the final diagnosis yesterday. These things take time—"

"Your Honor, this is a transparent effort to hold back vital information!"

"Okay," Judge Banks said loudly, "that's enough. It's lunchtime. I'll see you both in my chambers in one hour. Testimony will resume at three o'clock."

I felt Granny's hand on my arm. I was relieved; I had no stomach for seeing Matt Humberston dissected by the prosecuting attorney. I helped her out of the bench and out of the door. She was quiet as I settled her into the car, but when I went around to the other side and got in she said, "Mandy… whose fault you reckon it is? Quintus's death?"

"Well," I said, starting the motor, "I haven't heard all the evidence, but if I had to lay blame now I think I'd divide it between Matthew and Attaway. They planted the seed of all that hatred, and this is the flower. Sounds to me as though Attaway decided he didn't want Quintus to have the land."

"That's what I said."

"Yes, so he filled Matt full of stories that Quintus was out to get him, and then he met Quintus at the church and—" I halted. I thought Attaway had probably told Quintus that he wasn't a Fowlerand at all; and Quintus had gone off to find his only other relation, his cousin Matt, in a muddled half-drunk maudlin state.

"He never did nothing," Granny said.

I glanced over at her as I drove. "Who?"

"Attaway never did nothing."

"Sounds to me like he's done plenty."

"You don't know what I mean. I mean, Attaway never did nothing. He got other folks to do what he wanted. He talked. He pushed 'em the way he wanted, and watched 'em do the dirty work. His mind. Their hands."

"Granny," I said, hopelessly, "what is it you want us to do?"

Granny shook her head silently. I stamped on the accelerator in frustration.

"Don't go driving like no bat out of hell."

"Huh," I said.

"Was both of you gone last night?"

"What? Oh…yes, all three of us. Till about ten."

"Where to?"

"Out to dinner." I turned off Route 5 onto Little Croft Road.

"Attaway was up at the Tenant House, before either of you was home. I saw him walkin' around in the yard. An' then he went in."

"While we weren't there?"

"I saw him out m' window."

"I didn't even know he had a key."

"Yep. Said he wanted to help Giddy keep the place up, in case you two had house troubles."

"Then why did he want to go in while we weren't there?"

"I dunno." Granny knotted her old hands in her lap and leaned her head back, closing her eyes.

Chapter Twenty-six

Eddie's pickup was missing from our yard. I climbed the back steps, sniffing at the warm tomato smell of something cooking. Thomas was sitting at the kitchen table with his Bible and a stack of counseling books and a yellow pad of paper.

"Hi," he said.

"Hi."

"I put a pizza in the oven for us."

"Thanks. I'm starving." I went to him, sat on his lap, and buried my face in his shoulder. He put his arms around me. I let the sense of him soak into me; the sharp distinctive scent of his skin, the hard bone and muscle of his shoulder underneath my cheek, his hand at the nape of my neck. The pizza popped and bubbled in the oven.

"I ought to take that out," Thomas said, not moving.

I said into his shoulder, "Did you go see Tammy Watts?"

"Yes. I took Amelia Whitworth with me, like you said. We went in and I prayed for her, that God would deliver her from Satan's power, and she started screaming again, like I'd flipped a switch." He stretched backwards. I sat up reluctantly. "I'd gone back and read Acts and copied down what Paul said to the slave girl with an evil spirit. So I said, 'In the name of Jesus Christ, I command you to come out of her!' She let out this tremendous yawn and sat up and looked at me and then flung herself on top of me and started weeping all over my shirt—"

"I hope you got out from under her quick."

"Amelia peeled her off and made her a cup of coffee. We stayed and talked to her for a good while after that. Amelia's going to go pick her up every week for the women's Bible study, and Amelia says to tell you to make an appointment for her with your gynecologist."

"Is that what she said?"

"No, she whispered in my ear, 'Tell Amanda that Tammy needs to see her special doctor.'"

"Do you think she was really demon possessed?"

"I don't know what to think," Thomas said. "I don't want to pretend there's no such thing as spiritual evil. But I do think it might be very easy to duck overwhelming problems by chalking them all up to possession."

"Did you ask her about Matthew Humberston recommending she come to Little Croft Church?" That incongruity had been niggling at my mind all day.

"No. The time didn't seem right. Hop up and I'll get the pizza."

I drew up my own chair while he cut the pizza and poured Coke into glasses. The kitchen windows were dusk-dark; we were alone in the warm circle of light.

"Where's Eddie?" I said.

"He called from Richmond and said he'd met Joe unexpectedly at a job site, and that Joe and Jenny invited him back for dinner tonight. He and Joe seemed to hit it off."

"So we have a quiet evening?"

"I lit a fire," Thomas said. He smiled at me across the table.

I thought, later: Eddie wasn't in Richmond today. He was in the Little Croft courtroom, testifying to Attaway's misdeeds.

But I didn't want to bring Eddie up again while we were alone, with the Tenant House quiet and welcoming again.

Granny Cora greeted me Tuesday morning with "What have you folks been doing down at Little Croft Church, anyhow?"

"Why?"

"I hear Reverend Clement's been calling up spirits an' scolding them."

"Where'd you hear that?"

"Dorry Miles told me when she called this morning."

"Where'd Mrs. Miles hear it?"

"I don't know. I haven't got the time to sit around and gossip."

"Of course not," I said.

"Almost wish I'd come. Sounds a lot more interesting than all the talk, talk, talk that other preacher used to do."

"Thomas didn't call up any spirits, Granny. A woman who came had some sort of a fit, that's all. We're going to send her to see a doctor."

"Ah." Granny sounded disappointed. "Well, after you do my hair I got some more jam for you to take down to Miz Whitworth. She called this mornin' and said they'd eaten it all up already and could you come over with some more and the recipe. Giddy says the trial's all hung up arguin' about Matt Humberston's memory anyhow, so there's no point in us going down to the courthouse."

"Amelia Whitworth called you?"

"That's what I said, isn't it? Give Dog-dog some of that bacon fat an' let him in here with me. And then you get that jam and take it to Miz Whitworth afore she calls and pesters me some more."

~ ~ ~ ~ ~

Amelia Whitworth appeared on the porch as soon as I drove Granny's old car into the lane. She watched me walk up the old brick walk, her hands clasped anxiously beneath her bosom and her sharp thin face drawn into a complex of worry lines.

"Good morning," I said. "Granny said you wanted more jam."

"You keep the jam," Amelia Whitworth said. "I just wanted to talk to you without Miz Scarborough spreading it from one end of the county to th'other."

I followed her down the hall into the sunny red-and-white kitchen. She'd made cranberry muffins this morning, and she made me sit down and butter one and insisted on steeping me a cup of tea before she would settle down and talk. Finally she arranged herself on a chair across the corner of the table from me and folded her hands.

"I been hearing things," she said.

"What things?"

"John was down in Winnville last night, takin' the food from the church pantry, 'cause Ambrose Scarborough came down with the stomach flu."

"Yes?"

"Some of them wouldn't take it," Amelia said. "They've heard that we're having séances during church. Raising dead spirits and talking to the Evil One. And that's not all. They hear that we roll on the floor and weep. That would be young Mr. Winn's contribution, I believe."

I stifled the first urge to giggle. "People who were there will know better."

"Yes, but the folks who were there don't have anything at

stake," Amelia retorted. "When John came back, draggin' his chin on the ground, I made some phone calls. I give you three guesses where them stories got wings."

"Matthew Humberston?"

"The same."

"Now I know why Tammy Watts came to church."

"Well, she came to be delivered, I reckon. But Matthew's no fool. He saw a tool and took it to hand. Tammy's a cousin of his, over on his mama's side. He's known her all his life. Seen her do that screaming and foaming bit whenever life gets too much for her. Reverend Clement's a good boy, Amanda, but he don't know all that goes on behind his back."

"I know," I said gloomily.

"But I thought you ought to know. That knife in your tire, that was Matt Jr. As for the dog, I dunno; Matthew might have gotten himself in such a blue fury that he was lashin' out at any livin' thing. But Matthew's had time to think now. Reverend Clement's stepped over the line, far as Matthew's concerned. There's no way that boy's going to get off free, no matter what the jury decides, and Matthew's out for blood. He wouldn't bother with a dog. He wants Reverend Clement gone for good."

"What can we do about it?"

"Spread the truth," Amelia Whitworth said, "but it ain't nearly as interesting. Still, you might put the bug in Eddie's ear. He goes around the county, chattering like an old woman when he ought to be working. And he helped start this rumor, so he might as well help clear it up. And tell your grandma what really happened. She talks to half the people in the county before noon."

"What should I tell Thomas?"

"That's up to you. But if it was me, I might leave him out of it. What's he goin' to do now? He already spoke the words. And it won't help his pastoring none. If he could hear about Matthew's gossip and not be angry, he'd be holier than Moses."

I drove back to the Old House, turning this over in my mind. I was starting to shy away from discussing church matters with Thomas anyway. Back in Philadelphia, we had rarely discussed his pastoral problems; I had started coming to All Saints only after we got engaged, and the church had always been a world apart from our relationship with each other. And here, church and family were all mixed together in a big messy stew.

I met Great-uncle Attaway on Poverty Ridge Road as I drove back up to the Old House. His heavy face was set and angry. He veered off the road for me to pass without looking at me at all, and when I looked in my rearview mirror I could see him spin the pickup's tires on the dirt road as he pulled away.

When I got to the Tenant House, our car and Eddie's green pickup were both gone. I went noisily through the kitchen and tramped up the stairs to change clothes. I wasn't looking at Eddie's door. His room was dark and still, the door half open.

Something shifted suddenly in the darkness. I paused on the steps. The back of my neck prickled. I backed downstairs and stood at the bottom of the stairs with my heart beating hard in my ears. I wondered where Chelsea was.

I retreated to the hallway, near the door, and called, "Who's there?"

The door creaked. Feet shuffled out onto the landing.

"Amanda?"

"Eddie," I said. My heart slowly descended back into my

chest. "Eddie. What are you doing?"

"Just having a nap." His voice sounded odd. I peered up the stairs into the semidusk, wondering whether he'd been drinking alone up there.

"Want some dinner?"

"Sure." Eddie came down the stairs towards me. The hand he reached out to the wooden rail trembled. His face was salt white.

"Are you coming down with something?" I asked.

"No, no. I'm just fine." He reached the living room floor. A fine mist of sweat stood out on his forehead, and his eyes were sick. I couldn't smell alcohol on him.

"Where's your truck?"

"Over behind the silos. Thought I'd…thought I'd get it out of your way."

His eyes were rapidly shifting back and forth. I hoped Thomas would come home soon. I went back into the kitchen and made coffee and poured him a cup. He sat at the table and drank it, and I cooked while color slowly came back into his face. I'd gotten the meat into the oven before I connected his state with Attaway's visit. I wiped meat juice from the top of the stove and said casually, "Did my great-uncle come by?"

"No," Eddie said, his voice strangled in his throat.

"I met him on the road. I thought he might have come by to have a look around. He was worried about something in the house."

"Didn't see him." The blood had left his face again.

I took the scraps I'd trimmed off the meat out to Chelsea and looked behind the silos while she ate. Eddie's pickup was back there, concealed by the old mulberry grove that grew just past the farthest silo.

~ ~ ~ ~ ~

Eddie got out of the house early the next morning. He told us he'd found a part-time job, holding stop signs for the Virginia Department of Transportation. Thomas left shortly afterwards for his usual breakfast with the Ruritans, and I had the house to myself.

I sat at the kitchen table with my coffee and thought about Eddie, his evasions and his fright; and from there I went on to consider Attaway Fowlerand, scaring Eddie into hiding, coming in with his landlord's key while we weren't home. I had never bothered to lock doors, growing up, but with all our computer equipment sitting right in the living room we'd taken to closing the Tenant House securely. What did Attaway think he would find?

I got up and walked slowly through the rooms. The fireplace room was silent and full of morning shadows. Upstairs, our bed was unmade. I pulled the covers up and folded clothes and wandered back out onto the landing.

Eddie's door was closed. I pushed it open. His shades were drawn and the room was dark. The air inside was stale and unpleasant. His dresser drawers stood open, and his bed was a rumpled heap of blankets. I knelt down and looked through his drawers, lifting the clothes and replacing them in the same wrinkled piles. The gun was gone. As an afterthought, I slid my hand carefully under Eddie's pillow. An indentation showed where the .357 had lain, but the weapon itself was missing.

When I came home that evening, Thomas was sitting at the kitchen table with his sermon notes spread out in front of him.

"Hi," he called, when I closed the door behind me.

"Hey."

"You or Granny Cora hear anything from the trial?"

"Giddy says they're still hung up over Matt's amnesia. Some medical expert is coming down from D.C. They might not get back to the trial itself till Monday."

"Poor Matthew," Thomas said. "The suspense must be unbearable for him."

His voice was compassionate. I stood in the kitchen and watched him for a moment; the faint lines at the corners of his eyes had deepened to crevices, and a fair shadow of late-day beard was visible along his jaw. The light glinted on gray threads in his bright hair.

"Want to go out and grab something for dinner?" I asked.

"Sure."

"Is Eddie expecting me to cook dinner?"

"He hasn't been back today. I don't know where he is."

I went into the fireplace room. The light on the answering machine was blinking. I hit the button, and Eddie's voice said, "Hi. I might be a little late for dinner—going over to Joe and Jenny's to fix a pipe. See you in a bit."

"He's gone to Joe and Jenny's," I called, dialing the number.

"Again?" Thomas said.

The phone rang. Jenny picked it up a moment later and said, "Hello?"

"Jenny? This is Amanda Clement. Is Eddie there?"

"Sure," Jenny said. Her low attractive voice was slightly breathless. A moment later Eddie said, "Yeah?"

"Eddie, can you get some dinner before you come home? I think Thomas and I might go eat out."

"Okay," Eddie said agreeably. "I'll just eat here."

Thomas called from the kitchen, "Let me talk to Joe for a minute before you hang up. He said he might be able to have lunch this week."

"And Thomas wants to talk to Joe."

"Oh, he's not here right now."

"Not back from work?"

"No, I don't think he's getting back until late."

I paused, waiting for an explanation, but Eddie said cheerfully, "I'll leave him a message, okay? See you."

He hung up. I replaced the receiver slowly. Thomas said, "What?"

"Joe's not there."

"What's Eddie doing, then?"

"Apparently," I said, "having dinner with Jenny by himself."

We looked at each other. I didn't voice my reservations, but Thomas pushed his hand through his short hair.

"All right," he said. "I'll talk to him as soon as I get a chance. He probably doesn't realize how inappropriate that is."

Eddie came back late that night. I'd gone up to bed; I heard the two men's voices in the kitchen below, rising and falling inaudibly until nearly midnight.

Chapter Twenty-seven

Matt's trial was indeed suspended until Monday, and we lived through the weekend in a state of fragile peace. But the pews were even emptier on Sunday. I stood in the back and counted silently while Thomas preached. We'd started with forty Little Croft congregants back in late August. Now, midway through November, we had twenty-six. Thomas's seminary professors used to call that a Scottish revival, but the joke wasn't funny firsthand.

I heard tires crunch through the parking lot twice during the sermon; the Little Croft Sheriff's Department was still checking up on us. I could have told Jimmy White that he was wasting his time. Matthew Humberston had found a less direct revenge.

I tried to comfort myself with the presence of the faithful. Joe and Jenny were there, Amelia and John Whitworth were solid in their pew with Ambrose and Ida Scarborough just behind them. Eddie sat near the back and Tammy Watts, with the two silent toddlers, near the front. I watched the back of her head warily, but Thomas had constructed a sermon that didn't mention the Evil One.

When everyone had left, we picked up the scattered bulletins and put hymnbooks back silently. One of the doors was cracked open, and cold air blew into the musty warmth.

Eventually Thomas asked, "Did you see anyone new this morning?"

"No, not this morning."

"I didn't do my visitation this week. Ambrose and I went back by to see Tammy Watts on Wednesday and take her some food, and then I had my sermon…" He was folding a bulletin over and over in his hands. "No," he said after a moment, "I wasn't any busier than usual this week. I just didn't want to do it. I couldn't face the hostility. There were three families gone this morning. I should have expected it."

"Thomas, God isn't punishing you because you didn't do your visitation."

"I'm doing something wrong, Amanda."

"Why? Because the church isn't growing?"

"It's shrinking," Thomas said. "Ambrose told me this morning that I needed to get out more, because we can't meet the budget for last month."

I put the last hymnbook away. I didn't know what to say to him. I ventured, at last, "Thomas, I think Matthew is spreading rumors about the church."

"Like what?"

"Well…that we're doing cult-type things here. Because of Tammy Watts, mostly."

Thomas folded the bulletin one more time, his head bent in concentration. He said suddenly, "Where'd Eddie go off to?"

"He told me he was having Sunday lunch with Joe and Jenny again."

Thomas shook his head slightly and pitched the bulletin into the wastepaper basket that stood beside the back door.

"I did talk to him. I told him it wasn't appropriate for him to be there when Joe was gone. I told him it was important to avoid every appearance of evil. He agreed with me and promised that he'd only go with both of them there."

"He's over there an awful lot."

"What else can I tell him? To stay away even if Joe invites him?"

"Is Joe the one who does the inviting? She always speaks for both of them. He's usually a couple of thoughts behind."

"I don't know. I can't interrogate Joe and Jenny about which one does the social planning."

"But you could ask them if Eddie is interfering with their home life, couldn't you?"

"That's intruding."

"But Thomas, you're a pastor. You're supposed to know about people's home lives."

"I'm not going to shove my way in without being invited, Amanda." His tone was sharp with growing hostility. I picked up another bulletin, wondering why; he had never been shy about dropping in and chatting with people before.

"Thomas," I said, "why don't you want to find out what's going on?"

"Eddie is doing so well. I don't want to make him think I distrust him."

"But if he isn't doing well, wouldn't you want to know?"

"Yes, of course I would." But his voice lacked an edge of certainty.

I thought suddenly: You don't want to know. I remembered him after Eddie's spectacular conversion, striding down the sidewalk in front of Little Croft Church with energy and enthusiasm overflowing from every movement; and I heard his voice saying, *At last I feel like I'm doing something worthwhile.*

"Well," Thomas said, "let's go home. I've had enough of this place for one day. I need a nap and a walk if I'm going to face it again this evening."

~ ~ ~ ~ ~

The phone rang Sunday evening, just as we were changing wearily after the night service. Thomas looked at me with *I'm not home* written all over his face, so I went down and picked up the receiver.

"Hello?"

"Mandy?" Granny Cora's voice demanded.

"Yes? Are you okay?"

"You send Thomas up here. I want to talk to him." The receiver clicked down before I could open my mouth again. I went back upstairs and broke the news to Thomas. He sighed with resignation and dragged his clothes out again.

"You want to walk over with me?" he asked, buttoning his shirt back up.

So we walked to the Old House together in the November dark. The sun had set. The scent of frost lay over us. Thomas's fingers were cold in mine. The Old House was casting long yellow oblongs of light into the dark yard. Uncle Giddy was sitting on the front steps, smoking a cigarette, his rifle across his knees. Dog-dog was curled on the step beside him.

"Evenin'," Uncle Giddy said. The end of his cigarette glowed red in the dark. Against the bright door behind him, his shape was dark and featureless. He lifted a hand and stubbed the cigarette against the step.

"Foxes?" I asked.

"Yep. Been after my chickens. Thought they might come up after dark." Uncle Giddy shifted aside. "Mama's waitin' for you. She's in a right mood."

"Why?"

"Dunno. Uncle Attaway's been here all afternoon. Made her mad, I reckon."

"I'll stay out here," I said to Thomas. He nodded and went in.

"Want to sit?" Uncle Giddy asked.

"Sure."

He gave Dog-dog a shove with his elbow. "Get on down," he ordered. The old hound rose and wandered off into the shadows. Giddy shook out a fresh cigarette. "Want one?"

"No, Uncle Giddy." I sat down beside him. The step was cold underneath me.

"That's good," Uncle Giddy said, lighting the cigarette. "Hate to see a woman smoke. Your eyes are younger'n mine. Tell me if you see anything out there."

The gravestones were pale indistinct shapes against darkness, and I could barely tell the dirt slope of the field from the air above it. Giddy blew smoke invisibly into the night. The acrid smell drifted over me. Suddenly I was fifteen again, sitting on Granny's steps at the end of a family picnic, listening to sharp voices inside the house. Giddy had always retreated outside, sitting and smoking silently while his sisters cleaned up and bickered inside. Sometimes Quintus had sprawled on the frosted grass, waiting for Attaway to emerge and drive home, down the dark narrow roads to the old Fowlerand place on the river.

"Uncle Giddy," I said, "do you remember you were telling me how Quintus's mother died?"

"Sure." Giddy sucked in a deep breath. The cigarette tip brightened and faded.

"You'd been out hunting with Great-uncle Attaway?"

"Yep."

"What happened when Attaway woke up and found her?"

I thought for a moment that he wasn't going to answer,

but he took another pull on the cigarette and said, "He came thundering back down the stairs yellin', 'Call the doc! Call the doc! She took too many of them pills!'"

"Which doctor?"

"Oh, that was old Dr. White. He retired way back when your dad set up shop out here."

"Well...what pills was she taking?"

"Durned if I remember. All them women were taking pills to help 'em sleep, or calm 'em down, or keep 'em awake. Old Dr. White handed them things out like candy. All I know is Attaway came stalkin' over to the sink and yanked it open and found her whisky bottle there under the counter. Just had a tiny bit left at the bottom. Sheriff tested the whisky, an' it was okay—just awful strong to be mixing with sleepin' pills. She started drinking and took them pills and then went to bed and never woke up no more."

I felt breathless with discovery. "Attaway took the bottle down to the sheriff himself!" I could see it all. Attaway had poisoned his unfaithful wife and switched the whisky bottle on his way to the courthouse.

"Nope. I took it. I was a sheriff's deputy, remember? Me an' Jimmy White, we were deputies together. When he pulled that cabinet open I said, 'I'll just take that, Uncle Attaway,' an' I whisked it right out of his hand. I was a good deputy. Coulda stayed with it, but Daddy needed me to help out—"

"Yes, I know. So you took the bottle down to the sheriff yourself?"

"Yep. Richard Banks, he was still sheriff then. He had the whisky tested, and her bottle of pills, an' said it was an accident."

I put my chin in my hands and sniffed the air. Giddy had

stubbed out his cigarette, and I could smell dark earth and browning grass and a faint whiff of Dog-dog, who had flopped down just around the corner of the house.

"I always wished I'd gone in the house earlier," Giddy said. "I coulda stopped her, I reckon."

"What do you mean?"

"Well, we was hunting down by the river, and Attaway stuck me up on that old deer stand right down from the Banks house. The rest of 'em went all the way down on the other side of Potter's Field, and I sat and sat and sat till I got so cold I got down and went back to the truck an' drove back to the house for my coat. I'd left it in the living room, see, when I went to meet Uncle Attaway, 'cause I thought it would be warm out. I snuck in and got it, but the house was quiet. I figured Doris was upstairs sleepin'."

Headlights were coming up the lane; Eddie was returning from his long afternoon with Joe and Jenny. The pickup turned into the Tenant House yard and the motor cut off.

"There's your Winn, back from tomcattin' for the night," Giddy said, shaking out yet another cigarette.

"You're hard on Eddie. You and Granny both."

"He ain't done nothing his whole life but hang around where he ain't supposed to be. Looking for women or loose objects, whichever may come to hand. He stole my best hunting knife that very same night. Not but ten or so, he was, back in 1970, but already thievin' from the neighbors. He was pokin' around the Tenant House outbuildings when I came out with my coat, and I yelled at him to be off. Next mornin' my knife was gone from the shed where I left my deer-cleanin' stuff. I ask you."

"The night Doris died?"

"Yep," Giddy said. "Knew we were gone. His daddy was a no-good thief, and he taught Eddie all he knew. I ran him away, though. Hope your spoons don't go off in his pockets, Mandy."

I thought of Eddie in the shadows of his darkened bedroom, the loaded gun shaking in his hand, Great-uncle Attaway treading across the old pine boards towards the bottom of the stairs. I could almost smell the earth on his farming overalls. The scene was so vivid that the creaking of the screen door behind me startled me like a gunshot. I scrambled up.

"Ready to go home?" Thomas said. "Your grandma's in bed for the night. Evening, Mr. Scarborough."

"Aya," Giddy said, smoking peacefully.

We walked back through the darkness towards the windows of the Tenant House, which created a faint welcoming glow against the pitch black of the pine woods. Thomas reached for my hand. The screen door slammed behind us; Giddy had gone inside.

Thomas said, "Your grandmother's having a bad attack of conscience, but I can't tell why."

"She didn't say?"

"All she'd say was that Attaway was with them all, just before they died. Doris, and Peggy, and now Quintus. 'With 'em all,' she said, 'like the angel of death.' And she went on saying that, over and over. She gave me the shivers. I kept expecting to turn around and see him in the doorway."

"Attaway?"

"No, the angel of death."

"I didn't think Attaway had been with Doris right before she died," I said. "I thought he was away hunting all night."

"Why does it matter?" Thomas said. "When did she die?

Thirty years ago?" He heard his own impatient voice and stopped in the middle of the road. I looked back at him, surprised. He stood with his face tilted upwards. Above us, the stars glittered in a pure black space; the Milky Way lay across the sky like a river of gleaming sand. I could see a very faint light on his face.

"Amanda, I've been thinking."

He wants to leave Little Croft, I thought. The pit of my stomach ached.

"I keep coming back to that passage from Merton, about the Incarnation," he said. "Over and over. I've done just what he warns against...made Christ in my own image. I always think of Christ born into a warm home, raised by a father who loved him enough to treat him as his own. I never paid that much attention to the other parts of the story—the brothers who think he's possessed, the family that didn't bother to show up and intercede for him at his trial. I have to stay here and let that Christ—the Christ who was alone—be formed in me. I have to let go of the wish to belong."

His fingers in mine were like ice. A long silence stretched between us. I said eventually, "There's a star shadow behind you."

"I thought that was a myth."

"You've never been far enough away from lights to see it."

"No," he said. "It's dark out here."

We walked back to the Tenant House without words.

Chapter Twenty-eight

The house was empty when I got up Monday morning. Eddie was out holding highway signs on Route 5, and Thomas had gone early to church. Chelsea flopped at my feet, snoring.

I sat at the kitchen table, staring out the east window at the cold fields of winter wheat, and thought about the night that Doris died. Attaway had been hunting all night, never out of sight of the two Humberston cousins who went with him. Giddy had gone back for his coat and seen Eddie Winn, poking around the house. Eddie Winn, ten, skinny and quick fingered. Eddie, spending the next three decades in a drunken stupor, living on money that came from some mysterious source. Eddie was sober now, and Attaway was afraid of what he would say.

I took a swig of coffee, discontented with this train of thought. I was still in the dark. Great-uncle Attaway, I decided, must have ordered Eddie to do something, and he'd been paying him hush money ever since. But he could hardly have suggested that Eddie Winn murder his wife. My Little Croft blood inclined me to think the worst of Winns, but even a Winn could do limited damage at age ten.

Maybe it *had* been suicide. I had firsthand proof that Little Croft suicides were occasionally smoothed over into accidents; and Doris had undoubtedly been depressed. But I could still hear Matthew Humberston's voice, thick with conviction. *She wouldn't never have left Quintus to your care, Attaway. She wouldn't never have killed herself with her little boy there.* I recalled the sweet pretty face of the girl in Granny's old pictures. Doris would have known that her son was my grandfather's child, not Attaway's. Would she have left him to be raised by the man who hated him?

Chelsea rolled over on top of my feet and yawned enormously. I shoved her off and got up to pour myself another cup of coffee. I noticed suddenly that there was a paper-hat note perched on top of the stove. It unfolded easily to reveal Thomas's slanted writing.

Mandy: I talked to Eddie again this morning, over breakfast. He says he's never over there with Jenny alone and that Joe keeps asking him back. I think everything's okay. I'm off to work on my sermon and take Thanksgiving baskets down to Winnville. Pray for me. See you at dinner—T.

I folded the note and tapped it against the back of my hand; and then I got up and dialed Joe and Jenny's number. I wasn't due at Granny's for another half an hour, which meant I had fifteen spare minutes before she started calling to see where I was.

Jenny answered, her voice breathless as usual. I said, "Hi, Jenny, it's Amanda. Are you on your way to work?"

"Oh, I've got five minutes before I have to rush off. How are you?"

I thought again what an attractive voice she had; low and silky and warm with friendship. I said, "Well, my grandmother keeps me busy. How are you and Joe doing?"

"Oh, fine, fine. We need to have y'all over again."

"We'd like that. Er…Jenny, I wondered whether Eddie was…well, taking up too much of your time. He's lonely, you know, and he doesn't know too many people, so he might latch on to you."

"He's no trouble," Jenny said. The words were sunny and open. "We figure you and Thomas have him for dinner so much, maybe you'd like a chance to be alone."

"We do, but we could ask some other folks in the church to have Eddie over—"

"Oh, no. You know, Eddie has actually been a big help to me."

"He has?"

"Oh, yes. See, my dad was an alcoholic, and when I was growing up he was always drunk. I still have all sorts of grudges against my dad. And that was poisoning my relationship with Joe, you know? We were just having the worst time when we started coming to the church. I know we looked fine, but all we did was fight all the time during the day, and all I ever did at night was cry and cry. We hardly ever talked. I think I was feeling like Joe was my dad, in a way."

"You were? I mean…well, I'm sorry to hear that." I felt ridiculously inadequate. I couldn't tell whether she was baring a deep secret of her soul or mouthing recovery-group platitudes.

"Yes. But since we've known Eddie, he's helped me understand what it means to be an alcoholic. He's just been so open and honest about his own addictions. I've been able to let go of a lot of anger towards my dad. You know," Jenny said, her voice sweet and whispery, "Joe's a wonderful man, he really is, but he doesn't understand what it's like to be addicted. I think I really have an addictive personality too, just like my dad. And

I kept expecting Joe to be like my dad. Oh, I've found out all sorts of things about myself that I didn't know before. It's just so wonderful."

I wished I could see her face. The clichéd phrases grated on me like chewed metal. But that wasn't fair; lots of people lacked the vocabulary to paste the proper tags over sincere and profound emotions.

"And you know," Jenny said, winding up, "we're so grateful to you and Thomas and the church. We've come such a long way since we met you all. I guess Eddie has just absorbed some kind of wisdom, living in your house and listening to you and Thomas talk. He's told us lots of things that the two of you have said about getting along, and about addictions, and about forgiving people in your past."

"I'm glad we've helped," I said. I couldn't remember ever discussing those topics in front of Eddie.

"Anyway, we thought we'd have him for Thanksgiving dinner on Thursday. Give you and Thomas a chance to be alone for the holiday. And we're having four other people over, so it won't be any problem to have Eddie as well. Actually, it was Joe's idea. Well, I've got to run. Want to come for dinner next week? Friday, maybe?"

"Friday would be good."

"'Bout six? We can talk about it on Sunday. See you then. Have a good Thanksgiving. Bye!"

The phone clicked down. I hung up. I knew with irrational certainty that Eddie was lying to Thomas. Something was going on, something more serious than the annoying presumption that Eddie shared the pastor's wisdom because he lived in the pastor's house.

"Giddy says they're goin' back to trial this afternoon," Granny said, attacking her breakfast with enthusiasm. I had fixed her buttermilk pancakes and pacified her for the lack of butter on top by slathering them with syrup.

"You gonna eat?" Granny demanded.

"I'm just having coffee this morning."

"Can I have two more?"

I poured two more circles of batter into the battered iron frying pan. Whatever secret Granny held in her old memory, she had done her usual shoulder shrug with it; her obscure hints to Thomas had temporarily eased her conscience, and she was full of relish and energy again.

"Thankee," Granny said, watching the pancakes rise. "Giddy says they're doin' all medical stuff today at the trial. He got it from Palmer Black, up at the courthouse. I can't see no reason to go listen to them all argue about Matt Humberston's head. We might go up tomorrow if they do the closin' arguments. Today you can help me quilt that log-cabin pattern. You still remember how to quilt, or did you forget all that in Philadelphia?"

"I remember," I said.

"Where's your Winn this mornin'?"

"He's at work." At work, wearing a loaded gun under his sweatshirt, watching for Attaway's truck with frightened eyes.

"There he is again," Granny said, holding out her plate for the second batch of pancakes.

"Who?"

"Attaway. Up at the Tenant House pokin' around."

I bent down and peered out the window. A trail of dust showed where someone had driven up Poverty Ridge Road. I couldn't see the Tenant House, though. I went out onto the front steps and squinted. Attaway's truck was parked in front of the little pump house. Chelsea was frisking around it as though she'd just caught sight of her best friend. I could see Attaway's green cap moving against the dark wood of the sheds out back; he was hunting through the old outbuildings, through debris that hadn't been moved in years.

"What's he up to?" Granny called.

"He's looking through the old sheds next to the silos." I came back in and started to clear her dishes away.

"He ought to know what's in there. That's mostly his trash. Nat let him put it there, back when him and Doris were stayin' in the Tenant House, and he never did move it out."

"Maybe that's why he was in the Tenant House while we were gone last week. Looking for something he's lost." I squirted dishwasher detergent over the blue Currier and Ives pattern on Granny's plate. Picturesque rustics, frolicking through the snow with country cheer.

"Lookin' for what?" Granny demanded. "We cleaned that house out good afore Miss Clunie moved there, and again afore you came. There wasn't nothing left from Doris's day but spiderwebs and a couple pieces of furniture."

I finished the dishes and started to dry them. When we'd moved in, the closets and corners of the Tenant House had been bare. But the sheds out back were full of decades of farm junk: old engines, bits and pieces of combines and harvesters, tires, stacks of old newspapers, drums of discarded oil, sacks of concrete and fertilizer and feed.

Eddie, skulking in the early twilight, could have concealed anything back there, and whatever he'd hidden could easily have lain undisturbed for thirty years.

~ ~ ~ ~ ~

Attaway came by late in the afternoon. He stood in Granny's doorway, his light shirt streaked with dirt and his hands greasy with oil, and growled, "You need anything, Cora?"

"Not a thing. Come in and sit a while."

"Nope," Attaway said. He banged the screen door behind him. Dog-dog fled from him; he stalked down the steps, slammed the door of his pickup truck, and spun his tires in the soft dirt at the curve of the lane.

I walked back by those sheds that evening, on my way to the Tenant House's back door. They were old tin-roofed structures, leaning dangerously to the right, hung about with cobwebs and speckled with bird droppings. A cold and moldy smell breathed from the dark doorways. The sun was already below the western pines, and their shadows fell across the Tenant House and the silos and the sheds, plunging the whole place into chilly dimness. Beyond the whole little compound of shed, pigpen, and silos, the slope of hill ran down to the gray river, wreathed in an impenetrable tangle of vines and scrub trees. I didn't know what to look for, and even if I had, I wouldn't have ventured into those lightless shacks to find it.

We ate chicken and bread and sweet potatoes for dinner. Thomas was mostly silent. He'd gone visiting, he said briefly, and left the statement to stand alone. Eddie chattered about the highway project he was working in, about waste and fraud in the Virginia Department of Transportation, about the laziness of his fellow workers and the inconsiderate driving habits of the motorists he flagged down. I watched his dark animated face, so different from the gaunt drunkard who had first sat at our table, and thought: What were you up to, Eddie Winn, creeping around the banks of the Chickahominy while Doris Fowlerand died?

Tuesday morning's sky was a clear watery blue, but the WRVA radio news out of Richmond warned that a big storm was on its way. Maybe snow, six to eight inches; maybe ice, if the temperature edged above freezing. By the weekend, we could be buried in winter. I made a mental note to do Granny Cora's shopping soon. A hint of snow in southeastern Virginia created more panic than a hurricane warning. Grocery shelves would be empty of milk and bread by Friday, and gas stations would be jammed with folks filling cans to run their farm generators.

Meanwhile, Matt Humberston's trial was drawing to its slow and inevitable close. I drove Granny back to the courthouse and we listened to the final statements; Matt's future tossed into the air like a coin, innocence and guilt alternating as the lawyers argued.

"Matthew Humberston Jr. plotted to kill Quintus Fowlerand," Jeremiah Adkins said. He stood in his well-cut charcoal suit, swinging gold-framed glasses on his finger. "You've heard Thomas Clement testify to the hostility between the two men, a hatred that stems from a long history of feuds between the elder Matthew Humberston and Quintus's father, Attaway Fowlerand. From the dead man's own mouth, we have these words: 'Matt said he'd kill me. Told me yesterday he'd kill me. Tonight, said he'd been meanin' to kill me all his life and now he had the chance.' Premeditated murder, ladies and gentlemen. Murder growing from a family hatred that started with the death of Doris Humberston Fowlerand and ended, three decades later, with the death of her son."

He put the gold glasses on and covered the medical evidence, the time of death, and the contention that Matt had lost his memory. Scorn was heavy in his voice. He clasped his hands behind his back and balanced on the balls of his feet.

"From Matt Humberston himself, we hear that Quintus Fowlerand offered no threat," he said. "The two men sat and drank. How much did they drink? When admitted to the MCV emergency room, Matt Humberston had a blood alcohol level of three times the legal limit. Three times, ladies and gentlemen. He decided to kill Quintus; he nerved himself with alcohol; and then, holding a loaded shotgun in his lap, he saw Quintus Fowlerand—his lifelong enemy, the son of the man he held responsible for the death of a beloved aunt—slip away, sprawl into a pickup, and drive away towards home. His blood boiled with anger. A moment ago, Quintus had been in his power. Now he was escaping. And although Quintus Fowlerand was driving away from him, into his own land, on his own road, Matt Humberston followed him, cornered him, and shot him. Not in the head, ladies and gentlemen. His hands were shaking. He was afraid he would miss. No, Matt Humberston took the sure and easy shot. He shot Quintus Fowlerand in the chest; and Quintus Fowlerand, breathing blood, begging for a priest, took a full hour to die."

He let the last words linger in the polished courtroom air. The curious crowd had grown smaller in the two weeks since the trial began, but the hard courthouse pews were still half full. I could see Matthew Humberston in his front seat, staring at his feet with sharp concentration; and Matt beside his counsel, his face covered with both his hands.

"Ladies and gentlemen," Jeremiah Adkins said, "I don't ask you to forget the wrongs done to the Humberstons by the Fowlerands. I don't ask you to dismiss the years of hatred between these two families. I don't expect you to discount Matt Humberston's love for his father and his father's sister, or the loathing his father instilled in him for Attaway Fowlerand and Attaway's son. I don't even deny that Mr. Fowlerand may have—for whatever reasons of his own—set his son and Matt Humberston at each other's throats. But I ask you to remember these simple facts. Quintus Fowlerand and Matt Humberston sat together. They drank together. Quintus Fowlerand left. And Matt Humberston, with malice aforethought, chased him, cornered him, and shot him, while Quintus Fowlerand's gun lay in the grass beside the porch where he died. I ask you to remember, finally, that when Reverend Thomas Clement turned to Matt Humberston and cried out, 'He's dead and you killed him!' Matt Humberston said a single word: 'Good!'"

He sat down. Judge Banks popped a Tums into his mouth.

"Mr. Hall?"

Matt's lawyer rose from beside him. The incredulous shake of his head, the momentary speechlessness as he fumbled for words, the two thoughtful steps away from the table as he considered his opponent's charges: all were masterpieces of unspoken opinion.

"Well," he said at last. "It's a shocking story Mr. Adkins has told you there. A terrible, brutal story of a young man with no regard for life. A young man with a loaded gun and nothing to fear. There's only one problem, ladies and gentlemen. If this young man had nothing to fear, why did he end up brutally beaten? Why did he spend nearly a week in the hospital, struggling to hold on to life? Why have his doctors testified that his memory has been destroyed? Members of the jury, this is not the story of a vicious killer who chased an innocent man to his death. This is the story of a boy who found himself the victim of family quarrels, of his own uncle's manipulative hatred; a boy who followed his cousin down a long dark road, concerned for his safety, only to find himself surrounded by a ring of enemies bent on doing him harm."

"Huh," Granny said beside me. I looked at her sideways. She had turned her head. When I followed her gaze I saw Eddie Winn, standing in the back of the courtroom. The shrinking furtiveness had crept back into his face and body.

Matt's lawyer covered the medical evidence, the time of death, and the neurological reports in a calm and methodical voice. Jeremiah Adkins had raised his voice, seeking to build his case on the emotion of a young man dead; Andrew Hall spoke in low measured phrases, showing that a reasonable man could come to only one conclusion. He wrapped Matt's beating, Quintus's erratic behavior, and Attaway's lies into one strong cord. It would hold, I thought, as long as the jury didn't think too hard about Eddie's reliability. And only if the men and women behind the pine railing didn't know Quintus.

According to Andrew Hall, Attaway Pierman Fowlerand could no longer tolerate his son's partnership. Determined to get his land back, he primed Matt with suspicions of Quintus. Attaway had met with Quintus late the night he died and had threatened to hand his inheritance over to his Humberston relations. Quintus had rounded up the Fowlerand cousins, and his flight down Fowlerand Road had been a ploy designed to trap Matt at the old Fowlerand place. Matt had followed Quintus out of concern for his cousin—afraid that Quintus, drunk and weaving, would drive off Fowlerand Road into a tree—but Quintus had turned to taunt his enemy, as the circle of Fowlerand relations closed in.

I craned my neck so that I could see every corner of the courthouse, but Attaway wasn't there.

Andrew Hall was winding up. "Ladies and gentlemen, Attaway Pierman Fowlerand isn't on trial here. Matthew Humberston Sr. isn't on trial here. But I submit to you that these two men, feuding for thirty years over the death of Attaway's wife, were responsible for the events that led to Quintus Fowlerand's death. When Matt Humberston raised his gun to shoot Quintus Fowlerand, he was acting in self-defense. He had followed his cousin out of compassion. He found that compassion repaid with treachery, with betrayal, and with the threat of death. Matt Humberston pulled the trigger because he was in mortal fear of his life; and if Thomas Clement hadn't arrived with the police close behind him, Matt Humberston would have died at the hands of the dead man's relatives. My client is innocent of murder, ladies and gentlemen. He acted in self-defense. And his only mistake was to worry about Quintus Fowlerand's well-being, late at night, down at the end of Fowlerand Road."

He sat down. On the pew just behind him, Matthew Humberston stood up. He walked out the side door of the courtroom, his joints stiff and his neck as rigid as a pillar. Matt turned his head to watch his father go. I saw his round immature face, creased with the unfamiliar lines of frustration, and I thought: He doesn't remember. The amnesia wasn't Andrew Hall's invention after all. Matt had no idea what he had done down there at the dark end of Fowlerand Road.

Granny tugged my arm. "Alrighty," she said, over the

sound of the judge's instructions to the jury. "Let's go home."

I helped her out of the courthouse, across the brown grass and back to the parking lot. Eddie and his truck were both gone. I settled myself behind the wheel and said, "Mind if I go the long way home?"

"Why?"

"Just for a change."

"Long as I get home before my story starts."

So I drove across Route 5 onto 155, the road that wound around Little Croft's outskirts and eventually led to the interstate. Joe and Jenny lived on 155. I slowed as I came abreast of their house. The two-story house was set off the road, in a clump of pines, but I could clearly see Eddie's pickup truck parked half behind a concealing tangle of azaleas, and Jenny's little red sports car, and an empty garage where Joe's jeep should have stood.

Chapter Twenty-nine

I sat in the kitchen that evening and watched the sun set. I made tea and opened a book, but it lay unread in front of me. Chelsea curled blissfully at my feet, smelling of dog and dead groundhog. It was time to haul her into the bathtub again.

Thomas was late. I called the church office. The phone rang again and again until I hung up. Headlights finally glinted at the end of the lane; high and square lights, not the little round lights of our hatchback. I stood at the kitchen door and watched Eddie slam the pickup door and walk across the yard.

"Hey, Amanda," he said. "What's for supper?"

He had regained all his bounce. The shifty cringing drunkard had completely disappeared. He was rosy and satisfied and freshly washed, and as he put his foot on the bottom stair I felt a wave of nausea wash over me. I backed away from the screen door, and he walked through the hallway and into the living room, shucking his coat.

"Thomas back?"

"Not yet. Where've you been today?"

"Highway department," Eddie said cheerfully. "All day. Down on 295. Showered before I came back."

"I was at the trial this morning. Listening to the closing arguments with my grandmother. I guess you didn't see me, did you, Eddie?"

He turned and looked towards the kitchen door where I stood. His eyes narrowed against the light. Secrecy peered quickly from his face and disappeared.

"Yeah," he said. "I took a break to hear the lawyers myself. Wanted to know what they'd make of my story. Went back to the highway department right after. Sorry for what I heard, Attaway Fowlerand bein' your great-uncle and all. I'm sure he didn't want everybody to hear the lawyers pin the blame on him."

"I drove by Jenny and Joe's house on my way home."

Eddie cleared his throat. "I just dropped by to see how they were doing—they been havin' a hard time—" His voice groped at casualness and failed.

"Yeah, and you're making the most of it, aren't you? Didn't Thomas speak to you about being there when Joe is away?"

"He don't know what it's like," Eddie said, rallying himself. "I've just been tryin' to help, Amanda. I see him workin' so hard to show all these people the right way, but he don't know what it's like to be addicted to something and I do."

"I see. So you're a better marriage counselor than Thomas? And of course this counseling has to be done while Joe is away?"

"When Joe's around she can't talk about these things. She's scared of him, see."

"Why? Does he beat her?"

"Nope. But he hurts her emotionally, you know?" Eddie took several steps towards me, intent on his justification. "I'm just helpin' her get all her feelings out, so they don't damage her relationship no more. But she can't get her feelings out with Joe there. It's a bit like Thomas and you, see?"

"What?" I said, flabbergasted.

"Well, I been living here for a while, and I seen you look at him when he's workin' at something, like you want to tell him about your day with your grandmother, but you think he might not listen. Or you want to tell him somethin' about the church, but he's too down in the mouth. Wouldn't it be nice to have someone else to tell? Someone you knew wouldn't get uptight about what you were saying?"

He had advanced another two steps. I was suddenly aware of how unpleasantly close he was. I backed away and heard Chelsea scramble up from underneath the kitchen table. She came and sat beside me, cocking her head questioningly, her big tongue lolling and her furry body heavy and comforting against my leg. I'd never thought of Eddie as a man of force. He was an insinuator, a soft-voiced infiltrator, a thief of peace. But I felt ill. The hair at the back of my neck rose up.

"Eddie," I said, "I think you should go somewhere else for supper. I don't feel like eating and I don't know when Thomas will be back. Go away."

He cocked his head sideways. Chelsea suddenly growled at him, low and meaningful. I put my hand down on her head.

"Ah," Eddie said, "suit yourself. Wouldn't want anyone to think anything inappropriate, would we?" He snatched his jacket off the back of the sofa and headed for the door.

"Eddie," I said, "Great-uncle Attaway has a key to this house. He's been in here looking for something he lost. Know what it is?"

I saw his shoulders tighten and draw inwards, but he didn't answer. He slammed the screen door behind him and stalked across the grass to his pickup truck. Chelsea stuck her nose into my hand and drooled happily on my fingers.

"Stop it," I said mechanically. "Good dog. Good dog, Chelsea." I'd bought a package of hot dogs last trip to the grocery, and they lay unopened on the bottom shelf of the fridge.

I cut the plastic and dumped them recklessly out in front of her. She slurped them down, waving her tail happily at this unexpected treat. I washed my hands and sat down at the table and folded them. My fingers were trembling. I thought: Do I tell Thomas about this? About what? Eddie's truck outside Jenny's house? We'd been there before. About some imagined threat from Eddie? All he had done was stand in the kitchen doorway and talk.

Amelia Whitworth. The name brought her sharp common sense vividly to mind. I was relieved already. I got up and dialed the Whitworth number.

Amelia herself picked it up, halfway through the first ring. The matter-of-fact voice was colored with frantic worry.

"Yes?"

"Mrs. Whitworth? This is Amanda."

"Amanda. I'm sorry, dear, I thought—well, I've got to get off the phone, all right? What do you need?"

"I—" I stuck, hearing the hurry in her words, unable to explain myself in a few brief words.

"What is it?" she said, impatiently.

"Is everything all right, Mrs. Whitworth?"

She took a deep sobbing breath. It came through the line with startling clarity.

"No," she said. "No. My girl. My Amy. They found my babies, my two little boys, on the street up in Washington. A policeman found them. On a corner of the street. Little John, he was holding his brother's hand and trying to be brave, and both of them cryin', and no shoes on, and no coats…the policeman said their little hands and feet were red with cold…and anyone could have picked them up, anyone at all, and I'd never have seen them again—" She caught her breath on a sharp intolerable pain. "Their dad, he's disappeared, and can't nobody find Amy. Little John won't talk. Four years old, and he won't say nothing but 'Mommy fall down. Mommy fall down.' Jeremy won't do nothing but cry and cry. John's gone up to Washington to get them, and I'm waiting...waiting by the phone...Amy would call me. She would call me if she could—I got to get off the phone. Amanda, you call me later. Tomorrow. Next week. I got to go."

The phone clicked down. I put the receiver back slowly. Concentrating on Amelia's distress, I'd missed the sound of a car rounding the house and pulling into our yard. Heavy footsteps creaked on the boards of the porch. A knock sounded at the door. I left the chain on, cracked the door, and peered through.

"Amanda," Attaway Fowlerand said. "That Winn here?"

He filled the doorway, tall and thick and gnarled, like a tree battered by too many storms, rotten inside and ready to topple. The red rage had drained from his face; it was livid and set, and his pale blue eyes shone with purpose. I had never before been afraid of one of my relatives. I didn't want to let him in the door.

"No, Uncle Attaway," I said weakly. "He's gone out for the evening. I was just headed for bed."

I thought for a moment that he was going to push his way in. He swayed, very slightly, and thrust his cane down to steady himself. Tires crunched in the lane. Thomas's car nosed around the side of the house. I felt relief like water in my joints. Attaway whirled and stamped away, down the steps and past Thomas without a word. He left deep plowed furrows in the grass as he pulled away.

"What was that all about?" Thomas demanded, bounding up the steps.

"He's looking for Eddie."

"Where is Eddie, anyway? It's late."

"He's gone out for dinner. Thomas—"

"Sorry I'm late," Thomas said.

I took another look at his face in the light falling from the open door. His eyes glittered with some strong emotion, and lines were visible around his mouth.

"What's up?" I asked.

"Let's go in. I went down to Winnville late this afternoon," Thomas said, waving me through the door and closing it behind us, "because I wanted to see Tammy Watts again, check on how she was doing, and take them a Thanksgiving basket from the church. I thought it would be better to go when her husband was there. I'd never met him, and I didn't want him to think I was sneaking around behind his back. So I went in to see her. What'd you say?"

"Nothing," I said feebly.

"She was doing okay, but her husband was there and he was stewed. I've never seen anyone so out of it at five in the afternoon. Much worse than Eddie ever was. He started laughing at me, saying that Tammy'd been pulling this screaming stuff all her life and all it meant was that she needed to see a doctor for crazy people. Then he turned ugly. Said he thought I'd just come by to see if I could catch him gone." He opened the refrigerator, scanning the shelves hungrily. "Didn't we have some hot dogs?"

"Er—they're gone now."

"Yeah, I see." He pulled out some ham and cheese and started to put a sandwich together. I held my tongue. He was moving with quick jerky motions, forceful and angry. Thomas always ate when he was angry. "So when he started shouting, she hustled the kids out and left me there—which I don't really blame her for—and he never did do much except yell. I hate to tell you this, but you ought to know what's going on."

"What, Thomas?"

"Well, Matthew's been telling people that you and Eddie are fooling around. Seems his truck's here sometimes when I'm gone, and so the gossip has been that he waits until lunch and then you come back from Granny's—"

"Which she doesn't notice, of course."

"And you can guess the rest." He slammed his plate down. Fury throbbed in his voice and in the veins at his neck. "I wish I could call down fire on the lot of them," he said. "I know how the Sons of Thunder felt. It's as though you talk and do and explain and weep over people's griefs and put out your hands when they need help, and it all goes invisibly by unless there's some huge supernatural event to make them sit up and notice. No wonder James and John wanted to call down fire. They'd talked truth until their tongues were sore, and all the listeners stared at them and yawned."

"I have to talk to you," I said.

"What?"

"It's about Eddie."

Thomas sat down at the table. He put his hands against his eyes in a sudden gesture of weariness. "What is it?" he said.

I told him about Eddie's half-truths, his evasions, my conversation with Jenny, his car at the Moreheads', and finally his words to me. I wound up with, "I can't actually say that he made a pass at me, Thomas—I don't want to accuse him unfairly, but I know he had intentions of—"

"It's all right," Thomas said. He took his hands away from his eyes. "You're right, Amanda. I should have opened my eyes to this a long time ago, but I was afraid. He's the only person

I've had a real relationship with, besides you, since we came back here. I was clinging to him. But it's been an illusion all along. I knew that, somewhere deep down, but I wasn't willing to be alone." He looked down at the sandwich. "Guess I'm not really hungry after all."

Eddie didn't come back that night. In the morning Thomas packed his things and stacked the boxes on the back porch. When I asked him why, he merely said, "Even if he comes back, he can't live here again. You and I need to be alone."

I filled Thomas in on the Whitworth crisis; he called them, but the phone rang on and on without an answer. We tried Ambrose and Ida Scarborough, but when their answering machine cut on, I remembered that Ida had mentioned going to Florida to spend Thanksgiving with relatives.

Thomas showered and brought me a cup of coffee and put a CD on the stereo before he went over to the church to finish his sermon. I drank the coffee and listened to Bach: a swelling chorus of gratitude and glory. I felt indefinably dirty, smeared by the minds of the Little Croft gossips. Getting up and dressing seemed like a huge impossible weight. I couldn't budge.

So I stayed in bed, idly watching the thin November sunshine that poured in through the window, and let the surging triumphant melody build up around me like great strong castles of sound. Through the golden haze that fell all around me, I looked up into a glorious triumph of certainty: the other side, where God's presence was a searing light that burned bright and hot on the other side of a thin curtain. It glowed gold and dangerous through the rents and holes, bursting almost visibly from the straining seams.

I put out my hand and saw myself, as though I stood out-side the window, haloed in the falling sunshine. I lay on a disheveled bed in a tiny room. The plaster had faded into dingy yellow, and dust collected in the corners. The last singing harmony died away. Tears filled my eyes and ran down from the corners, puddling wet and cold on my neck. The castles blew away into gray powder, an illusion of mold and wishful dreaming.

I got up and showered and walked over to the Old House. The wild sumac growing up against the wooden fence had dropped its leaves, and the naked wooden stems had blackened with the last frost. A thin film of mud coated the rutted road to the grave-yard. At the top of the slope, Uncle Giddy was bent double among the tombstones.

I went up Granny's steps. She was sitting in her television chair, watching the door. As soon as I pushed the screen open she said, "They're still thinkin' about it."

"Who?"

"The jury. Attaway called me from th' courthouse."

"I'd be surprised if they reach a verdict before the week-end," I said. "They'll break for Thanksgiving tomorrow, and they may not get back to deliberations until Monday. And all that medical stuff about Matt's head injury—that'll take them a while to plow through." Granny's white hair had slipped from its pinned coils. I looked around for her hairbrush. "So there's not much we can do but wait, is there? Where's your comb?"

"If they don't pin the murder on Matt good and hard, Attaway'll know it's because they believed your Winn. He'll know they blame him for Quintus's death. He'll be even madder than he is now."

"What do you think he'll do, Granny?"

Granny's voice dropped. I had to lean forward to hear her.

"I don't know," she whispered. "Listen, Amanda. I got to tell you something." The old hand fastened on my arm. "Listen. I only seen Attaway this mad a couple of times before. That day...that day before Doris died...he came up here ravin' like a lunatic, sayin' he'd been made a fool of. Nat was gone away, an' I was cannin' tomatoes. I couldn't leave the canner. You know, you take your eyes off a canner and it'll explode. I was watching the dial, and Attaway was bangin' around in those back rooms and mumblin' and mutterin', and finally he came out and left. I looked, later. After Doris died. My pills were gone. I'd had a whole envelope, and there was only two left in the bottom. I swear there was more than that."

"What kind of pills?"

"Sleepin' pills. I got 'em from Dr. White. I used to take a pill every once in a while, not real often, so I had lots left."

"You think Attaway took them?"

"He was so mad," Granny whispered. "Next time he got mad like this, Peggy died. An' then he shouted at Quintus, and Quintus died. He's mad at that Winn boy, Amanda, and y'all are standing in his way. He don't even think of you as a relative no more. You're just in the road, and he wants to get by."

Giddy's footsteps sounded on the porch. Granny let go of my arm at once. Her voice returned to its normal strength, but her blue eyes fastened on me, urgently repeating the caution.

"You get your foxes?" she demanded.

"Got two," Giddy said. "Maybe the others'll leave." He propped his rifle in a corner and flopped down into a chair.

"Where's your Winn, Amanda?"

"Gone for the day," I said.

"He better stay away from Uncle Attaway," Giddy said. "I ain't never seen a man boil so hard inside. He been up and down this road all day, tryin' to catch your Winn at home. Mama, you ready for dinner?"

Chapter Thirty

E ddie didn't come back Wednesday night either. Thomas prowled restlessly around the house until late, but the lane stayed empty. Eddie had gone to ground like an animal smelling danger.

I woke up, past midnight, and saw moonlight pouring through the window. I got up and followed the sweep of light to the glass. The yard was bright as morning. The silos glittered and the tin roofs of the sheds shone above the pitch-black doorways. Beyond the steep drop-off of the backyard, the Chickahominy lay like a path of poured silver. A woman was standing in the middle of the yard, staring off to the river. She was wearing a nightgown, and I couldn't see her face. I wondered with irritation why Chelsea hadn't barked; and then I saw the baby, crawling towards the slope. I tried to shout, but she didn't move. She watched the baby inch its way towards the river, her hands limp by her sides, until it put one chubby hand into empty space and tottered, wailed, slid downwards.

I woke up in the moonless dark of a cloudy night. Thomas was breathing noisily beside me. I huddled under the covers, close to his warm solid body, and decided that hot chocolate wasn't worth the long dark trip down to the silent kitchen.

On Thanksgiving Day, I got up at six to put the turkey in the oven.

The year we married, we had planned to travel down to spend our first Thanksgiving with Thomas's mother. But she had gone back to the psychiatric care facility two days before the holiday, and my parents had bought us two last-minute plane tickets to Virginia. Since then, we had always come back to Little Croft for Thanksgiving and eaten a meal that never varied. Turkey, dressing made with homemade bread and baked in square glass pans, sweet potatoes with a crumble of brown sugar and butter on top, homemade rolls, string beans with almond slivers. A ceremonial glass of wine at each place, ruby against the white tablecloth. And on the sideboard, the inevitable four pies made from Granny Cora's recipes: pumpkin, apple, lemon chess, chocolate chess like fudge in a crust, with pecans laid carefully in the bottom of the pan.

The Fowlerand Thanksgiving dinner this year was being cooked by Roland's hefty wife and served in the drafty dining room of the old Fowlerand place. We'd been invited, but thanksgiving would not have risen in my heart as I sat at a table with Granny and Giddy, with Attaway and Roland and Pierman.

So I armed myself in an apron and put the turkey in the oven while the November morning was still dark outside the windows. I made each pie, sweeping flour from the counter after each crust was safely in its pan. I cooked the sweet potatoes, the string beans, put the rolls on to rise. I put a white tablecloth on the kitchen table and poured us each a glass of wine.

Past Thanksgivings lingered in my memory: the glass doors giving on to the deep beech woods, early afternoon sun slanting through and lighting the polished glass into crystal, the warmth of family and the numinous beauty that stood for the presence of God. But this Thanksgiving Day was gray and sunless. The winter storm was stretching its first tentacles of cloud across the sky.

Thomas had put on a tie for Thanksgiving dinner. While he carved the turkey, I ran upstairs and changed into my deep red dress. We blessed the meal and ate, holding hands under the table. And it seemed that ghosts were all around us; not Doris and Peggy and Quintus, but the family we had come cheerfully back to Little Croft to find.

Friday, I made turkey sandwiches without salt for Granny, and Matt Humberston's jury went back to work. Granny had post-Thanksgiving indigestion, so Giddy went down to the court-house, late afternoon, for a report. He came back with the news that the jury had asked the judge whether they could continue deliberations on Saturday. The foreman was certain they could come to a verdict before the day was over, and none of them wanted to sit on the trial over yet another weekend.

"Don't blame 'em," Granny said, and sent me out to buy her broth and antacids. I drove to Mercysmith under the thickening clouds and fought the frantic hordes of storm-panicked shoppers. The milk shelves were empty, and every bag of salt was gone.

Saturday morning, I drank my coffee at the kitchen table, looking out at the fields. An occasional flake of snow fluttered down past the window. The sky was low and gray, loaded with unstable clouds. Snow was ready to cascade down on us at the slightest shift of wind. Eddie's belongings still sat on the porch by the back door.

Thomas came down, peered out to see whether Eddie's

boxes had disappeared, and started to make himself toast.

"Let's drive up Route 5 and go visit one of the plantations," I said. "Evelynton, maybe. They'll be decorating for Christmas. We could make turkey sandwiches and pour a thermos of coffee and wrap up warm."

Thomas agreed. We bundled up in boots and gloves, put leftover turkey on bread, and drove to Evelynton, stopping at the bottom of Courthouse Hill for a bag of chips and a box of cookies from Charlie Winn. The morning had that subdued and breathtaking beauty peculiar to a cloudy November day. We walked through Evelynton's halls, admiring the Christmas wreaths and the spiced pyramids of Christmas fruits and candies; and we sat on Evelynton's cold, high hill and looked out at the pewter waters of the James River. The gray wind blew up into our faces, and beneath us the brown grass smelled of winter. I leaned into the curve of Thomas's arm.

"I love you," he said, half under his breath.

"I'm sorry," I said. "For all the mess. I keep waiting for it to go away...so that I can feel God here, the way I used to."

He didn't answer, but his arm tightened around me. We sat in silence; and later we drove towards home in the same quiet. Halfway back, he put his hand out and I took it. As we came up on Courthouse Hill, Thomas slowed and gave me a sideways questioning glance. I nodded, and he turned right and drove up to the courthouse parking lot. The consciousness of Matt's ongoing trial had run underneath my thoughts all morning, like a strong sideways current beneath the tide.

The courthouse itself was mostly empty when we peered through the doors. A lanky middle-aged man in a sweater was sitting in a back pew, scribbling and yawning. Matthew Humberston was up at the front. He was facing his son's empty chair, and his dark head was between his hands. We backed out silently.

"Want to wait for a bit?" Thomas said. "See if the jury comes back in?"

I nodded. He said, "I'm going to the men's room. Meet you back here in a few minutes."

When he had disappeared, I tried the door of the little office building next door. It opened onto a bare hall with a wooden bench set next to a water fountain. The frosted-glass doors of empty offices were closed and locked all along its length. Down near the far end, a single door stood open.

I walked down and peered cautiously through. Jimmy White sat writing at a desk beneath a small cloudy window. He glanced up and said, "Afternoon, Amanda. You waitin' for the verdict?"

"We thought we'd wait for a bit."

"Your great-uncle's been in and out of here all day."

"Can I talk to you for a minute?"

He pointed at an empty swivel chair. I sat gingerly down, feeling it creak beneath me.

"Back when Peggy Fowlerand died," I said, "you said you thought my grandmother had something eating at her."

"I remember," he said. His dark eyes were shielded. He leaned back, twiddling a pencil between capable fingers.

"Well, I want to tell you what my grandmother knows. I have to start back at the beginning, back when my great-aunt died." I told him about Granny's fears and hints; about Great-uncle Attaway's fury before Doris died, and about the missing sleeping pills.

He nodded. "I remember old Dr. White. I was a deputy back when Doris Fowlerand died. I went and talked to Dr.

White about her prescriptions. You can't imagine how different it was out here back in 1970. Dr. White did all his own dispensing. He used to order them phenobarbital capsules in big old buckets, like ice cream containers, and he didn't keep no records to speak of. Folks come in with trouble sleeping, hysteria, high blood pressure, you name it, and he'd scoop a bunch of tablets into an envelope and hand it over. Never write a word. And that stuff was mighty addictive, too. But it wasn't phenobarbital killed Peggy Fowlerand. She didn't have no drugs in her at all."

"No, but Doris—"

"You seriously telling me you think your great-uncle murdered his wife with your grandmother's sleeping pills?"

"There's more," I said. I told him about Uncle Giddy's trip back to the Fowlerand place the evening Doris died. I told him about Eddie Winn as a boy, skulking around while Doris slipped into a coma; about Eddie's present terrors, and Great-uncle Attaway's trips to the Tenant House, and his carbon-copy furies before Peggy's death and Quintus's murder.

"You got a big mess there, Amanda," he said when I'd finished. "You tryin' to sweep it all into a neat pile?"

"I'd just like to clear it up so that we can get on with the church work."

Jimmy White brooded for a moment. His big, heavily muscled body was perfectly still, except for the fingers that twisted his pencil around and around. Feet squeaked on the polished floor outside. The pencil broke. Jimmy White sat up. "'Scuse me," he said. "That'll be my deputy. The jury's coming back in."

I went back outside. The courtroom doors were propped open. A sprinkling of spectators had materialized on the front porch. Thomas was standing in the middle of the lawn, looking around him. I went up and slipped my arm through his.

"Where'd you go?"

"To speak to the sheriff."

"Are we going in?"

I nodded. We followed the last of the thin crowd in through the courtroom doors and sat unobtrusively in the back. Matthew hadn't moved, but Matt was back in his chair with his lawyer behind him. Judge Banks sat behind the bench. The jury was rustling itself into the box. I squinted, trying to see whether they were looking straight at Matt or not. It was hard to tell from the back. They looked respectable and middle-aged and uncertain.

"Have you reached a verdict?" Judge Banks asked.

"We have," said the foreman. He was a small round man with glasses, immensely self-conscious. Jimmy White took the verdict from him and handed it to Judge Banks, who flattened it and read it with practiced blankness.

"The defendant will rise."

Matt stood up. I could see his back, with the dark curls falling down onto the collar of his suit jacket. Behind him, Matthew Humberston rose as well, as if drawn by invisible wires. Judge Banks opened his mouth and then thought better of it.

The foreman cleared his throat. "On the charge of murder in the first degree, we the jury find the defendant, Matthew William Humberston Jr., not guilty."

Matthew took three steps forward, but the little man wasn't finished.

"We the jury find the defendant guilty of murder in the second degree…"

The man with the writing paper departed swiftly from the back row. Matt's expensive lawyer put his hands on the table in front of him, palms down, and dropped his head. Thomas was gripping my arm so tightly that it hurt. I put my hand over his, and he relaxed his fingers.

Matt turned completely around to look at his father. His face was stiff with sheer terror. Matthew Humberston dropped his hand on his son's shoulder. I saw the hand shake, like an old man's, and when Matthew turned his head I saw that Matt's terror had passed into his face.

Judge Banks was saying something about sentencing. A deputy walked up to Matt, blocking him from view. I pulled on Thomas's arm. We went silently out of the courthouse and drove home.

Thomas called Ambrose Scarborough and John Whitworth that same night. Second-degree murder wasn't the worst possible verdict, but he didn't think Matthew would see it that way. The Scarborough answering machine picked up Thomas's first call. He hung up with a grimace.

"They must be staying in Florida over the weekend," he said. "I don't blame them, with this weather." He dialed the Whitworth number, but it rang and rang without answer. Thomas put the telephone back. "Well," he said, "I guess I'm top dog for the weekend. I'll tackle it Monday morning."

The telephone rang at midnight. I woke up with my heart in my throat. Thomas stumbled down the stairs ahead of me, and I listened to his voice.

"Calm down," he said. "I can't understand you. Joe, I can't hear what you're saying. Joe—" He held his hand against his free ear, his face tight with concentration. "Are you sure that's what it said?...Okay. No, I can come over now. You just wait. Make yourself some coffee, Joe. Eat something." He blocked the receiver for a moment and hissed at me, "Jenny's left him. He found a note on the table when he came back from a late job."

I walked to the back porch and peered through the storm door. Eddie's boxes and bags were gone.

"Did you pack his gun?" I asked.

"The .22?"

"No..." I climbed the stairs to Eddie's room. I hadn't been in it since before he left, and the rumpled blankets and sheets were still on the bed. I picked up the pillow. The loaded .357 still lay underneath it.

Chapter Thirty-one

Thomas dressed swiftly and left; I stayed up in the cold hours of Sunday morning, putting wood in the fire and making coffee and reading the same psalm over and over. Outside, I could hear rain pattering softly into the dirt. The air was still two degrees above freezing, but when I stepped out onto the back porch around six to feed Chelsea, my feet slipped on ice.

Thomas came back at six-thirty, red-eyed and unshaven. He accepted the huge mug of coffee I poured him and went to shower. I sat on the closed toilet lid and listened to him talk through the sound of running water.

"She left him a note," he said, lathering his hair. "On the table. Told him he'd almost broken her spirit, that she was afraid of what he might do next and she was getting out just in time. She'd packed most of her clothes; her drawers were almost empty. Joe spent four hours weeping hysterically. Amanda, I know he isn't the brightest guy in the world, but I do think he tried his best. See my razor?"

I handed it around the curtain.

"Thanks. So I finally got him calm enough to eat something, and then Eddie called. Around six. I answered the phone. I think he was startled to get me, 'cause there was a long silence, and then he said, 'Reverend Clement?' and I said, 'Eddie, what do you think you're doing?' and he said, 'I'm saving Jenny from an abusive marriage, that's what,' and gave me a whole earful of psychobabble." The water cut off. He reached for a towel and wrapped himself in it.

"He's never heard a thing I've said, Amanda. And I introduced him to them. I've ruined that couple's marriage. I didn't let Joe talk to Eddie on the phone; I finally got him in bed. He'd been up for twenty-four hours. I called Joe's dad in Dinwiddie, and he's going to drive over and sit with him."

"Thomas—" I began, but he shook his head.

"I have to preach in three hours," he said. "I can't even remember what my sermon's about. I can't talk about this anymore right now, or I won't be able to say a word this morning. I'm going over to the church to practice through it once, okay?"

"Be careful," I said.

"I'm driving slow. The road's only iced in patches, and mostly I can see them. Do you mind fixing some breakfast? And a whole pot of coffee."

"Of course."

"If this keeps up, by afternoon the whole place'll be under a sheet of ice."

He left, and I pulled out coffee-cake ingredients and a dozen eggs and a package of bacon. I had barely measured out flour and sugar when I heard Thomas's car in the backyard again. The motor cut off and the door slammed. I went out into the hallway, pulling my bathrobe around me. He came in the back door with a cloud of frigid air. Water glistened on his hair.

"The church is locked," he said.

"What?"

"Locked. Usually one of the deacons goes over early and unlocks it and turns the heat on, but I guess with everyone gone, no one had the job. It's dark and cold over there…and when I tried to unlock the front door, my key wouldn't turn. Do you have some kind of oil I could put on the lock?"

"Sewing machine oil? In the junk drawer."

I went back up and changed into jeans and a sweatshirt while he sorted noisily through the drawer. He looked at me in faint surprise when I reappeared in the kitchen. I said, "I'll go back over with you."

Chelsea was curled up with her groundhog on the back doormat. We stepped over her and drove to the church. Patches of ice already covered the curves of Little Croft Road.

In the wet morning dark, the white building loomed up like a rock on a misty coast, hard and impregnable. The key slid into the front door lock but wouldn't turn. We squirted oil, shook and jiggled, tried the back door. Nothing worked. The Little Croft Church windows were high and narrow, the bottoms just at Thomas's fingertips when he stretched his arms up. He braced his feet against the boards and managed to hook his arms over the sill of the window closest to the front of the building, but several unsteady heaves at the sash yielded no movement. The windows were wedged. His feet slipped; the church's sides were wet with freezing rain.

I went back around to the front door lock and knelt down to examine it closely. Bits of sawdust were still scattered on the bricks at the threshold. The white paint of the door had been scratched and touched back up.

"Thomas?" I called.

He came back around the corner of the building, dusting his hands.

"This lock's been changed."

He stooped beside me and examined the lock, and then went silently around to the back. In a moment he reappeared.

"The back too," he said.

"What do we do? Call a locksmith?"

"No. Not a locksmith. Let's check the fellowship hall."

We went back together to the little low building behind the church. Its doors were tight shut, but the rickety windows yielded to Thomas's hand. He heaved himself up, slithered through, and fell with a crash inside.

"Ow," he said from the other side of the wall.

"You okay?"

"Just fine. Come around to the door."

I went around and waited at the little hall's front until the door opened. Thomas said, "The room at the back is big enough to have church in. Come help me put some chairs in it."

I walked back down the narrow hall with him. We arranged folding chairs in two short semicircles on the carpet. The room at the back was cramped and dim, but a woodstove sat in one corner. Thomas went out to the woodpile behind the hall, and I found paper and matches. We lit a fire and banked it up to burn all morning. The room began to warm. Gray rain drove against the windows.

"Let's wait on the front steps for people to show up," Thomas said. "It's useless to pretend this isn't happening, so we may as well tackle it head on."

"We'd better dress warm if we're going to stand out in this ice," I said.

We stood on the top step, Thomas with his Bible and sermon notes, me with a handful of bulletins. As church members arrived, Thomas answered the constant "What's the matter,

Reverend?" with the same simple sentence: "Mr. Humberston has changed the church locks."

When eleven o'clock came, we had twenty or so people standing around us, huddled in a cluster underneath the protective overhang of the church's porch. Twenty instead of the original forty: Tammy Watts, her eyes shadowed with weariness and a toddler on each side; the little old pianist clutching her books against her chest; two families who lived around the Loop, a farmer and his wife from a turf farm on the other side of Poverty Ridge, the owners of a small public boat dock just down the Chickahominy.

Thomas said, "Let's pray," and they looked at each other and at us and then bowed their heads uncertainly.

"Loving Father of us all," Thomas said, "we come this morning to worship you, as you have commanded us. We don't have our building to meet in. We're missing some of our brothers and sisters. We're facing hostility and hatred. Protect us this morning. Send your glory to this place."

Glory, I thought. Old, old words from the prayer book flitted through my mind. *O Almighty God, who hast built thy Church upon the foundation of the Apostles and Prophets, Jesus Christ himself being the chief Corner-Stone. O Almighty God, who hast knit together thine elect in one communion and fellowship, in the mystical body of thy Son.* I thought of the church, the army of God, shining and terrible as a host with banners; and I looked at the bewildered little cluster of folks shuffling their feet in the dirt.

"Let's go around to the back," Thomas said.

We trooped around to the fellowship hall, hunching our shoulders against the cold rain. We sang an a cappella hymn in wavering voices, and Thomas preached. I watched from the second row; they were really listening to Thomas, their faces intent with concentration. The little old pianist was nodding her head slowly. The public dock owner was writing notes in the margin of his Bible. Tammy Watts sat silently with tears creeping down her cheeks, the toddlers clinging to her hands. I thought again: the church of God, terrible as an army with banners, and this time the thought didn't seem quite as ridiculous.

It would be pleasant to say that the little service in the fellowship hall ended victoriously, all of us overwhelmed with the power of God and the presence of the Holy Spirit. But we were tired in body and in spirit, discouraged and apprehensive. The room was cramped, the light was lousy, we'd slept a bare two hours the night before, and no glory fell on us from the heavens. Just as Thomas reached the benediction, the lights in the cramped room flickered once, twice. In Little Croft, a third flicker inevitably meant that a line had finally come down; and in his apprehensive pause between the prayer and the amen, the lights blinked once more and then went out.

The rain was falling harder. As we stood at the doorway shaking hands I could see that the bare maple branches behind the church were glistening with a coating of ice. Thomas drove very slowly home on glazed blacktop. A four-wheel-drive truck came rocketing by us, spraying sleet and water behind it, and we slid to the edge of the ditch before Thomas eased us back onto the pavement. The houses, spaced wide along Little Croft Road, sat gray and silent at the ends of their lanes.

The Tenant House windows were dark. Chelsea huddled on the back porch with her nose against the door, and when

Thomas pushed it open she rocketed into the hall and made for the fireplace. The steps were solid ice. Our rooms were gloomy with rain, the corners veiled in shadows. Water pounded on the tin roof and rolled down into long icicles at the edges.

"I'll put some wood on the fire," Thomas said, "and you can find the candles."

He headed for the fireplace room, and I heard the sound of crumpling newspaper as he persuaded the fire back to life. I dropped my wet coat on a chair and went through to the kitchen. The candles were on a top shelf, but I couldn't remember which one, so I pulled a chair over and rummaged through all the high places. Eventually I found the box in the cabinet over the refrigerator. I was balanced at the very edge of the chair, leaning precariously and groping with my left hand, when the floor squeaked upstairs.

"Thomas?" I called.

"Yes?" Thomas said, from the fireplace room.

"Where's Chelsea?"

"In here."

I held my breath, perched insecurely on the teetering chair. The boards in the ceiling creaked again and paused.

"Thomas," I said, more quietly. "Someone's upstairs."

I heard Thomas's feet walk gently to the hallway and stop. We both stood still, waiting. Above us, a door closed; the gentle rub of edge against jamb was almost lost in the clatter of rain.

"Amanda," Thomas said, barely in a whisper, "come out here." I got down from the chair and crept across the floor. He was standing in the hallway, his head tilted up. He formed the word "Who?" with his lips. I shook my head. Granny's frightened words sounded loud in my ears: *He don't even think of you as a relative no more. You're just in the road, and he wants to get by.*

"Where's the gun?" Thomas mouthed. I pointed up at our bedroom.

"Flashlight?"

"Batteries are dead."

"Well, that's not much use, is it?"

"I'll get a candle," I whispered back. The day had darkened into something like twilight, and the upstairs hall was murky. I walked silently back into the kitchen, lit a candle, and came back. Thomas took it from my hand.

"I'll go first," he said.

"Wait!" I slipped back into the fireplace room and got him the poker. Chelsea was sprawled blissfully in front of the flames. I exhorted her in a whisper to rise and defend us, but she yawned a huge pink yawn and rolled onto her back.

Thomas took the poker in his right hand and the candle in his left. Another board creaked upstairs. I followed him silently along the hallway, up the steps. At the top of the steps we waited, until a stealthy rustling sounded from behind Eddie's closed door.

"He's in there," Thomas whispered. "You push the door open."

"Who's in there?" I mouthed back at him.

"Whoever it is. Open the door." He half raised the poker. In his eyes was a faint, unmistakable gleam; finally he had a real and unambiguous enemy to defeat. I thought: Even Great-uncle Attaway wouldn't plug the pastor on his own stair. I pushed the door open.

Eddie Winn scuttled away from the candle's light. He was damp with rain, his hair slicked down all over his head, and I could hear him breathing. Thomas lowered the poker.

"What are you doing back here?" he demanded.

"Nothin'," Eddie said weakly. He shrank back behind the closet door. Something hard and metallic fell on the floor and rolled away, rattling noisily on the bare boards. Chelsea started barking below us.

"It's too late now!" Thomas yelled down the stairs. "Hush up!"

She whined and scuffled on the floor. Eddie was down on his knees, collecting his treasures with shaking hands. I knelt down beside him and pushed his arms away; he was gathering up hollow-point bullets that had spilled out of their flimsy cardboard box. I swept them away from him.

"Where's the gun?" I demanded.

"In my pocket."

"Give it to me." I pulled at his jacket. I had a creeping fear that he might suddenly erupt into violence, but he seemed passive, stunned and pliant. I felt the smooth cold metal barrel in his pocket and yanked it away from him. The chambers were empty.

He raised his head, blinking up at Thomas. Thomas still had the poker in his hand. Behind the candle flame, he loomed up dark and huge, and his morning with Joe lent an extra edge of wrath to his voice.

"Where's Jenny?"

"In Richmond. At a hotel."

"I can't believe you even came back here. After making a pass at Amanda—"

"I never did. And you ain't supposed to judge me. The Bible says you're supposed to love the sinners."

"Yeah? Well, the apostle Paul once told a whole group of

sinners that he wished they'd go and—"

"Let's go downstairs," I said firmly, "and talk about this. Eddie, are you coming or do we have to drag you down?"

He shambled out of the closet. Some intense fear was disabling him; he didn't protest again, or even ask for the gun back.

"Have you seen Joe?" Thomas demanded again when we were sitting at the kitchen table. He had propped the poker close at hand; Chelsea wandered in and sniffed at it and sprawled on the floor underneath the table.

"No," Eddie muttered.

"Why'd you come back?"

"To get my gun. I never meant to run off with her, Reverend Clement. Honest. I just went over for—for a while—to visit. I knew Amanda would tell you...well anyway, one thing led to another, and then she said she wanted to leave right then, and I didn't have my gun with me, but I need it." His voice was growing more desperate.

I tightened my fingers around the gun in my lap and said, "Why?"

"To protect me, that's why."

"From my great-uncle?"

Eddie hunched his shoulders. The whites of his eyes stood out, rimming the dark pupils.

"We could call Great-uncle Attaway and ask him to fill in the blanks."

"He's already here," Eddie whispered. He swallowed, and his Adam's apple bobbed in his gaunt throat. "I came back to get m' gun. Knew y'all would be gone, and I got to have my gun. Thought Attaway was in Richmond. He came drivin' up while I was upstairs, poked through them sheds back there for hours and finally went on down to your grandma's, just as you was coming up the lane. I couldn't get out. I couldn't get out."

"What does he want?"

"The bottle."

"What bottle?"

"You ain't gonna turn me over to the sheriff?"

"You're probably going to hell," Thomas said, "so Jimmy White ought to be the least of your concerns."

"Thomas…"

"All right," Thomas said. "What bottle?"

"That whisky bottle," Eddie said. The secret, thirty years buried, rose up out of his soul with the relief of a long-dammed spring. "The whisky bottle Doris had. He tol' me to bring it back to him, and I didn't. Giddy caught me, see, and I threw it over the hill."

"Wait a minute," Thomas said. "He told you to do what?"

"Told me to go in and get the bottle," Eddie said eagerly. "While Doris was sleeping. I used to do errands for him now and then. Only spending money I ever had. See, he told me Doris drank too much when he was gone, an' he was worried 'cause she was there alone with the baby. He told me he'd be gone all night, and to go in and get the bottle that was mostly full and put a mostly empty bottle there instead. That way she couldn't get too drunk with him away."

"So you did it?"

"Soon as I saw her go upstairs. She'd already had a lot, I reckon, 'cause she was weavin' a bit and the baby was cryin' out. The window was open, so I could hear. I went in an' got the bottle—it was half full—an' put the other one there instead. Just had a little puddle in the bottom. I was supposed to take the half-full one back to Attaway."

"And then what?"

"Went back out," Eddie said, twisting his hands together, "went back out, and here came Gideon Scarborough up the lane. I didn't want him to see me. Attaway, he told me nobody ought to see me with that bottle, so I pitched it over the hill. When I saw Attaway later he yelled 'cause I didn't have the bottle. He scared me." For a moment his voice was childish. "His eyes got real wide and kind of shone, and his voice came up from the bottoms of his feet, an' so I ran off. An' when she died, I figured I just got there too late to stop her from drinkin' too much…and Attaway, he got nice again, gave me work now and again, plenty of money—"

"Plenty of money to buy liquor?" Thomas said.

"I ain't drinking, not now."

"And you've been thinking about this? About Attaway and Doris?"

"My mind cleared up some," Eddie whispered. "Cleared up, after you came by. After I quit drinking. I ain't thought about Doris Fowlerand for years, till I quit drinking, and then…then I lay awake at night and thought and thought."

"You thought," I said slowly, "that my great-uncle had something to do with his wife's death?"

"He was so mad when I didn't bring him the bottle. And then I thought, now that I'm not drinkin', and everybody knows it, what if—what if—"

"He knows you're sober and decides to find out what you've remembered?" Thomas inquired.

Eddie nodded, looking out the kitchen window. Through the dull sheets of rain, I could see Great-uncle Attaway's pickup, parked in front of Granny Cora's house.

"You threw it down the hill," Thomas said. He looked over at me.

"It's been thirty years," I protested.

"It could have lain down in those vines—"

"It didn't break," Eddie said. "I told Attaway it broke, down there on the hill. He believed me then. I dunno whether he would now. It didn't break. It went into the brush silent, and it stuck there."

"You never went back for it?"

"I never went near that hill again. Not the hill, nor the room where she died. Gave me the shivers."

I said to Thomas, "You're not really going to go down there in the rain, are you?"

"Best time to do it. No snakes in November, not with all this ice." He rose, and Eddie shrank back. He said, quite kindly, "Don't worry, you little roach, I'm not going to hurt you. But you can sit right there till we get back."

"Old Attaway—"

"Old Attaway's iced in," Thomas said. "He's been sitting up there because the roads are too slick to drive on. How'd you get here?"

"Walked on the old road in the woods out back," Eddie mumbled.

"Well then," Thomas said, "you can walk right on back without your gun, or sit here and wait till we've had a look down the hill."

Eddie started to get up. Chelsea raised her head and fixed him with a meaningful eye. The hair bristled on the back of her neck. Eddie sat back down again hurriedly.

"Better late than never," I said, rising from my chair. "Let me get a pair of gloves and my heavy coat and I'll come with you. There's a lot of vine grown up over that hill in the past thirty years."

Chapter Thirty-two

More than once in the two hours that followed I thought: This is ridiculous. It's broken; it rolled into the river; it's buried under silt and mud; Eddie's lying and it never existed. The slope to the river was gentle here, covered with bent trees and wreathed in ivy. Thirty years ago these could have been saplings, the ivy just beginning to creep into the brush.

We hunted systematically back and forth, with rain soaking into our winter coats. I found all sorts of ancient debris hidden underneath that ivy. The ice was thick on it, and I had to crack the frozen leaves apart with gloved fingers before I could reach down to the ground. An antique rubbish heap, full of broken bottles, occupied me for a good forty minutes. The ivy was full of sharp things, too: rusty pieces of a baby carriage, an old iron tractor seat, and a set of worn-away harrow tines. I had to feel carefully, digging into the top layer of ground with fingers growing more and more numb.

Somewhere in the middle of the slope, where I knelt surrounded by vines that wrapped around my ankles and dirt that clung to my fingers, a truth came to me; not with a blinding Damascus light but with a clear gray certainty. I too had remade Christ in the image of my own desires. I'd wanted to sweep away the mess so that God could be seen, and I had seen the Jesus who stalked through the temple with a whip, making a space to worship God. But I'd forgotten Christ crucified: dying with Peggy, looking at God's turned back through

Quintus's eyes, suffering with Doris as evil men put him to death. I saw not the healer, but the man who stood in a tangle of human sins and said, "Father, forgive them" before he died. He was here, in this mess, where I crouched and dug for a long-buried truth.

I was beginning to shake with cold when I groped beneath the ivy and found the neck of a bottle: a smooth, unbroken cylinder, three-quarters buried. I worked dirt away from it with both hands, holding my breath. My gloves felt down its length, waiting for a crack, a jagged edge.

"Thomas!"

He looked up from his place farther down the slope.

"Come look at this."

Together we unearthed it. The label had rotted completely away, but the cap had been on it tight. It was still a quarter full of muddy liquid. Thomas held it up, squinting in the dim light.

"Is this it?" he asked.

"It's the right shape. But Thomas…"

"What?"

"Nothing will happen," I said slowly. "Even if the liquid can be tested, which I don't know…anyone could have thrown it here. There's no label, no mark, nothing to show that this is the bottle Eddie threw over. Even if he would say so in court."

Thomas studied the thick viscous stuff in the bottle. "No," he said at length. "I know. But your great-uncle and your grandmother are together at her house, and Eddie's at our house, and I want all the secrets told. Then, maybe, we can go back to work. I don't think secrets inhabit God's kingdom very comfortably, Amanda."

I thought of my own secrets, the family skeletons I'd concealed in the name of compassion, in the name of protecting my husband's ministry, in the name of sparing his feelings. And I thought: *Oh, she's a Fowlerand, right enough. She sits on those secrets like all of you, smilin' and white on the surface and with her very bones rotten underneath.*

"All right," I said. "Let's walk up and talk to Attaway. It won't sweep the mess into a neat pile, but at least we can get the truth out in the open."

"Eddie's got to come too." Thomas strode up the slope, his tall figure purposeful and his fair hair dark with water.

I followed him back to the kitchen. Chelsea had gone to sleep across the kitchen threshold. Eddie was still huddled on his chair, eyeing her.

"We're walking up to Cora Scarborough's house," Thomas said, "and having this out. And you're coming too."

Eddie moved like a snake uncoiling. His thin body whipped from the chair, across Chelsea and through the door. The back door banged. Feet slid on ice. Chelsea raised her head and cocked her ears. I went out into the hall and peered through the back door. Eddie was sprinting away across the glassy field towards the overgrown path that led through the back of Poverty Ridge Farm, out to Winneck Road. His feet splayed sideways as he ran, and his arms waved wildly.

"I've still got his gun," I remarked.

"Well," Thomas said, "I guess we keep it. Let's go."

We picked our way down the road towards the Old House. Thomas stripped off his glove and took my hand, and I curled my fingers into his warm palm. My throat was oddly dry. The spattering rain around us was mixed with snowflakes, and a white film had begun to layer itself over the ice beneath our feet.

We went carefully up the steps, and Thomas rapped at the door.

"Come in," Granny said.

We stepped in. The Old House was almost completely dark; candles made pools of light in kitchen and sitting room. Granny's old oil lantern sat on top of the silent television, casting a ring of yellow light into the room. Dog-dog slumbered in the middle of the rag rug. At one edge of the ring of light, Granny sat in her recliner; at the other edge, Attaway leaned back against the old brown sofa. I thought the rest of the room was empty until Giddy shifted in the green plush chair, beyond the reach of the light.

"Y'all need any water?" he asked. "Mama had me draw a couple of pitcherfuls just afore the lights went out."

"No," Thomas said, "we're all right."

"William Adkins called," Giddy said, settling back. "Says a tree came down right across the wires at the end of his lane. Take 'em all day to get out here, as bad as the roads are."

"Your phone out?" Granny inquired.

"I don't think so," I said.

"What are you doin', then, walking around in this weather?" She leaned forward to see Thomas's face in the dusk. "I heard that Eddie run off with someone's wife. That true?"

"Yes," Thomas said resolutely, "I'm afraid so. I was wrong about Eddie. I thought he'd reformed."

"That Winn's always been drowning his sorrows," Attaway said. "Can't stand to live without his sweets. He's off alcohol now and onto women."

I looked at him where he sat on the brown sofa, his shoulders back and his feet apart, the cane driven firmly between his feet and his hands folded on top of it. His hands were in the light, but his face was in shadow.

"Mr. Fowlerand," Thomas said, "Eddie told us a story."

Attaway stared at us from the shadows. I saw the faint glitter of his eyes between the narrowed eyelids.

"He told us that you had him go up to the Tenant House the night your wife died. You told him to take away the bottle of whisky under the sink and bring it to you, and to put another bottle in its place. You counted on the fact that he was just a boy and wouldn't hear the whole story, how Doris died because sleeping pills were mixed with her alcohol. But just to make sure, you paid Eddie for his trouble. He drank that money, and his memory got worse and worse."

Giddy's long figure sat straight up. "What?"

"Winns," Attaway said, low and dismissive. "Give that man a bottle of malt liquor, and he'd see more visions than a saint."

I looked over at Granny. Her old hands were tight on the green plush seat, and she was staring at her brother with narrow concentration.

"He told us he threw the bottle down the hill," Thomas said.

Attaway was silent.

"We climbed down the hill, just now. We found it." He drew the dirt-encrusted bottle from the inside of his jacket. "It's still a quarter full."

Attaway stiffened. His hands whitened over the head of his cane, and his narrow eyes opened wide. They shone in the shadows with a flat blue light, and his voice rose up from deep in his belly.

"No!" he said.

"Attaway," Granny Cora said in a whisper.

"Hush up, Cora."

"Attaway," Granny said again. Her voice was stronger. "Attaway, I knew you took my pills. That day you came up here, ravin' about Doris, and went back into my rooms. You took them pills and put them in her whisky, 'cause you knew Quintus wasn't yours."

"Mama!" Giddy said, appalled.

"Cora," Attaway said. "Hush your mouth, Cora." He was shaking with strong emotion, but his voice was tight and controlled again.

Granny shrank away from him. I went over to her and took her hand. The old dry fingers dug into mine. She said, "Amanda, I ain't got anyone to watch over me."

"You've got me," I said. "I'm not going anywhere." I left my hand in her grasp. She stared over at her brother, clinging to my fingers.

"It's true enough," she said. "I knowed then it was true, but I wouldn't tell myself so. I knew Nat's face, and I seen it in Quintus. I took a picture once, with Nat and Quintus lookin' the same way. Quintus looks as though Nat spat him out of his mouth. You ask Amanda. She's got the picture back at the Tenant House." I could hear in her voice the vast relief of guilt released.

"Cora," Attaway said.

"It's true, I tell you. You think Doris was the first woman my husband romanced? I always knew when he wandered. I could see his eyes change, go all dark and deep. And when did you know, Attaway? When she lit up like a candle for the first time, with that prettiness you did your best to wipe out? When she got pregnant at last? When Quintus was born and you looked at his face?"

Attaway raised his stick and crashed it down on the floor-boards. Dog-dog woke up and scrambled away, whining with fear. Giddy was standing up now, looking from his mother to his uncle in bewilderment.

"He always beat me," Attaway spat out. "Always in every-thing. We were both buyin' land, and he was always there first. He always got the best price, the best piece. He married you and got all that land from Daddy. An' then he had the four children to carry it on. Four children, Cora! An' I never had the one. We waited and waited. I built up all that land. I got nothing but dust waiting for me, Cora. Reverend Clement here, he talks about a land in the sky, but I know there ain't nothing for me but what I leave behind with my name on it. And nobody had my name. And finally my child was born, and I looked at his face and I saw Nat Scarborough laughin' at me, one last time."

"You killed her!" Giddy said. "Uncle Attaway, you killed her! That bottle I took up to the courthouse—"

"That bottle you got there ain't nothing but one o' Doris's long-ago empties. The woman looked away from me and it made her wretched. She could no more stay away from a whisky bottle than a wasp from light." His hands were clenched on his cane. In the candlelight, I could see the blood beating hard beneath the weathered skin of his face and neck. His lips were folded tight.

"And Quintus?" I said.

"Huh," Attaway said.

"What about Quintus. You wanted him to die, didn't you?"

"I seen too many detective programs to spill my guts to you, Amanda."

"What about Peggy?" Granny demanded. "You was there, right before she died. Just like with Doris. Did she talk to you?"

Attaway stared over her head.

"You know she was pregnant with Nat's grandchild? Did you, Attaway? Generations goin' on, all with your name and Nat Scarborough's face."

"Oh, she told me," Attaway said. "No mystery about that. All glowin' with it, just like Doris was when she told me, an' I waited all that time to see another man's baby."

"What did you tell her?"

"Nothin'." Attaway glared across at his sister.

Granny, still holding my hand, cried out, "You told her you'd take the land, didn't you? Poor little girl, all shining 'cause she was going to have a family and a farm at last, and you told her no grandchild of Nat's was going to get your land? What did you say, Attaway? Why'd she drive off that road?"

"Weak-minded girl," Attaway said. "Ignorant." He closed his mouth.

I said, "You told her that if she had a baby, you'd cut Quintus back out of the land and ruin him?"

"He can't do that," Giddy protested.

"Peggy wouldn't know that. And Great-uncle Attaway didn't know Quintus had destroyed his will. Did you?"

Attaway heaved himself up to his feet. Thomas and I both stepped backwards. His big shadowed figure was threatening, larger than life, and his old face was black in the dim light.

"What are you gonna do about it, then?" he said to Thomas. His voice sneered, dripping with disgust. "Take that old bottle down to Jimmy White? He'll laugh at you, that's all. And Peggy's death had nothing to do with me. Wasn't my fault if she drove off the road in a fit of gloom. Girl was never more than half there anyway. Wasn't my fault if Quintus went drinkin' with Matt Humberston when Matt was full of suspicions. You ask Jimmy White and he'll tell you so. There ain't no court can call me to account."

"There is," Granny said, half in a whisper.

Attaway turned his head and looked down at her. "You're a woman, Cora. You always thought there'd be happy endings to everything. Ain't you old enough to be over that now?"

He walked forward into the center of the lamplight, and as he did he diminished in size. The wavering shadows died away behind him. He stared balefully at Thomas.

"What is it you're after?" he said. "The land? You and Winnie and Giddy and Matthew can fight about it all you like, but it'll come back to me at the end. Go get your fancy lawyers and see. There's never anyone got the better of me."

"I don't care about the land," Thomas said.

"You think you're so smart. I made this whole county think you were my man. I can make them think you're a drunkard, or a thief, or a womanizer. Whatever I please. I can do all that and you'd best remember it. I'm goin' home, Cora. I been drivin' these roads for seventy years. Ice don't make no matter to me now."

He stumped across the room, down the steps and into the darkening night. Giddy stood perfectly still. Granny's hand still lay in mine. We watched, silent and motionless, as the headlights of Attaway's pickup cut on. Snow drifted down through the yellow-white beams. The truck pulled cautiously around the house. The sound of its motor died slowly away as Attaway drove off down Poverty Ridge Road.

"He'll go off the road," Granny Cora said hoarsely.

Giddy made a derisive sound in his throat. "Not likely. Devil takes care of his own."

Thomas reached out and set the whisky bottle on the TV. We all stared at it, as though the glass might speak to us.

"Amanda, darlin'," Granny said at last, "will you come up here and sleep tonight?"

"Yes, of course I will."

"I will too," Thomas said. None of us wanted to be alone, in the powerless dark.

Thomas and I didn't sleep much that night. We lay curled together in the narrow single bed that occupied Granny's spare bedroom, listening to the occasional sharp ping of ice on the roof.

"It might all fall apart this week," Thomas said softly.

"We can't leave, Thomas. Not now. Even if you lose the church, Granny's going to need me."

"She's family," Thomas said. "We'll stay as long as she needs us. As long as you want to."

"I want to stay," I said. "This is home."

Chapter Thirty-three

The lights came back on just after sunrise. We ran water through spluttering pipes, checked to see that Granny's heat was back on, cut on the lights, and went sleepily back to the Tenant House to shower. Thomas sat down in the kitchen with his Bible and sermon pad in front of him, gazing out the window. The church was still locked, and in any case Little Croft Road was almost impassable. Six inches of snow had fallen on top of an inch and a half of ice; a crippling Virginia blizzard. The clouds were blowing away, and the midmorning sun lit the farm into dazzling whiteness. I could barely look out the windows.

John Whitworth came down the lane around eleven, in an old pickup skidding unsteadily from side to side. He crept around the corner and stopped in front of the house. Thomas went to the front door to welcome him.

"Thank you," John said, stamping his way up onto the porch. "'Fraid if I pull into that backyard of yours I might never get back out. You got power, then?"

"Yes, and a fire lit. Come on in and have something hot to drink."

"Well, I will then," John said. He stepped out of his knee-high rubber boots at the door and laid his jacket carefully across them. "No need to shake snow all over your livin' room. Thank you, dear." He took the cup of coffee I offered him and sat in the rocking chair next to the flames. I sat on the edge of the hearth; Thomas stood behind me, his hands clasped at his back.

John Whitworth took a sip of the coffee. His long melancholy face was neatly shaved, and his cloth shirt was pressed. The whites of his eyes were bright red. He'd missed a strip of beard just under his chin.

"Well," he said again. "I hear y'all been stirring up all kinds of storms. I been by Matthew's place already this morning. Asked him why he had to go and change the locks. The man's not thinkin' straight, Reverend Clement, but he's done a lot of talking, here and there."

"I have to make a confession," Thomas said.

"What's that?"

"I did testify against his son, but I can't say I did it for the right reasons. I was angry at Matthew. I didn't want to let him push me around. If I hadn't been angry…I don't know what decision I'd have made."

"Might've been the same one?"

"Well, yes."

John Whitworth rubbed his chin, his fingers discovering the unshaven strip beneath it. He said with apparent irrelevance, "I been in Washington. Lookin' for my daughter. We found her, did you know?"

"No!" I said. "How is she? Is she all right?"

John shook his head. "Matthew Humberston lost his son this week. I might lose my girl. That man she married, he beat her till he was tired and dumped her in an alley." The laconic country voice shook, suddenly. He dragged his hand across his face. "They flew her down to MCV. She's in a coma. Don't know when she'll come out of it. Amelia and me, we got her boys back at the house."

"Can I do anything?" Thomas said.

"You can visit Amy for me some. They say at the hospital she can probably hear us, and she ought to be talked to. I go when I can, but I got to work to keep her there, and Amelia's got the little boys. They don't want her out of sight an' she don't think they ought to see their mother like this."

"I'll go visit her today."

"I do appreciate that, Reverend. There's two things I want to say to you now."

I could see Thomas bracing himself.

"Don't go lookin' like a dog's about to be kicked." John's voice was mild. "I called Ambrose this mornin', down in Florida. Matthew waited till we were both gone afore he pulled his stunt with the locks, 'cause he knew we'd never go along with it. Reverend, I can't say you've done much to build this church up yet. But afore you put new paint on a door, you've got to strip off the old and sand it; otherwise the new peels off. We're willin' to let you finish your sanding job afore we start judging your paint job. See what I mean?"

"Yes," Thomas said.

"Second thing is a message from Amelia. She wanted me to tell you this. The police, they're still looking for Amy's husband. Amelia says if she found him, she'd try to kill him with her own two hands. Sounds funny, don't it?" One corner of John's mouth twitched in grim amusement. "She's such a little thing, and always been so proper. But when she saw Amy all battered up like that—well, she went into a rage like I never seen. Thought for a bit that Amy's doc would have to give her some-thin' to calm her down. I got up this mornin', and she was sit-ting in a chair rocking little Jeremy back and forth. He'd been up screaming. She said, 'Tell Reverend Clement I understand

Matthew now. I understand what he did to his boy, teachin' him to hate the Fowlerands like he did. It wasn't the right thing to do, but I understand it. Tell Reverend Clement the man's hurtin' inside, worse than I am. My girl might get better, but his boy's always gonna be crippled.' That's what she said. I better get home now."

He set his coffee cup carefully on the hearth and rose, cracking his shoulders backwards. "Mercy, I'm tired," he said. "Been up almost two days. Guess I need to get them locks changed back."

"John," Thomas said, "will you come with me?"

"Where?"

"To visit Matthew. And Matt in jail, if he'll see me."

"I reckon I will. Soon as the road's a bit clearer, we'll go up and see the man." He paused at the door. "By the way, there's a piece of land down near us up for sale. Plenty of room for a nice house. Off the road, like, so children could play without gettin' around cars. Thought you might like to come down and have a look at it. Well, I'm gettin' along home now."

We stood on the porch and watched him drive down the road. Over at the Old House, a door slammed. Giddy's voice said, "Hellfire and blazes!"

"What is it, Uncle Giddy?" Thomas bellowed, pitching his voice to carry the distance.

"Two more o' them foxes!" Giddy yelled back. "Look out there!"

I squinted across the blinding snowfield. Up on the hill, the naked arms of the tree stretched out black over the mounded gravestones. A small dark shape flitted among them and disappeared.

"Moved in from across the road!" Giddy bellowed.

"Thinks I cleared out the dens for them!" The door slammed behind him and cut off his voice.

"He'll never get those dens cleared out there."

"No," Thomas agreed. "Looks like a long war." He stretched his long arms upwards. "Well," he said, "as long as I can't go anywhere, I may as well work on my sermon. And I need to call Joe again, go over and see him as soon as the roads are cleared up, and get back to Ida about her Christmas program. This week is the first Sunday in Advent, did you know?"

"I'd sort of lost count," I said.

"Me too. But I'm back on track now. I'm preaching about the Incarnation. The presence of God in very human flesh."

I took the bottle up to Jimmy White, later, and poured out the whole story. He listened with his eyebrows rising higher and higher.

"I'll be," he said, when I'd finished.

"What can you do?"

"Darned if I know," Jimmy White said. "Reckon I'll have to get some advice. Might take a long time to figure this one out."

"I'll be here, if you need me to repeat any of this. We're not going anywhere."

"You done good, Amanda."

"I didn't clear up the mess."

"You're here with your grandma," he said. "You done good."

The phone rang early, that first Sunday of Advent. I was up, clumsily twining pine around the Advent candles that I'd fixed on a flat board. I was never very good at crafty things, but Amelia had asked me to see to the decorations until she got the boys into a routine. Amy had opened her eyes, that Friday; not for long, but the doctors were hopeful.

I picked up the phone and said, "Yes?"

"Mandy?" Granny's voice said.

"Yes? Are you okay?"

There was a little pause. "Thought I'd go to church with you, if you'll come drive me over."

"Granny, I'd love to."

"Don't 'spect there'll be much worth hearing. But I figure, I might ought to hear Reverend Clement preach at least once, all things considered."

"He might surprise you."

"Maybe so. Anyhow, maybe you'd be kind enough to come on up a bit early and help me get my hair brushed out straight."

"I'll be up in half an hour."

"I'm right thankful."

She hung up; and so I called Thomas at the church and told him not to worry about coming back over to pick me up. I walked up to the Old House with my candles in my hand, got Granny ready for church, and helped her down the steps into the front seat of the car.

"Thankee," she said. She was silent until we rounded the curve just before Little Croft Church, when she said suddenly, "I haven't seen Attaway since that night."

"No. We haven't either."

"He always did work in the dark," Granny said. "I daresay he'll still cause you trouble, Amanda. He's got his teeth. But somehow they don't seem so sharp when the sun's out.

Reverend Clement go over to see Matthew?"

"He and John went together."

"Do any good?"

"He wouldn't see them. He came to the door and locked it in their faces. They went on down to the jail, but Matt sat with his face in a corner and wouldn't turn around."

Granny meditated on this, while I parked the car carefully in a dry patch. The week's snow had turned to slush and mud.

"I reckon Reverend Clement messed up there," she said at last.

"I don't know. The story's not over yet."

She got out, squinting her eyes at the morning light. I helped her up the steps and into a back pew, and she watched the Little Croft congregation assemble. Joe wasn't there; his father had taken him back to Dinwiddie for the weekend, but Thomas was due to see him again on Monday. Amelia came in with the two little boys clinging to her, John behind her; both of them thin and weary, but with hopeful eyes. Tammy Watts was there, the children trailing behind her and staring wide-eyed at the greenery. Thirty people gathered for the festival of Christ's birth.

"You got some work to do," Granny observed.

"We've got all the time in the world," I said.

She shot me a sharp glance as the organist began to play. The congregation rose all around us and started to sing in wavering voices: *Let all mortal flesh keep silence, and in fear and trembling stand!*

"Amanda," she whispered, "you better help me stand up."

I leaned down, and she hoisted herself up on my arm.

"That's better," she said. We stood together and listened to the hymn roll to its magnificent final verse.

Rank on rank, the host of heaven
Spreads its vanguard on the way.
As the Light of Light descendeth
From the realms of endless day,
And the powers of hell, they vanish
As the darkness fades away.
Alleluia, alleluia, alleluia, Lord Most High!

Granny leaned hard on me, and I braced my feet to bear her weight. The last notes rose and dissipated. The light came through the plain glass windows and turned my little Advent wreath all gold and green and scarlet, so that the candle flames were lost in the greater glory of the sun.

I had dreamed of river breezes and wide silent fields, back before we came home. I didn't dream the rest: the ancient sins and resentments that twined into our present, Quintus Fowlerand's bloody death and the coils of bitterness that would tighten around us. I saw the pictures, not the reality.

But now the pictures have three dimensions. Now I see the beauty of Little Croft, and the dark reality of evil lying behind it, and the presence of God. The three sides of my home, inseparable until all things are set in order.